The Clinician's Guide to Alcohol Moderation

The Clinician's Guide to Alcohol Moderation examines alcohol use around the world and teaches a range of behavioral health care providers how to help clients practice alcohol moderation.

Excavating the current treatments available for alcohol moderation, the book offers step-by-step processes of engaging clients and their families, self-assessments, and alcohol moderation tools. In addition to using it in conjunction with *Practicing Alcohol Moderation: A Comprehensive Workbook*, readers would benefit from the *Alcohol Moderation Assessment* which predicts who may be able to successfully drink in moderation as well as developing and monitoring an Alcohol Moderation Plan. The text uses recognized alcohol moderation resources throughout the world and real-life case studies to address typical clinician, client, and family member questions. It challenges the traditional recommendation that drinkers experiencing problems are "alcoholics."

This guide is a resource for all who overdrink or know people who struggle with their alcohol use. Through its medium, a broad range of health care providers receive a step-by-step process on how to practice alcohol moderation, how to put tools into practice, case examples, and answers to the most commonly asked questions.

Cyndi Turner, LCSW, LSATP, MAC, is the Co-Founder and Clinical Director of Insight Into Action Therapy and Insight Recovery Centers. She is a harm reduction therapist who has been in the addiction treatment field for almost three decades. Cyndi co-developed and facilitates the Dual Diagnosis Recovery Program©, is a clinical supervisor for licensure, expert witness, topic expert contributor for GoodTherapy, therapist for players involved with the NFL Program for Substances of Abuse, and is a nationally recognized trainer on alcohol moderation.

The Clinician's Guide to Alcohol Moderation

Alternative Methods and Management Techniques

Cyndi Turner

Routledge
Taylor & Francis Group

NEW YORK AND LONDON

First published 2020
by Routledge
52 Vanderbilt Avenue, New York, NY 10017

and by Routledge
2 Park Square, Milton Park, Abingdon, Oxon, OX14 4RN

Routledge is an imprint of the Taylor & Francis Group, an informa business

© 2020 Taylor & Francis

Library of Congress Cataloging-in-Publication Data
A catalog record for this book has been requested

ISBN: 978-0-367-21797-6 (hbk)
ISBN: 978-0-367-21798-3 (pbk)
ISBN: 978-0-429-26616-4 (ebk)

Typeset in Bembo
by Apex CoVantage, LLC

For those who challenge the status quo

Contents

10 Alcohol Moderation Tools

Acknowledgments

Writing can be a lonely process, but it cannot be done without the help of others. There are many who supported me along the way. I want to extend my appreciation to them here:

Thank you to my girls: Kaitlyn and Jacklyn. You knew when to leave Book Mommy alone and when to crack her up with a witty comment or help with a chore. I can't wait to see how you each will impact the world.

To my husband Mike. I appreciate your support of my writing two more books, especially when you knew what an undertaking it would be.

To Craig James, my business partner and friend of twenty years. You ran the day-to-day operations of our baby, Insight Into Action Therapy, so I could take the time to write and encouraged me when I questioned myself.

To Angie Harris, my business partner for Insight Recovery Centers. You took the lead on the startup operations of our intensive outpatient program when I was too overwhelmed to think.

To Amanda Devine, my editor at Routledge. You sought me out and asked: Do you have another book in you? And then you convinced me to write a third, *Practicing Alcohol Moderation: A Comprehensive Workbook* to accompany this one.

To the World's Greatest Beta Reader, Bill Schmidt, reader of almost 300 manuscripts, who is also my father. Your copyediting, feedback, and words of encouragement were invaluable.

Thank you to my colleagues Angie Harris and Matt Christian for your beta reading services. Angie, you reminded me of how to send my message to a skeptical audience, and Matt, your attention to detail kept my message consistent.

Chelsea Sievers of Level 27 Media: It was amazing to see how you put my words into images. Thank you for your patience with my perfectionism.

I am grateful for all of the harm reduction clinicians who have laid the groundwork before me. Your research has given validity for alcohol moderation as a more effective treatment option for the majority of those struggling with their drinking.

Dr. Bill Miller, I appreciate your taking time to comment on my manuscript and offer further research ideas and connections.

Finally, thank you to all of the clinicians who picked up this book and are willing to challenge the status quo. May you be armed with research, tools, and compassion to fight for the right kind of treatment for your clients. You have the ability to impact the lives of many.

Foreword

Cyndi Turner had an unusual advantage when she emerged with her master's degree in the 1990s to work in the alcohol treatment field: she had learned almost nothing in her training about substance use problems and addiction. So she had to rely on two old standbys—common sense, and what she knew to be true about helping people in general.

And everything these two sources of knowledge told her repudiated what she was taught to do as an alcohol treatment professional.

- Where the standard of practice in the field was to treat clients with alcohol problems as liars trying to put one over on clinicians, Cyndi knew implicitly to gain the confidence of her clients in order to form a therapeutic alliance.
- Where the main inputs from therapists were threats and scare tactics, Cyndi was nonjudgmental with and supported clients.
- Where her colleagues emphasized how badly clients had screwed up their lives, Cyndi recognized that they were at life low points and urged them to identify positives and successes.
- Where the governing therapy ideology instructed counselors and clients that their negative drinking was independent of and superseded the rest of their lives, Cyndi instead explored with clients the interplay between drinking and their overall lives.
- And where total abstinence was the *only* goal of standard treatment, Cyndi reached the obvious conclusion that drinking less and less often was an improvement worth noting, rewarding, and building upon.

In short, without realizing it, Cyndi discovered and implemented for herself every modern development in the alcohol and addiction treatment tool kit: cognitive behavior therapy, environmental support and rewards in treatment, motivational self-directed therapy, and—most remarkable of all—harm reduction, or treatment that recognizes intermediate goals in functioning other than complete abstinence.

And clients and their families quickly recognized that Cyndi was an effective helper—one who understood the value of common sense and the usefulness of ordinary therapeutic and psychological principles. You know, the truisms discarded by 12-step and disease therapy.

So, after several decades of almost practicing in hiding, Cyndi began to write about what she was doing that made such sense and worked so well. The current result is *A Clinician's Guide to Alcohol Moderation*, to share what she has discovered without requiring everyone to reinvent the wheel.

And, indeed, in reviewing decades of work on Harm Reduction and alcohol moderation, including mine and that of other psychologists like Alan Marlatt (now deceased) and Bill Miller, Cyndi realized that major research and mental health groups had been reinventing this wheel alongside her, and even decades before she started working.

It is a tribute to Cyndi's thoroughness and intellectual integrity that she summarizes the results of *every* relevant major American research project, from the Rand Report to Project MATCH to NLAES, NESARC the Substance Abuse and Mental Health Services Administration (SAMHSA), DSM-5, the National Association of Social Workers, and the Surgeon General. To find encapsulated in a clinical guide such a complete, but clear, review is a blessing to be savored.

And what does this research tell us? That people get better all the time in conducive settings with pragmatic and client-centered assistance, that this improvement covers the landscape in terms of the types of solutions people engage in, but that the changes are *real* and have a real beneficial impact for people's lives. Among the ways people improve are to abstain, to achieve genuine moderation, to drink in protected settings and in ways that reduce negative consequences such as accidents, violence, sexual assaults, lost jobs, and homelessness—as I say, the entire waterfront.

But, overall, nonabstinence solutions abound. Which is good to see and know, since relatively few people will abstain, although a vast treatment industry is organized around this artificial, difficult, and usually unobtainable goal.

Which is where Cyndi Turner has entered the fray, as a remarkable one-person counterweight to an alcoholism treatment system most notable for its ineffectuality and failure. Cyndi, in a soft-spoken, modest yet detailed way, instructs counselors, therapists and would-be helpers on how to assist people, real people, to moderate their drinking.

> While I address how much and how often my clients consume alcohol, I have found that it is much more important to explore *why* a person drinks. In that way, I avoid a power struggle and give the client real tools to manage the symptoms and struggles that are contributing to the drinking. If I look at abstinence as the primary goal and measure of success, I would be missing the underlying issues. While completely refraining from alcohol is a necessary and life-saving goal for some, many other measures for positive outcomes also exist. A different way of determining success can be seen in the way I helped a client named Sarah.

Cyndi "focused on teaching [Sarah] coping skills to manage her trauma, identifying cognitive distortions, and developing a safety plan. Once these elements were in place, alcohol was no longer a problem for her." In other words, as a sensitive therapist, she worked with her client to develop a manual for her life going forward.

Cyndi Turner is a bold advocate for people with drinking problems who is ready, willing, and able to take on the vast bureaucracies of AA, all the various outposts of the 12-step treatment industry, and the medical, brain-disease model—all of which she confronts, sympathetically but decisively, in detail.

She begins with a client-centered assessment:

> My job is to figure out where they fit and what their goals are. It's help-ful to state that just because one uses alcohol or other drugs does not mean they are an alcoholic or addict. . . . I make it clear that I don't like those words and won't use them, unless that is what they chose. They determine what alcohol means in their life. By doing this I have conveyed the message that I don't make any judgments. I also tell them that what I care most about is *why*. I want to understand why they are using alcohol and what it does for them so that we can personalize a plan for their unique situation.

Cyndi gets into every detail of the therapeutic relationship, including her own relationship with alcohol:

> I never reveal my background with alcohol or drugs. If I did, then the session becomes about me. If I say that I have had a problem, the person wonders what my recovery was like, if I am going to push my beliefs and experiences on them, or if I am healthy enough to help them. If I say that I did not have a problem, I run the danger of their think-ing I will judge them or could not understand their experience. The therapy is about them, not me.

Cyndi then details every aspect of her therapeutic interaction with clients. This is a manual that finds no detail, no feeling, no aspect of the counseling relationship too small or insignificant to consider. *It is a true user's guide for counselors in alcohol moderation.*

Included in her approach is a four-month period of abstinence. Among other purposes, this offers people a chance to discover living:

> The idea is to get out and do something. People may not like nine out of ten things they try, but the tenth one may become a new hobby or passion, and they may make some great friends along the way. As a therapist, one of the few times I give homework is to have fun. I require my clients to pick an activity and report back. Many struggle with this, but once they do something, their happiness is priceless.

No aspect of the moderation counseling process is left unexamined. This includes involving the family, the people most impacted by the client and their drinking. As with every aspect of this process, Cyndi presents a detailed self-care plan. She leaves no stone unturned.

In this remarkable document, Cyndi Turner takes on the world. Rather, she takes on a range of worlds: the world of alcoholism treatment, the world of research on alcohol problems, the therapeutic world, worldwide drinking—and, most importantly, the world (or worlds) her drinking clients face.

She is their advocate, their helper, their appreciator, and their biggest rooter. She is not their savior. But by following her manual, individual counselors can rescue themselves from decades of America's futility in dealing with people's alcohol and related problems. Indeed, the guide Cyndi Turner provides can serve as a manual for the entire world of addiction provider services.

And we'd be a better society if Cyndi Turner's guide were implemented society wide.

Stanton Peele, PhD
Founder of the online Life Process Program for addiction coaching
Author (with Zach Rhoads) of *Outgrowing Addiction: With
Common Sense Instead of "Disease" Therapy*

Introduction

I didn't know that I was practicing harm reduction. I was just doing what worked for my clients. Having completed my master's degree in the 1990s, I didn't learn much about substance use disorders. The little that I was taught was that people who use drugs or alcohol are "addicted", need inpatient treatment, should go to Alcoholics Anonymous (AA), and had to admit that they were powerless. If they did not do these things, they were in denial and had to hit bottom before they could be helped.

To earn my degree, I had to complete two year-long internships. The first one was in a county mental health agency. There I learned how to complete assessments. My supervisor told me that my clients were liars and that I should double or quadruple how much they told me they were drinking. The next year I interned in a hospital-based setting. My job was to educate the "lying addicts" about how bad the drugs and alcohol they were using was for them. The idea was that if they just knew how bad it was, they would stop. I did not feel right for two years. I couldn't believe how I was being asked to interact with people who were at one of the worst points in their lives. I questioned my career choice.

Once I completed graduate school, I spent six years working at a group practice that treated adolescents, young adults, and adults who had court involvement as a result of their substance use. Here my job was to remind them about the bad choices they made and how it was only going to get worse if they did not stop using drugs and alcohol. My co-counselor's job seemed to be to catch them in a lie and threaten to tell their parents or probation officers. If my clients got better, it was only out of fear and for a short period. I focused my individual sessions on my clients' goals. We talked about their substance use, but in a nonthreatening, exploratory way. I did not judge, but offered a different perspective when they seemed open to it. My clients started getting better. My supervisor wondered what I was doing.

After becoming a Licensed Clinical Social Worker and Licensed Substance Abuse Treatment Practitioner, I began seeing clients in a private practice setting. There was less paperwork, fewer rules and regulations, and no one to report to as long as I was practicing within my ethics and licensing guidelines. I talked to my clients like people, not as criminals whom I had to convince that they had to stop what they were doing. I found that mostly people were at a low point in their lives and were using alcohol to cope. I got to know who they were, outside of their substance use. When we did introductions in the groups I lead, I began asking them to end on something positive, like a skill they had or something they were proud of. I was shocked: uncomfortable silence. Nothing from this cocky 17-year-old who came off like he did not have a care in the world? The young adult said everything was fine in his life, except for getting caught. Why couldn't the adult who seemed to have it all say something good about herself? Many of them had been in other programs and attended self-help meetings. They were used to being seen as the screw-up and accepting a label that was fraught with stigma and negative messaging. Something was very wrong. I could see the good in each person, but they were conditioned not to. That is not what treatment is supposed to do.

Those who had been in multiple programs seemed to have the lowest views of themselves. I praised them when they went from drinking every day to a few times a week. I asked how they did it when they cut their alcohol use in half. The voices of past supervisors said I should discharge them: you can't drink while in treatment. But my internal voice knew that this was the very reason that they were in my office. I could not turn them away.

As a result of my more accepting approach, celebrating successes, and willingness to understand why people drank, many of my clients voluntarily continued therapy with me. Once they satisfied their court, job, parent, or spouse requirements, they would ask me: Can I keep drinking? Instinctively I knew that many of them could consume alcohol without consequences. Some needed a few modifications. But isn't that what therapy is for?

I felt like I was practicing in secret. I even wondered if I was doing something wrong. But thousands of people who first entered my office depressed, unhealthy, and ashamed were now happier and more productive. And many of them continued to drink alcohol, although in a much different way from when they started.

Can someone who experienced a problem with alcohol keep drinking? Can they drink at a level that does not cause them problems?

About ten years ago I decided that there must be a way to determine this. I began doing research and developed the *How Do I Know if I Can Keep Drinking Quiz*. Professionals who referred their clients to me for alcohol treatment were wondering what I was doing as their clients were experiencing positive change. Clients sent their friends, family members, and neighbors. The individuals and families that I was working with asked me for more, so I wrote *Can I Keep Drinking? How You Can Decide When Enough Is Enough*.

After practicing for nearly two decades, almost in secret, going against the traditional treatment model, I found out that I'm not alone! There was even a name for what I was doing: harm reduction! I knew I needed to educate others. The people I was working with were getting better. Why isn't everyone doing this?

The first book was published in 2016. I wanted to educate and train others who had likely received old-school training. What I was doing was working. Why isn't alcohol moderation being taught in graduate programs and medical schools? Why are there no continuing education credits on this?

I began submitting proposals to speak at local and national conferences. I was rejected more times than accepted. The rejections often stated that there was not enough research. Not true. Harm reduction has been widely studied, researched, and accepted in other countries for decades. Even though the United States is one of the richest and most educated countries in the world, it is archaic in how drug and alcohol use is treated. The rejections also said that alcohol moderation was not appropriate for addiction. My point exactly! We need to treat the whole spectrum of alcohol use. What about those dealing with mild to moderate alcohol use disorders? There are four times as many people struggling with their alcohol use as there are those dealing with an addiction.

I found that little information and few tools on alcohol moderation exist. With the new addition of the *Diagnostic and Statistical Manual of Mental Disorders-5* now diagnosing substance use on a spectrum, my argument is that treatment needs to occur on a spectrum as well. Why are clinicians taught only how to deal with the most serious alcohol user?

A goal of this book is to give you the history of how harm reduction came about and why many won't accept it as a viable treatment option. You will learn how to determine who is a candidate for alcohol moderation, how to develop a moderation plan, and how to practice the tools.

Get ready for a paradigm shift in the way you treat alcohol use disorders. You will learn the skills to help individuals get the right kind of treatment.

1 Recovery

What's Missing?

How do you define recovery? Well, it depends upon who you ask.

A primary care doctor might say that it is giving the body time to heal after an illness, injury, or surgery. If you are a behavioral health care provider, your response will likely have more to do with substance use disorders. You may even include mental health disorders and the impact on the family. If an individual just completed an inpatient treatment program, a primary counselor might say that it is what you do to "stay clean." A discharge planner might say that recovery involves not using drugs or alcohol and going to AA meetings. Some might include going to an intensive outpatient treatment program or sober living house. The individual's response will be influenced by the treatment program. Family members' definition may be affected by what they read on the internet. Those who participate in mutual support meetings usually define recovery through abstinence from the substances that rendered them powerless.

What does recovery mean to you?

In 2011, the Substance Abuse and Mental Health Services Administration (SAMHSA) announced its definition of recovery:

> A process of change through which individuals improve their health and wellness, live self-directed lives, and strive to reach their full potential.[1]

Have you noticed what is missing?

The 2016 Surgeon General's Report on Alcohol, Drugs, and Health says that there are numerous definitions of recovery in relation to substance use disorders. The report states:

> All agree that recovery goes beyond remission of symptoms . . . "abstinence" though often necessary, is not always sufficient to define recovery.[2]

There it is. Abstinence from alcohol or drugs is not necessary to be in recovery! This is such a controversial topic in the field that this concept is rarely taught in schools, presented at conferences, or available as continuing education. Most people assume that in order to be in recovery, you cannot use alcohol or drugs. Did your definition include something about substances?

I cannot stress enough that experts agree that abstinence from mood-altering substances is a factor in recovery but is not sufficient to define recovery.

Get ready for a paradigm shift—specifically, a shift that should change the way you work with people who struggle with alcohol use. You have an opportunity to help many more people with the methods you will learn about in this book. But, before we do that, we need to look backward before we can move forward.

As I mentioned in the Introduction, I have successfully been treating thousands of individuals with alcohol moderation. But I don't want you to take my experiences as the foundation for why it works. I want to give you a brief summary of the research from the last 50 years. You may have a negative reaction. I know I did.

RAND Reports

The concept of alcohol moderation as a viable treatment was first introduced in 1976. Have you ever heard of the RAND Corporation studies? I've been in the addiction treatment field for over 25 years, earned two degrees, and complete 70 hours of continuing education to maintain my two licenses and national certification. I just stumbled across them as I was researching for this book.

The RAND Corporation completed the first report in the early 1970s. RAND is an acronym for "Research and Development." The study was funded by the National Institute for Alcohol Abuse and Addiction (NIAAA). They studied over 2,000 men who had been patients at 44 NIAAA funded treatment centers. They found that after 18 months of treatment, approximately 22% of the men were consuming alcohol at moderate levels. The researchers concluded that it was possible for some alcohol-dependent people to return to non-problem drinking.[3,4]

The results caused so much controversy that attempts were made to discredit the study. Thomas Pike, a board member of the National Council on Alcoholism, attempted to have the report suppressed. A press conference was held on July 1, 1976, condemning the outcomes. The NIAAA's rationale was that if "alcoholics" heard these results, they would be lead to relapse and death. So they hid scientific results.[5,6]

Are you angry? I am. This feels like censorship. Shouldn't we allow people self-determination? They took away the opportunity to have a discussion with individuals who were struggling with their drinking and to provide education. Think of how many people continued to suffer because we were not given an opportunity to learn about these results. We were not allowed to be trained in a viable treatment option. Many people avoid getting help because they are not ready to give up alcohol for the rest of their lives.

Due to the enormous amount of controversy and attacks on its validity regarding the original RAND Report, a second set of studies was completed and released in 1981. Over this four-year study, the researchers responded to all of the criticisms. They broadened the study, increased the sample size, refined definitions, analyzed subgroups, and increased the time the subjects were studied. The researchers upheld their original findings that controlled drinking is viable for all types of drinkers.[7]

The most egregious event that happened regarding the reports was that the Director of the NIAAA, John DeLuca, and his assistant, Loran Archer, gave their summary of the results. They stated that abstinence should be the goal of treatment and that AA participation gave the best prognosis. Neither of these were in the report's results, and neither of those two were researchers qualified to interpret the data.[8]

Sobell Study

In the 1970s addiction researchers Drs. Linda and Mark Sobell conducted one of the most controversial studies regarding controlled drinking. They compared two types of treatments. One group received a behavior modification program that focused on moderation. The other group received the standard hospital-based treatment of the time that had a goal of abstinence. They published their results, along with one- and two-year follow-ups. They found that the moderation group functioned better than those in the abstinence group. The Sobells found that with a brief intervention that focused on teaching moderation skills, alcohol-dependent users could safely attempt controlled drinking.[9]

The treatment community was so outraged that the Sobells were attacked for years. An article in *Science* received attention in the treatment community as well as the general media. The results were so shocking that the Sobells were accused of fraud.[10] However, in 1982, the prestigious Addiction Research Foundation of Ontario (now part of the Centre for Addictions and Mental Health) and four additional panels cleared them of all fraud or wrongdoing, finding their studies to be accurate.[11]

G. Alan Marlatt

Throughout the 1980s G. Alan Marlatt, one of the most respected addiction researchers of our time, pointed out that providers are treating alcohol use as a progressive disease that can only be treated with abstinence. He fought public opinion about how people struggling with alcohol problems should be treated. He pushed for effective treatment to be the criteria for obtaining funding for programs and recommended early intervention. Marlatt also encouraged the use of the term *moderation training* rather than *controlled or responsible drinking* as a way to combat stigma related to alcohol use.[12]

Project MATCH

Project MATCH was one of the largest and most expensive studies ever completed on alcohol treatment. It was funded by the NIAAA and cost over US$30 million. The hypothesis was that matching patient characteristics to the type of treatment would yield better outcomes. The study compared three types of treatment: Cognitive Behavioral Therapy, Motivational Enhancement Therapy, and 12-Step facilitation (Alcoholics Anonymous).[13] All participants were voluntary. Given that all participants were receiving treatment, the validity of the study was later questioned as there was no control group.[14]

The results found no significant difference between the three treatment modalities. The misinterpreted message that came out of the study was that treatment works. As a result, government agencies began promoting: Treatment Works! Months. AA was lumped into the group with the assumption that if treatment works, AA must also work. Many have mistakenly quoted Project MATCH as a way to show the efficacy of AA, but that argument is based on a misinterpretation of data.[15]

Box Matter 1.1

DID YOU KNOW? It is illegal to require individuals to attend Alcoholics Anonymous meetings. In 2007, the Ninth Circuit Court of Appeals ruled that it was unconstitutional for judges to mandate that people attend 12-step meetings. The ruling was based on the Establishment Clause of the U.S. Constitution, which is referred to as the separation of church and state.[16]

Effectiveness of Alcoholics Anonymous

Since the mid-1930s when AA was founded, it has been the go-to recommendation for individuals struggling with alcohol use. Doctors, judges, probation officers, treatment providers, and lay people all recommend it as if it is the one and only treatment that can save drinkers. The program is a lifesaver for many. I recommend the program as an option for some of my clients, not as a requirement. However, there is little scientific evidence to support its efficacy.

In 2006, the Cochrane Collaboration, a health care research group, reviewed studies going back to the 1960s. They concluded that there were no studies that demonstrated the effectiveness of AA for reducing alcohol dependence.[17]

In his controversial book, Lance Dodes, MD, a Harvard University psychiatry professor, found that AA is helpful only about 5–10% of the time.

He states that it is the camaraderie that AA offers, not necessarily the 12 steps, that is helpful. He points out that if the success rate is 5–10%, we may actually be harming 90% of people by forcing them to attend meetings.[18]

Longtime experts in the field, Drs. Hester and Miller studied the top alcohol treatments. They came up with a list of almost 50 different methods. The doctors focus on the need for providers to practice with "informed eclecticism." This means that clinicians should have a spectrum of treatment approaches that are matched to the client's needs. There is no one-size-fits-all, or even ones that fit most. Their evidence shows that the most effective treatments include honest but non-confrontational feedback from a health professional about alcohol use, medication such as Acamprosate or Naltrexone, Motivational Interviewing, and moderation training. AA is at the bottom of the list, ranking 38th out of 48 treatment approaches. Some of the approaches that rank worse than AA include seeing a video of oneself while intoxicated, watching educational programs, and confrontational techniques.[19]

Keep in mind that AA is not treatment. While the 12 steps are helpful in addressing problematic behavior, the program does not treat the underlying reasons of why a person might be using alcohol. It is a peer-led program by individuals who are also struggling with their alcohol use with no oversight.

Institute of Medicine

In 1990 the Institute of Medicine of the National Academy of Sciences performed a study to explore the effectiveness of how systems were dealing with alcohol problems. The report indicated that for every one person dealing with an addiction to alcohol, there were three people who were experiencing serious health problems as a result of their drinking. They realized that the majority of drinkers could stop or moderate their consumption if they were given a brief education and tools to do so. The report also noted that the majority of treatment programs required total abstinence, but that this did not make sense for 75% of the population experiencing problems related to their alcohol use. The report called for more programs for those experiencing problems.[20] Over 30 years later, little has changed in the treatment community. Most treatment is still geared for the most severe alcohol user.

National Longitudinal Alcohol Epidemiological Study

The National Longitudinal Alcohol Epidemiological Study (NLAES) was conducted by the U.S. Bureau of the Census. They wanted to determine outcomes for individuals who had met criteria for alcohol dependence. It was a large study, with 4,585 adults that included alcohol users who had been alcohol dependent at one time in their lives, from recent use to as long as 20 years in the past. They found that more than half (57.8%) of participants were able to change their patterns so that they no longer met criteria for alcohol abuse or dependence.[21]

This again should have changed the way we treat alcohol use disorders. More than half of the most severe alcohol users can moderate their drinking. This is challenging, as the desire of many drinkers is to be able to keep drinking. Many of my clients have said: "I want to be normal." What they mean is that they want to be able to drink like most people do—being able to stop at having one or two and not have any consequences from their alcohol use. It is a simple solution to tell an alcohol-dependent drinker that they should never drink again. It takes a lot more work, skill level, and risk tolerance to work with an alcohol user to find the solution that works for his or her unique situation.

World Health Organization

The World Health Organization (WHO) performed a study on 1,490 heavy but non-dependent drinkers at ten different locations around the world. They wanted to see the impact of a brief intervention on drinking habits. After receiving an assessment, participants received education about alcohol. Nine months after the intervention, drinkers reduced their consumption by about a third.[22] This again shows that with information, most drinkers can bring their drinking patterns to safer levels.

NESARC Study

The National Epidemiologic Survey on Alcohol and Related Conditions (NESARC) is the largest and most comprehensive look at alcohol use in the United States. They conducted a yearly survey of 43,000 people age 18 and older from 2001 to 2005. The findings should have changed the way we treat alcohol use disorders.

The results indicate that most drinkers can change their drinking habits with non-confrontational education about the risks and impact of their alcohol use. Most people who use alcohol will never reach the point of addiction. With information, most individuals can make informed choices about their consumption, make lifestyle changes, and reduce the consequences of their alcohol use.[23]

The most significant result from the study was that while 30% of adults will experience an alcohol use disorder at some point in their lives, about 70% of them will be able to return to safe consumption patterns.[24]

Doctor Recommendations

Since 2000 the NIAAA has recommended to physicians that they direct patients to one of two goals when patients express concerns about their drinking: abstinence if they are dependent on alcohol and moderation if they are not.[25] It is interesting that this recommendation has been around for decades, yet it is rare for a clinician to be trained in or ever be aware of alcohol moderation as a treatment option.

The United States is decades behind other countries on this approach. Parts of Europe and Canada have been practicing moderation, while much of the United States believes that alcohol is so dangerous that abstinence is the only option.

National Association of Social Workers

In 2014, the National Association of Social Workers (NASW) put out the NASW Standards for Social Work Practice for Clients with Substance Use Disorders. They clearly state that in accordance with the *Diagnostic and Statistical Manual of Mental Disorders* (5th edition), substance use is no longer viewed as an either/or phenomenon, that it is viewed as existing along a continuum. And—wait for it—"the harm reduction approach is consistent with the social work value of self-determination and 'meeting the client where the client is.'"[26] Skeptics of moderation accuse me of being unethical. In reality, those who do not practice harm reduction may be violating their code of ethics.

Surgeon General's Report on Alcohol, Drugs, and Health

In 2016 the Surgeon General came out with a groundbreaking report, *Facing Addiction: The Surgeon General's Report on Alcohol, Drugs, and Health.* In addition to removing abstinence as a requirement for recovery, there were many significant findings.[27] The report definitively states that there are many paths to recovery. It recognizes that people chose their path based on many factors, including cultural values, socioeconomic status, psychological needs, the severity of their substance use disorder, and age.

The report included a special section entitled "Key Findings: Recovery: The Many Paths to Wellness." As a treatment provider for a quarter of a century, I cannot stress how significant this is. It should change the way we educate and treat people with alcohol use disorders. The report noted that recovery should be person driven, that individuals define their own goals and unique paths.[28] People should not have to fit into a program. Rather, the program should be designed for their individualized needs.

One of the key findings is that remission, defined as the reduction of symptoms from the diagnostic threshold for substance use disorders, is more common than was traditionally thought. Evidence shows that about 50% of adults who once met criteria for a substance use disorder are currently in stable remission.[29] In the United States, this is approximately 25 million people! Remission can take several years, with multiple episodes of treatment and levels of support. Many mistakenly believe that residential treatment is the cure, yet ongoing outpatient treatment is often what is most effective in the long run.

You may have heard the term that alcohol use is "chronic, progressive, and fatal." It can be, but only for a very small percentage of the population. There is great fear that if we teach alcohol moderation, drinkers will get out of control. This is the same mistaken belief regarding teaching safer sex practices. The fear there was that if we teach young people about using condoms, it will put sex into their brains and they will go out and have intercourse. Education does not make people engage in behaviors. It keeps them safer if they chose to do so.

An additional finding was that alcohol misuse and alcohol use disorders can be easily identified through screening and that less severe forms can be addressed through brief interventions.[30] The Surgeon General gives us evidence that less severe alcohol use should be dealt with in outpatient settings; yet when most providers hear that someone is struggling with alcohol, they recommend abstinence and AA. Why are providers still giving this recommendation? Most people know they are not "alcoholic", so they avoid all forms of treatment. Health care professionals need to meet the person where they are and tailor the treatment to their needs. There is a huge gap between the traditional recommendation and the actual need. Why does this still occur?

The Surgeon General defined a recovery-oriented system of care. This includes a network of services to address the full spectrum of substance use problems. Consumers should have a menu of treatments that include alternative treatments and services.[31] Why is alcohol moderation not more widely taught?

Think about what you were taught in school. Is your clinical practice accommodating these findings?

There are several reasons why abstinence remains the status quo. The reasons should make you question how your chosen profession is being represented in the larger population.

A $35 Billion Industry

Addiction treatment is a $35 billion industry. Private equity firms, venture capitalists, and all levels of investors all view addiction treatment as a lucrative place to put their money. There are two main reasons why the industry is seen as a desirable investment.[32] One is due to the Mental Health Parity Act of 2008, which required insurance companies to offer the same benefits for behavioral health care as they do for physical health care. The other reason is Obamacare, where more people have health insurance. Both ensure a diversified revenue stream from multiple payors for the facility owners. The goal of many investors is to purchase smaller companies, centralize and automatize the process, and then sell it as a larger company as a lucrative exit strategy. But we are working with people in crisis, not a product that can be made cheaper.

An additional reason why addiction treatment is seen as a desirable investment sector is because the consumer is dealing with a potentially relapsing condition that may require multiple treatment episodes with several levels of care. The longer someone stays in treatment and the higher the level of care, the greater return the investor earns on his or her money. It pays more to label someone an "alcoholic." The "alcoholic" needs detoxification and residential treatment that requires 24/7 care. They will then step down from this level of treatment and go to partial hospitalization for a few weeks, then intensive outpatient for several months, then outpatient for longer. Investors see long-term use of their services, which equals larger profit.

In subsequent chapters I will show how there are about four times as many people dealing with a mild to moderate alcohol use disorder than a severe one. Alcohol moderation does not yield a good return for investors as it can be treated on an outpatient basis. The money is in the severe alcohol user who uses the services listed in the above example.

Why Alcohol Moderation Is Not Practiced

Practicing alcohol moderation requires a flexible professional. The clinician must be able to practice a variety of treatment modalities and be trained in mental health as well as substance use disorders. The provider is adapting the treatment to the consumer, not the consumer morphing to the program. It is easy to say that a client must be alcohol free. That's a clear goal. There are rules, and the consumer is supposed to follow them. With alcohol moderation, the goal changes based on what the client desires. The practitioner who supports alcohol moderation does not give up. They find another way to reach the person. They don't kick people out of treatment because they continue to drink or have a relapse. The provider must be compassionate yet direct. He or she needs to be able to tolerate risk, as clients often continue their alcohol use despite consequences.

Education

It is easier to teach a method that has clear rules and guidelines. New clinicians want to know "how" to provide therapy. It's overwhelming to realize that it takes years to learn the nuances of working with people. I believe that this is why so many are taught that if a person drinks, they are an "alcoholic" who needs abstinence and AA. It is much harder to teach students that if a person drinks, the steps you take depend on many factors. The client will be in charge of the treatment, and it is your job to help them reach the goals they define.

Challenging a Higher Power

AA has been the primary recommendation for individuals struggling with alcohol use for decades. It is a spiritually based program. To challenge a recommendation that relies on a Higher Power is akin to challenging God. It is hard to challenge the status quo; it is even harder when challenging it is akin to heresy.

Call for Change

It is time that we get people the right kind of treatment. For over 50 years, research has shown us that alcohol moderation is an effective treatment option. New clinicians need to learn the tools to practice it effectively. Read on to learn how to practice alcohol moderation.

Notes

1. Substance Abuse and Mental Health Services Administration (2012, February). *What's recovery? SAMHSA's working definition.* Publication ID: PEP12-RECDEF.
2. U.S. Department of Health and Human Services, Office of the Surgeon General (2016, November). *Facing addiction in America: The surgeon general's report on alcohol, drugs, and health.* Washington, DC: Health and Human Services.
3. H. B. Braiker & M. J. Polich (1977). *Some implications of the RAND alcoholism and treatment study for alcoholism research.* Santa Monica, CA: RAND Corporation.
4. R. Hodgson (1979, October). Much ado about nothing much: Alcoholism treatment and the rand report. *The British Journal of Addiction to Alcohol and Other Drugs.* 74(3): 227–234. DOI: 10.1111/j.1360-0443.1979.tb01343.x.
5. D. J. Armor, M. J. Polich & H. B. Braiker (1976). *Alcoholism and treatment.* Santa Monica, CA: RAND Corporation.
6. S. Peele (1997, September 16). *A brief history of the national council on alcoholism through pictures.* Amsterdam: The Stanton Peele Addiction Website.
7. S. Peele (1996). Denial—of reality and of freedom—in addiction research and treatment. *Bulletin of the Society of Psychologists in Addictive Behaviors.* 5(4): 149–166.
8. J. E. Brody (1980, January 30). Drinking problem dispute. *New York Times,* p. 20.
9. M. B. Sobell & L. C. Sobell (1973). Individualized behavior therapy for alcoholics. *Behavior Therapy.* 4(1): 49–72.
10. M. L. Pedery, I. M. Maltzman & L. J. West (1982, July 9). Controlled drinking by alcoholics? New findings and a reevaluation of a major affirmative study. *Science.* 217(4555): 169–175. DOI: 10.1126/science.7089552.
11. M. B. Sobell & L. C. Sobell (1984). The aftermath of the heresy: A response to Pendery et al.'s 1982 critique of "Individualized behavior therapy for alcoholics." *Behavior and Research Therapy.* 22(4): 413–440. https://doi.org/10.1016/0005-7967(84)90084-6.
12. G. A. Marlatt (1987). Research and political realities: What the next twenty years hold for behaviorists in the alcohol field. *Advances in Behavior Research and Therapy.* 9(2–3): 165–171. https://doi.org/10.1016/0146-6402(87)90013-0.
13. Project MATCH Research Group (1997). Matching alcoholism treatments to client heterogeneity: Project MATCH posttreatment drinking outcomes. *Journal of Studies on Alcohol.* 58: 7–29.
14. R. Cutler & D. A. Fishbian (2005). Are alcoholism treatments effective? The Project MATCH data. *BMC Public Health.* 5(75). https://doi.org/10.1186/1471-2458-5-75.
15. S. Peele (1997, May–June 2). Bait and switch in project MATCH: What NIAAA research actually shows about alcohol treatment. *Psych News International.* (2) Retrieved from https://peele.net/lib/projmach.html.
16. B. Egelko (2007, September 8). Appeals court say requirement to attend AA unconstitutional. *San Francisco Chronicle.* Retrieved from https://www.sfgate.com/bayarea/article/Appeals-court-says-requirement-to-attend-AA-2542005.php.

17. F. M. Amato & M. Davioli (2006). Alcoholics anonymous and other 12-step programmes for alcohol dependence. *Cochran Database of Systemic Reviews*. (3). Art. No:CD005032. DOI: 10.1002/14651858.CD005032.pub2.

18. L. Dodes & Z. Dodes (2015). *The sober truth: Debunking the bad science behind 12-step programs and the rehab industry*. Boston, MA: Beacon Press.

19. R. K. Hester & W. R. Miller (2002). *Handbook of alcoholism treatment approaches: Effective alternative* (3rd ed.). Needham Heights, MA: Allyn & Bacon.

20. Institute of Medicine (IOM) (1990). *Broadening the base of treatment for alcohol problems: Report of a study by a committee of the institute of medicine, division of mental health and behavioral medicine*. Washington, DC: National Academy Press.

21. B. F. Grant (1997). Prevalence and correlates of alcohol use and DSM-IV alcohol dependent in the United States: Results of the national longitudinal alcohol epidemiologic survey. *Journal of Studies on Alcohol*. 58(5): 464–473.

22. World Health Organization Brief Intervention Study Group (1996). A cross-national trial of brief intervention with heavy drinkers. *American Journal of Public Health*. 86: 948–955.

23. D. A. Dawson (1996). Correlates of past-year status among treated and untreated persons with former alcohol dependence: United States. *Alcoholism: Clinical and Experimental Research*. 20(4): 771–779.

24. Hasin, D. S. & Grant, B. F. (2015). The national epidemiologic survey on alcohol and related conditions (NESARC) waves 1 and 2: Review and summary of findings. *Social Psychiatry and Psychiatric Epidemiology*. 50(11): 1609–1640.

25. Hasin, D. S., F. S. Stinson, E. Ogburn & B. F. Grant (2007). Prevalence, correlates, disability, and comorbidity of DSM-IV alcohol abuse and dependence in the United States: Results from the national epidemiologic survey on alcohol and related conditions. *Archives of General Psychiatry*. 64(7): 830–842.

26. National Association of Social Workers (2013). *NASW standards for social work practice for clients with substance use disorders*. Washington, DC: National Association of Social Workers.

27. U.S. Department of Health and Human Services, Office of the Surgeon General (2016, November). *Facing addiction in America: The surgeon general's report on alcohol, drugs, and health*. Washington, DC: Health and Human Services.

28. *Ibid.*

29. *Ibid.*

30. *Ibid.*

31. *Ibid.*

32. A. Kodjak (2016, June 16). Inventors see big opportunities in opioid addiction treatment. *NPR*. Retrieved from www.npr.org/sections/health-shots/2016/06/10/480663056/investors-see-big-opportunities-in-opioid-addiction-treatment.

2 What Is Alcohol Moderation?

Alcohol Moderation Defined

Alcohol moderation has been called low-risk drinking, controlled drinking, and moderate drinking. There are several definitions, all very similar:

The U.S. Department of Health and Human Services and the U.S. Department of Agriculture Dietary Guidelines for Americans 2015–2020 states that moderate drinking is up to one drink a day for women and up to two drinks a day for men.[1] They further stress that individuals should be: of legal drinking age; not pregnant; not planning to drive or participate in activities that require skill, coordination, or alertness; not suffering from certain medical conditions; and able to control the amount they drink.

The American Heart Association's Guidelines recommend an average of no more than two standard drinks per day (28 g/day) for men and no more than one standard drink/day (14 g/day) for women.[2]

The National Institute for Alcohol Abuse and Alcoholism's (NIAAA) definition of low-risk guidelines for alcohol is: no more than three drinks at a time for women/four for men with no more than 14 drinks a week for women and 21 drinks a week for men.[3]

Most countries around the world agree that a low level of alcohol on a healthy adult carries minimal risks. Alcohol in Moderation compiled a worldwide list of Sensible Drinking Guidelines put forth by each country's public health department of their government.[4] In general, they all support the idea that healthy adult men should have no more than two drinks a day, while women should have no more than one in a day, and none if pregnant or breastfeeding. Some countries such as Indonesia and India recommend avoiding alcohol altogether, while Belgium, Malta, and New Zealand recommend some days of abstinence a week, and Mexico recommends drinking with food.

People may wonder how these guidelines are developed. Experts review data regarding alcohol consumption and then analyze the negative outcomes. The data encompasses hundreds of studies on tens of thousands of people over a period of years. These outcomes are grouped into chronic

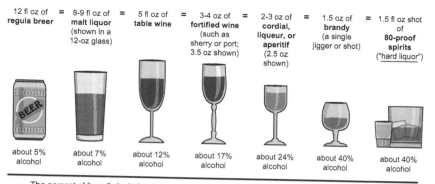

The percent of "pure" alcohol, expressed here as alcohol by volume(alc/vol), varies by beverage.

Figure 2.1 What counts as a drink?

and acute. The chronic outcomes analyze the long-term effects of alcohol use on disease, mortality, income, and quality of life. The acute outcomes look at the effects of being intoxicated, such as accidents, injury, sexual assault, and aggression. The overall data are then based on the normal distribution curve that predicts that 68% of the population will fall within one standard deviation on each side of the mean. The recommendations are based not on emotion or opinion but on the statistical analysis of large amounts of data.[5]

Moderation Management (MM) is a behavioral change program and support group network for people who are concerned about their drinking and want to make positive lifestyle changes. The program is supported by the National Institute for Alcohol Abuse and Alcoholism and is listed on SAMHSA's National Registry of Evidence-Based Programs and Practices (NREPP). MM defines a moderate drinker as someone with the following characteristics:

- Considers an occasional drink to be a small, though enjoyable, part of life.
- Has hobbies, interests, and other ways to relax and enjoy life that do not involve alcohol.
- Usually has friends who are moderate drinking or nondrinkers.
- Usually does not drink for longer than an hour or two in any particular occasion.
- Usually does not exceed the 0.055 percent BAC (blood alcohol concentration) drinking limit.
- Usually does not drink faster than one drink per half hour.
- Feels comfortable with his or her use of alcohol, never drinking in secret or spending a lot of time thinking about drinking or planning to drink.[6]

Four to One

In 2019, the U.S. Census Bureau recorded approximately 329 million people living in the country.[7] Studies show that the majority of individuals (seven of ten adults) drink at low-risk levels, with 37% always drinking at low risk and 35% not drinking at all.[8] They point out that about one-third of the population consumes alcohol at levels that put them at risk of alcohol-related consequences. It is important to note that while 28% of the population is drinking at risky levels, only about 6% is drinking to the point that they would meet DSM-5 criteria for a severe alcohol use disorder.[9] The other 22% falls into the mild to moderate (AUD) category where there is a dearth of treatment options.

To put these numbers in perspective: 6% of the American population is about 20 million people—enough to fill the entire state of Florida. While that is a huge number, the majority of treatment is geared for them. However, an even more staggering number is 22%. That 22%

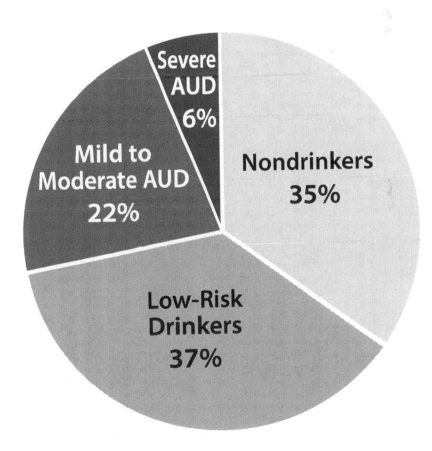

Figure 2.2 Four to One

represents the number of people who are struggling with a mild to moderate alcohol use disorder. This represents over 70 million individuals. That's about the amount of United States residents who live in the Central Time Zone.

I ask you to do simple math. Why is most treatment focused on the much smaller number of 20 million, and not the 80 million? This is what is happening in the treatment community. The training, education, funding, and facilities focus on the more severe user, leaving those who are not physically dependent on alcohol with few treatment options.

Many people avoid seeking help because they do not want to be labeled as an "alcoholic", attend AA meetings, or accept abstinence as the sole goal of treatment. Giving up drinking is not the only answer for dealing with alcohol-related problems. We need to offer more options. It is especially important to address our clients' mental health and environmental factors. If we only focus on alcohol as the issue, we are providing inadequate treatment.

The Importance of Why

While I address how much and how often my clients consume alcohol, I have found that it is much more important to explore *why* a person drinks. In that way, I avoid a power struggle and give the client real tools to manage the symptoms and struggles that are contributing to the drinking. If I look at abstinence as the primary goal and measure of success, I would be missing the underlying issues. While completely refraining from alcohol is a necessary and life-saving goal for some, many other measures for positive outcomes also exist. A different way of determining success can be seen in the way I helped a client named Sarah.

Sarah was a 22-year-old college senior who had been charged with two citations for being drunk in public and was on academic suspension for a low grade point average. Some treatment providers would look at her drinking as the problem. However, upon completing a thorough mental health and substance-use-disorders evaluation, I discovered that Sarah had been sexually assaulted in her freshman year but had never told anyone about it. She was using alcohol to deal with her post-traumatic stress symptoms of insomnia, anxiety, and hypervigilance. Drinking a few beers helped her to fall asleep and not worry about the recurring nightmares of the assault. Taking a few shots before a social gathering helped her forget how anxious she was around the opposite sex, where she now felt all men were predators.

Rather than placing Sarah in the typical mixed-gender substance use education group, I had her participate in several months of individual therapy with me. Our sessions focused on teaching her coping skills to manage the trauma, identifying cognitive distortions, and developing a safety plan. Once these elements were in place, alcohol was no longer a problem for her.

Had Sarah enrolled in a traditional treatment program, she may have been required to attend AA meetings, where she could have become a victim of "thirteenth stepping." This is a practice where some men in AA meetings prey upon vulnerable women and encourage sexual activity as a distraction from alcohol. Additionally, well-intentioned members who mistakenly focused only on her drinking as the problem rather than addressing the trauma she had experienced would have further exacerbated her victim role. This young woman could have walked away with a label that would not have addressed the underlying issues. Instead, through individual therapy she developed other coping skills that dealt with the mental health issues that were causing her to drink.

Spectrum of Alcohol Use

Whenever I begin a substance-use-disorders evaluation, I let my clients and their family members know that I believe in a spectrum of alcohol use. Not everyone who drinks alcohol and experienced a consequence has an alcohol use disorder (AUD). Most people fall on a continuum of alcohol use throughout their lifespans. An increase in alcohol use is typically gradual. No one becomes an "alcoholic" on their first sip.

No Alcohol Use: On one end of the spectrum of use are people who do not drink at all. As noted previously, more than 35% of people do not drink any alcohol at all. Some people just don't like the effect, feel out of control when drinking, have had a family member with a drinking problem, don't want the calories, or feel it is against their religious beliefs or negatively affects their health.

Experimental Use: This first stage is often driven by the curiosity of what alcohol does and what it tastes like. This often occurs during the teenage years. First-time alcohol users often want to see what all the fuss is about. After trying alcohol, some people decide they can take it or leave it. Others will have too much, pray to the "porcelain god," and not drink again for a long period of time, having gained a better understanding of their limits.

A very small percentage of first-time drinkers will describe their first intoxication as "meeting my best friend," "finding the answer to my problems," or "something I couldn't wait to do again." It is like flipping a switch in the brain where it continues to seek the same pleasurable response. This group of drinkers may experience addiction if their alcohol use continues. The experimental use of alcohol becomes dangerous when curiosity is quenched, yet the person returns for more.

Occasional Use: Occasional users are not preoccupied with drinking, but they will often drink in social situations. Adults may consume alcohol when they go out to eat, attend a party, celebrate an important event, or want to relax on some weekends. Teenagers may consume alcohol as part of an event like homecoming, prom, or a concert. This type of drinking is often not a problem; however, younger drinkers tend to drink more for effect and to binge drink to become intoxicated. This increases the odds for poor decision making and cell adaptation. This is addressed further in Chapter 7.

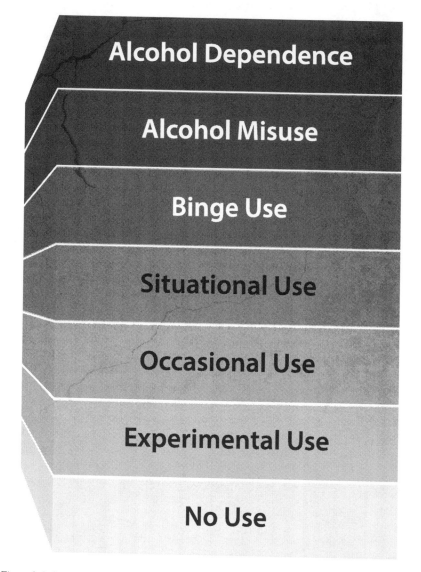

Figure 2.3 Spectrum of Alcohol Use

Situational Use: Situational use is also not generally a problem. However, the amount and frequency of alcohol use begin to increase. What was once special-occasion drinking now becomes more consistent and associated with specific events such as every weekend, parties, birthdays, sporting events, clubs, and other such things.

Binge Use: A binge drinker is someone who consumes a large quantity of alcohol, usually five or more drinks in two hours for men and four or more drinks for women, with the intent of becoming intoxicated. Binging can be a part of normal experimentation as less experienced drinkers do not yet know how alcohol affects them. The person who experiences the consequences of drinking too much and refrains from use for a period of time will most likely not develop a problem. The individual who experiences a consequence yet does the same thing the very next night, weekend, or party may begin to develop an AUD.

Alcohol Misuse: This consumption pattern tends not to occur every day and is not a concern every time a person drinks; however, it is beginning to cause problems. Most alcohol users will slow down or stop drinking when they have had a fight, developed a health problem, or received a legal charge. People developing an AUD tend to continue their drinking patterns despite having recurrent problems. A good way to define alcohol misuse is this:

If it causes a problem, it is a problem.

The person who misuses alcohol tends to drink in a larger amount than others and does so more frequently. At this stage, many either minimize the existence of a problem or deny alcohol's impact. They may say such things as "I can stop anytime I want," "It's not like I drink every day," or "I'm not as bad as _____."

Alcohol Dependence: At this stage, alcohol use has become a serious problem and meets DSM-5 criteria for a severe AUD. As mentioned previously, only a very small percentage of the population, about 6%, is physically dependent on alcohol. Severe AUD is what many people picture when they think of someone with a drinking problem. This 6% may be who individuals compare to in order to validate that they do not have a drinking problem. This small percentage includes people who drink every day, need alcohol to function, have suffered severe consequences like DUIs (driving under the influence), and have lost something of importance or value to them like a spouse, child, job, house, or health.

This person tends to drink on a regular basis and in large quantities. The individual has developed tolerance, meaning increasing amounts are necessary to achieve the same effect. This person may also experience withdrawal symptoms such as delirium tremens ("the shakes"), seizures, hallucinations, delusions, heart attack, and stroke if denied alcohol. These are dangerous, can be life-threatening, and require medical attention.

People can vacillate on the Spectrum of Alcohol Use over a lifetime. What causes a problem at one time of our lives may not be an issue in another. For example, many individuals in their early 20s drink more than people in their 40s. Does this mean they all have an AUD? No. A 25-year-old typically does not have as many responsibilities as a 40-year-old. The younger person can stay out late on the weekend as long as he doesn't make unhealthy decisions when out and gets a ride home if necessary. However, if a 40-year-old stays out until three in the morning, he may neglect his spouse, kids, lawn, or household chores.

Which One Are You?

I begin each of my presentations with an activity. I find that it challenges people's perceptions about who is actually drinking and highlights the concept of the Spectrum of Alcohol Use. Based on the percentages that the research tells us, I hand each of the audience members a card. On it may be a picture of a water, donut, cucumber, or pickle. The images each represent a type of drinker.

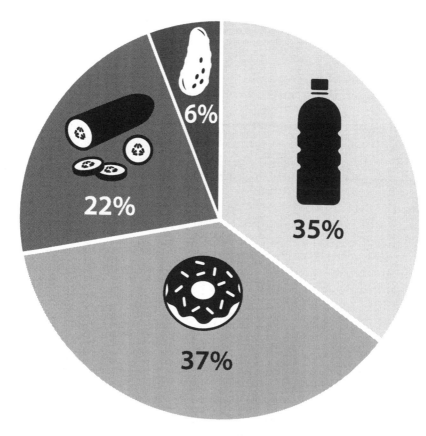

Figure 2.5 Types of Drinkers

The first of the four types of drinkers are waters. They represent 35% of the population. They are the nondrinkers. Many heavy imbibers do not believe that they exist. I often talk about how our normal is what we see. If you spend time with drinkers, you may assume that most people drink. But about a third of the population does not drink at all. Waters generally do not like the taste, want the calories, or like the feeling of intoxication or hangovers. They might have a family member who has a problem, so they abstain. Drinking might be against their religious beliefs, or they would rather eat than drink their calories.

The next group of drinkers encompasses what I call donuts. Donuts represent 37% of the population. The majority of alcohol users fall in this category. Sometimes they order a glass of wine or a cocktail when they go out; sometimes they have water or a soda. Donuts may open a bottle of liquor and forget that it is in their cabinet. They can take it or leave it. If they have too much one night, they will not drink again for a long period of time. They rarely drink to the point of intoxication or experience any consequences from their consumption. The idea is that having an occasional donut will not hurt you, but having multiple donuts every day will eventually lead to serious consequences.

> "Having an occasional donut will not hurt you, but having multiple donuts every day will eventually lead to serious consequences."

The third type of alcohol user is what I call cucumbers. They represent about 22% of the United States population, or about 70 million people. The individuals in this group are starting to experience problems as a result of their drinking. I say: "If it causes a problem, it is a problem." Cucumbers may have received a legal charge like a Driving Under the Influence or a Drunk in Public. This group may not learn from their mistakes. They might drink too much one night and do the same thing the very next time. Friends and family are starting to get concerned. Relationships, work, mood, and motivation might be starting to be negatively affected. But, they are not physically addicted. Clinically, we would say that they are struggling with a mild or moderate alcohol use disorder. Without a change to their drinking patterns, they could move on to the next category: pickles.

Pickles are cucumbers that have consumed alcohol so much and so frequently that their bodies are likely physically addicted to alcohol. Some say that their insides have become "pickled." As you may hear in an AA meeting, you cannot go back from being a pickle into a cucumber, no matter how badly you want to. However, numerous studies described in Chapter 1 demonstrate that even those in this group benefit from alcohol moderation.

Pickles are often referred to as "alcoholics," or suffering from a severe alcohol use disorder. They represent only about 6% of the population. This group and their loved ones will experience devastating consequences. They will have higher rates of depression and anxiety. Pickles will often get into legal trouble, and their actions will negatively impact their jobs, motivation, goals, family, and finances. Pickles experience problems in many areas of their lives. The good news is that the majority of treatments available are geared towards their recovery.

During the activity I ask each group to raise their hands when I call out the corresponding water, donut, cucumber, or pickle. When a roomful of over a hundred people sees the raised hands of how many people abstain from alcohol use, they are shocked. They are even more surprised to see the percentages of cucumbers who can benefit from a brief intervention like outpatient therapy and education versus the pickles who may truly require abstinence and higher levels of treatment. I am pleased to hear when audience members recognize that while they may be a pickle and choose lifelong abstinence, some of their clients may be cucumbers who need a different type of intervention. Alcohol itself is not the problem; it is how it affects the individual.

Binge Drinking

Most people who drink excessively are not alcohol dependent. In 2014 the Centers for Disease Control and Prevention in collaboration with the Substance Abuse and Mental Health Services Administration found that nine out of ten heavy drinkers are not dependent on alcohol. What was even more groundbreaking was that, with the help of a medical professional's brief intervention, most individuals can change unhealthy habits.[11]

Severe alcohol use disorders (AUDs) where physical dependence tends to occur is most common among excessive drinkers. About 10% of binge drinkers will have a severe AUD, but only 1% of non-binge drinkers will meet criteria for a severe AUD. Binge drinkers do have a higher chance of developing an AUD; however, 90% of binge drinkers will not develop a problem.

The fact that nine out of ten drinkers who binge drink and do not have a severe AUD is not an endorsement for excessive drinking, but it does mean that we must treat drinkers individually. Requiring abstinence often backfires. The individual knows that he can stop drinking and does not identify with what is discussed in traditional self-help meetings. The danger of recommending a strict protocol is that the person will avoid any kind of treatment. We miss out on an opportunity to help a person understand why he is choosing to consume alcohol excessively, explore the potential risks of drinking, and teach the tools to decrease the amount, frequency, and impact of alcohol consumption. I would rather have an ongoing therapeutic relationship with someone who is struggling than tell them they cannot drink and have them never come back for help.

Current research repeatedly shows that we need to change how we treat alcohol use disorders. The *Diagnostic and Statistical Manual of Mental Disorders* (DSM-5) in its 2013 update recognized that substance use disorders occur on a spectrum from mild, to moderate, to severe. Yet, there are not typically therapeutic options that take into account this spectrum. Most treatment remains abstinence-based. My hope is that this book proves that alcohol moderation is a necessary treatment option for the majority of drinkers experiencing problems and provides a foundation for how to practice alcohol moderation.

Why People Avoid Getting Help

Moderation Management (MM) reports that nine out of ten drinkers will not seek help.[12] The estimate that 90% of the people who are having problems with alcohol will not seek help is a very concerning statistic to me. It is sad that so many people will continue suffering because of the mistaken belief that if they are having a problem with drinking, they must be an "alcoholic" and therefore can never drink again. This is even sadder because the drinker is interconnected with many systems: family members, friends, neighbors, and coworkers. One person struggling with alcohol can literally affect hundreds of people, which in turn affects thousands. In theory, this would mean that every person is either directly or indirectly affected by alcohol.

I do not see how applying what works for only a small percentage of drinkers to all drinkers experiencing problems is an effective treatment strategy. We don't treat everyone who has chest pain as if they were having a heart attack. Doctors examine their patients, order tests, and collect more information before they make a diagnosis and provide treatment. Behavioral health care providers need to individualize their recommendations and treatment. Doctors also don't perform open-heart surgery on someone who only has heartburn. Similarly, alcohol treatment should be done in the least restrictive environment.

When people get sick from diabetes, cancer, or heart disease, we don't necessarily get mad at them. Instead, loved ones may help them change their diet, research treatments for them, or begin an exercise program with them. We don't get angry and leave them to fend for themselves. We work to help them find different ways to cope. The same should be true for people struggling with alcohol.

Notes

1. U.S. Department of Health and Human Services and U.S. Department of Agriculture (2015). *2015–2020 dietary guidelines for Americans: External* (8th ed.). Washington, DC: Office of Disease Prevention and Health Promotion.
2. American Heart Association (2014, August 15). *Alcohol and heart health*. Retrieved from www.heart.org/en/healthy-living/healthy-eating/eat-smart/nutrition-basics/alcohol-and-heart-health.

3. National Institute of Alcohol Abuse and Alcoholism (2016, May). *Rethinking drinking: Alcohol and your health.* Bethesda, MD: Department of Health and Human Services, NIH, National Institute on Alcohol Abuse and Alcoholism.
4. Alcohol in Moderation (2018, Updated September). *Sensible drinking guidelines.* Retrieved from www.drinkingandyou.com/site/pdf/Sensibledrinking.pdf.
5. P. Lincoln (2013, September). *Low-risk drinking guidelines: Where do the numbers come from?* Retrieved from https://ireta.org/resources/low-risk-drinking-guidelines-where-do-the-numbers-come-from/.
6. F. Rotgers, M. F. Kern & R. Hoeltzel (2002). *Responsible drinking: A moderation management approach for problem drinkers.* Oakland, CA: New Harbinger Publications.
7. United States Census Bureau (2019, March 11). Retrieved from www.census.gov.
8. Substance Abuse and Mental Health Services Administration (2018). *Key substance use and mental health indicators in the United States: Results from the 2017 national survey on drug use and health* (HHS Publication No. SMA 18-5068, NSDUH Series H-53). Rockville, MD: Center for Behavioral Health Statistics and Quality, Substance Abuse and Mental Health Services Administration. Retrieved from www.samhsa.gov/data/.
9. National Institute on Alcohol Abuse and Alcoholism (2019, March 20). *Alcohol and your health.* Retrieved from www.niaaa.nih.gov/alcohol-health/overview-alcohol-consumption/alcohol-use-disorders.
10. World Health Organization (2014). *Global status report on alcohol and health—2014 ed.* Retrieved from www.who.int/substance_abuse/publications/global_alcohol_report/msb_gsr_2014_1.pdf.
11. M. B. Esser, S. L. Hedden, D. Kanny, R. D. Brewer, J. C. Gfroerer & J. C. Naimi (2014). Prevalence of alcohol dependence among US adult drinkers, 2009–2001. *Preventing Chronic Disease.* 11: 140329. http://dx.doi.org/10.5888/pcd11.140329.
12. Moderation Management (2019, March 27). Retrieved from www.moderation.org/about_mm/whatismm.html.

3 History of Alcohol Use and Treatment

This chapter offers a brief history of how alcohol use has been viewed and the treatments available. It shows how we are still practicing with outdated philosophies that have been proven to be unscientific, have been designed for a limited population, and are not effective for the majority of people struggling with their alcohol use. Public perception regarding those who struggle with their drinking has drastically improved; however, treatment philosophies have yet to catch up. As a result, millions of people are not getting the right kind of treatment and may be unnecessarily suffering.

Temperance Movement

The disease model is called the American Model in most parts of the world.[1] Alcohol use increased three times in the United States during the period 1790 to 1830. This was due to a shift in consumption from fermented beverages to distilled spirits.[2] With greater availability of alcohol, use increased, as did its potential of negative impact.

The temperance movement began in the late 19th and early 20th centuries focused on the moral, economic, and medical effects of overindulging on alcohol, which eventually led to Prohibition. The temperance movement was happening during women's suffrage and religious movements in both the United States and England, and increases in immigration to the United States. One of their goals was temperance—to reduce the amount and frequency of alcohol consumption. They also warned against "spirits," mistakenly thinking that they had a stronger alcohol content than beer or wine. Spirits were distilled beverages like rum, gin, or whisky—what we now call liquor. Heavy drinkers and drinkers of spirits were seen as a menace to society who should be locked away in facilities. Eventually in 1920, the United States passed the Eighteenth Amendment to the Constitution, which banned the manufacture, transportation, and sale of alcoholic beverages except for religious of medicinal use. Interestingly, the amendment did not ban consumption of alcohol.

Prohibition was terrible. Most Americans were consuming healthy levels of beer and wine. However, when access became limited, people began rapidly drinking hard liquor in underground bars. Consequences from drinking increased and alcohol use became seen as evil. Drinkers were viewed as having moral failings. These beliefs set the stage for the acceptance of AA.

Alcoholics Anonymous

During the years 1920 to 1933, the United States was going through Prohibition. People believed that alcohol was a dangerous poison. They thought that if someone drank it long enough, he or she would eventually develop an addiction.

In 1935 Bill Wilson and Dr. Bob Smith founded AA during the post-Prohibition era in America, when heavy drinking was looked at as a moral failure and the medical profession treated it as incurable and lethal.[3] People welcomed a different view of how to handle heavy alcohol use. The only requirement to join AA is the desire to stop drinking. One of the primary ways it helps is through self-help groups, but also with sponsorship, fellowship, accountability, and 12-step work.

AA was intended for the most severe alcohol user. However, it has become the go-to recommendation for all alcohol users. Interestingly, in countries that never made alcohol illegal, AA has not strongly influenced treatment programs. There, alcohol moderation has consistently been a logical, accepted lifestyle and treatment option.

Box Matter 3.1

DID YOU KNOW? Bill Wilson, the co-founder of Alcoholics Anonymous, was in the hospital experiencing delirium tremens, sedated with morphine and on a hallucinogenic drug called belladonna, an experimental treatment for addiction of the time. In his hospital room, he reportedly called out to God to loosen the grip of alcohol. He described a flash of light and a feeling of serenity that he had never felt before and quit drinking for good as a result. He incorporated this idea of serenity and surrendering into the 12 steps. He described it as an intense religious experience where he came to believe that God was his Higher Power. Was it a spiritual awakening or a hallucination?[4]

Jellinek Curve

In the 1940s, E. M. Jellinek was hired by an AA member to perform research on alcoholism (as it was called during this time period). He is credited with coming up with the disease theory of alcoholism. Listen to how he developed his theory. He conducted a small study with a few subjects who responded to a questionnaire that he advertised in an AA magazine. The subjects were mostly white males in their 50s who had been drinking heavily for years. The results of the study would never be considered reliable or valid by today's standards.[5]

Based on the limited data from the small sample size, Jellinek came up with a theory. He believed that that drinkers went through stages of alcohol use that become progressively worse. This eventually became known as the Jellinek Curve. This is where the idea that alcohol use is chronic, progressive, and fatal was developed.[6]

Jellinek's study greatly impacted how people who struggle with alcohol use are treated. As a result some credit him with the idea that people struggling with alcohol use have a disease.

While Jellinek did help the medical profession begin to look at alcohol as a treatable issue rather than an incarcerable problem, the study shifted perceptions. It took what was true for a miniscule segment of drinkers and applied it to all drinkers. The general population, educational institutions, and treatment programs still operate as if all alcohol use is chronic, progressive, and fatal. Decades of data in multiple countries have proved otherwise, yet the field has not caught up to the reality.[7] I even know of many treatment facilities that still require participants to write out their personal Jellinek Curve prior to being able to graduate from the program.

Drunkenness as an Odious Disease

The idea that those struggling with their alcohol use could actually be the result of a disease was first coined by Benjamin Rush in the 19th century. These origins may not sit well with you, either. Dr. Rush was a physician who studied "chronic drunkenness" and also was a member of the Continental Congress and a signer of the Declaration of Independence. During this time drinking sprits was seen as a sin. He published the pamphlet *Inquiry Into the Effects of Ardent Spirits Upon the Human Body and Mind*. In it he said that drunkenness was an "odious disease" and that "habitual drunkenness should be regarded not as a bad habit but as a disease."[8]

Rush also distinguished between temperance and intemperance. Temperance was drinking in moderation, while intemperance led people to do horrible things such as fraud, theft, and murder. He said that it led people to have disease-like qualities like tremors, madness, and physical illness, which should be punished in such ways as whipping, bleeding, and purging them with toxic substances. It is important to note that all of this was his opinion. None of it was based on scientific evidence. He also believed that "black people" had a skin disease akin to leprosy that was inherited and that they could be cured of their "negroidism."[9]

Disease Model of Addiction

National Institute on Drug Abuse (NIDA) defines addiction as:

> a chronic, relapsing disorder characterized by compulsive drug seeking, continued use despite harmful consequences, and long-lasting changes in the brain. It is considered both a complex brain disorder and a mental

illness. Addiction is the most severe form of a full spectrum of substance use disorders, and is a medical illness caused by repeated misuse of a substance or substances.[10]

The American Society of Addiction notes that addiction is characterized by:

A. An inability to *a*bstain.
B. Impairment in *b*ehavioral control.
C. *C*raving.
D. *D*iminished recognition of significant problems.
E. *D*ysfunctional *e*motional response.[11]

I cannot stress this enough—only severe alcohol use disorders should carry the label of addiction. Addiction is very different from problematic alcohol use. People dealing with mild and moderate alcohol use disorders are not physically addicted to alcohol. Clinicians need to accurately diagnose then treat accordingly.

Even though there are challenges with the Disease Model, including addiction as a disease was significant. Problematic alcohol use began to be treated as a health care problem for which treatment is warranted; thus, insurance companies will cover services and the government can provide funding for prevention and assistance. Another major benefit to the Disease Model was that it shifted perception away from the idea that those struggling with alcohol use are bad people who are morally weak. People began to accept that the undesirable behaviors that people displayed from chronic alcohol use were less about a simple vice than about a more complex disease.

Brain Disease Model of Addiction

In 2015, Dr. Nora Volkow and Dr. George Koob, directors of the NIDA and the National Institute for Alcohol Abuse and Addiction (NIAAA), reported that the brain disease model of addiction is strongly supported by scientific evidence.[12] Additionally, the most recent Surgeon General's Report states that there is well-supported scientific evidence that addiction to alcohol is a chronic brain disease that has potential for recurrence and recovery.[13]

I'm not even debating either of these, because we are not talking about addiction in this book. Alcohol moderation is generally not for those struggling with a physical addiction to alcohol. The aforementioned reports have to do with addiction, those diagnosed with a severe alcohol use disorder. This is the 6%, the pickles described in Chapter 2. A clinician's job is to assess, diagnose, and treat based on what the client is experiencing. It is not to apply what may be appropriate for a minority to the majority of alcohol users. Treatment programs use the buzzwords "individualized treatment." You need to consider if this is an accurate description for your treatment if all who attend the program are expected to be alcohol free and participate in 12-step meetings.

Minnesota Model

The 12-steps began to get incorporated into treatment with the Minnesota Model. Prior to this time treatment for alcohol use involved only detoxification and simple custodial care. The Minnesota Model, developed in the late 1940s, combined the philosophies of three treatment programs, Hazelden, Pioneer House, and Wilmar State Hospital, all of which were located in Minnesota. They believed that people experiencing problems with alcohol were dealing with an involuntary, primary, chronic, progressive, biopsychosocial disease for which abstinence from all mood-altering substances was required. The model believes that recovery is achieved through the 12-steps of AA and immersion in a community of shared experiences. It was helpful that a multidisciplinary team began providing treatment to address the many needs of its clients, but it was believed that forming less formal relationships with clients was beneficial. Thus, people who were themselves in recovery became part of the treatment team.[14]

The model offered a shift away from the idea that "alcoholism" was a moral failing and offered an environment where people struggling with alcohol use could get help and retain their dignity. However, there is minimal research that supports the effectiveness of the Minnesota Model, although many programs are still using it.[15]

Florida Model

The Florida Model also incorporates 12-step into treatment. Remember that AA is about fellowship. It is peer-led by individuals who are also struggling with their own alcohol use. Treatment is health care given to a person who has a problem. Treatment is rendered by a trained provider who has received education, demonstrated a specific skill set, and is monitored by a licensing board.

During the 1980s managed care reduced coverage for the traditional 28-day inpatient program. As a result, the Florida Treatment Model was developed. A goal of the model is to make treatment less institutionalized by offering more real world experiences in a group home setting. After a detoxification period, treatment is offered on an outpatient basis. Clients receive services such as individual, family, and group therapy and medication monitoring in one location. At the end of the day, clients return to residential living. The benefit is that this model can be more affordable and that clients learn how to cook, clean, and shop for themselves, attend 12-step meetings, and live among people also in recovery.

The origins of the model had good intentions. However, this model has become fraught with financial greed. Sober living facilities pop up without any real oversight. Clients and their families are seen as a way to make money and are taken advantage of when they are at their worst point in their lives.[16] While there are many quality programs, it is up to the consumer to check to see who the owner and operators are, if they have criminal backgrounds, or any education or experience in the field of substance use disorders. There are currently some efforts to have some type of licensing by each of the states, but they still remain largely unregulated.

Just Say No

Just Say No was an advertising campaign that was part of the United States' War on Drugs. It was popularized by former First Lady Nancy Reagan in the 1980s. The anti-drug campaign focused on a zero tolerance policy on substance use. Federal support for treatment declined and the number of people incarcerated for drug and alcohol offenses rose dramatically.[17]

This policy once again viewed alcohol and drug problems as a lack of willpower on how to handle drug and alcohol problems. It simplifies substance use and makes it look like it is just about willpower. Thankfully, this campaign was short lived, and we now focus on "Just Say Know" where we deliver unbiased, accurate information about substances.

American Society of Addiction Medicine (ASAM) Patient Placement Criteria

During the 1980s, treatment for those dealing with an alcohol or drug issue was inefficient and expensive. As a result, the American Society of Addiction Medicine and the National Association of Addiction Treatment Providers developed a national set of criteria for providing outcome driven, results-based care for addiction treatment, originally known as ASAM-PPC and now referred to as ASAM criteria. It was revised in 1996, 2001, and 2013. The 2013 criteria were updated to be compatible with the *Diagnostic and Statistical Manual of Mental Disorders*, 5th edition, that was released early that year. The 2013 criteria have special sections for treatment in the criminal justice system, older adults, parents receiving treatment concurrently with their children, pregnant women, and those in safety-sensitive occupations. There are also sections on gambling and tobacco use disorders.[18]

ASAM criteria offer guidelines to standardize the way individuals are placed into, transferred in, and discharged from treatment. Simply put, the criteria help to determine at what level a client might be the most successful. There are different placement criteria for adolescents and adults. ASAM criteria can also aid in developing an individualized evaluation and treatment plan. The criteria offer a way to use a strengths-based, multidimensional assessment over five areas of treatment that are based on the amount of direct medical care required, the structure, safety, and security needed, and the level of intensity of the treatment provided. It looks at a potential client's needs, obstacles, liabilities, strengths, assets, resources, and support structure.

The criteria also use six life areas called dimensions to assess an individual for service and treatment planning. A clinician, who has typically gone through two full days of training, examines how each one affects the other. The six dimensions include:

Dimension 1: acute intoxication or withdrawal potential. It looks at an individual's past and present substance use and risk of life-threatening withdrawal symptoms that might need to be medically monitored.

Dimension 2: Biomedical conditions or complications. This area looks at physical and medication health status and risks that should be addressed.

Dimension 3: Emotional, behavioral, or cognitive conditions or complications. This dimension addressed thoughts, emotions, behaviors, and mental health issues.

Dimension 4: Readiness to change. The fourth area assesses what motivates a person to make a change and readiness to do something different.

Dimension 5: Relapse, continued use, or continued problem potential This explores areas regarding ongoing substance use and identifies risk factors.

Dimension 6: Recovery/living environment. The final dimension explores the living situation as well as people, places, and things that may affect recovery.

Based upon the individual's unique presentation in each of these areas, a level of care is then determined. There are five broad levels with a graduated increase in intensity:

- Level .05: Early Intervention, often involves brief education.
- Level I: Outpatient Services, which run less than nine hours a week.
- Level II: Intensive Outpatient and Partial Hospitalization programs, which range from 9 to 20 hours a week.
- Level III: Residential and Inpatient Treatment, which requires an individual to have 24/7 care.
- Level IV: Medically Monitored Intensive Inpatient Treatment is the highest level of care where the person has 24-hour nursing care that is monitored by a medical team.[19]

Alcohol moderation would typically fall along the lines of .05 to a Level I care. There are also some Level II IOPs beginning to work with clients who want to reduce their use to safer levels rather than strictly requiring abstinence. These are the least restrictive options and are typically the most cost effective. The ASAM criteria are a positive step forward in the treatment of AUDs. It begins to address the complexity and varying treatment modalities possible for those struggling with alcohol use.

Third Wave

As you can see, we have shifted from a Moral Model to a Disease Model in the way we view alcohol use disorders. Some argue that we are entering a "Third Wave" for alcohol use treatment.[20] While it was certainly an improvement to view AUDs through a medical lens, it limits how services are provided. As noted above the Disease Model looks at excessive alcohol use as an addiction, yet we know that four times as many people are dealing with a mild to moderate AUD than a severe AUD. It also puts the medical provider in charge of treatment. This is all despite the numerous studies that have shown that the best outcomes for treatment occur when the client choses the goals.[21]

The Third Wave incorporates mindfulness, Dialectical Behavioral Therapy, Motivational Interviewing, Acceptance and Commitment Therapy, and harm reduction models. It acknowledges that alcohol use involves many factors, and thus treatment should attempt to address all of these areas with the client. It includes a biopsychosocial spiritual model that includes medical, social, and environmental factors.[22] Potentially the most controversial tenet of harm reduction is that it does not require abstinence from alcohol for people to get help. Harm reduction models will be discussed more in the next chapter.

Notes

1. P. Denning & J. Little (2017). *Over the influence: The harm reduction guide to controlling your drug and alcohol use* (2nd ed.). New York: The Guilford Press.
2. W. White (2000). Addiction as a disease: Birth of a concept. *Counselor.* 1(1): 46–51, 73.
3. General Service Office of Alcoholics Anonymous (2019, April 23). *Historical data: The birth of A.A. and its growth in the U.S./Canada.* Retrieved from www.aa.org/pages/en_US/historical-data-the-birth-of-aa-and-its-growth-in-the-uscanada.
4. G. Glaser (2015, April). The irrationality of Alcoholics Anonymous. *The Atlantic.* Retrieved from https://www.theatlantic.com/magazine/archive/2015/04/the-irrationality-of-alcoholics-anonymous/386255/.
5. T. J. Falcone (2003). *Alcoholism: A disease of speculation.* Amsterdam, NY: Baldwin Research Institute.
6. T. Powers (2015, September 13). Recognizing the stages of alcoholism: The Jellinek Curve. *The Fix.*
7. D. J. Hanson (2019, April 16). *E. M. Jellinek: Disease theory of alcoholism promoter: Crook & liar?* Retrieved from www.alcoholproblemsandsolutions.org/e-m-jellinek-disease-theory-alcoholism-promoter/.
8. B. Rush (1808). *An inquiry into the effects of ardent spirits upon the human body and mind: With an account of the means of preventing, and of the remedies for curing them.* Philadelphia: Thomas Dobson.
9. D. J. Hanson (2019, April 17). *Beginnings of temperance in America.* Retrieved from www.alcoholproblemsandsolutions.org/beginnings-of-temperance-in-america/.

10. National Institute on Drug Abuse (2018, July). *The science of drug use and addiction: The basics.* Retrieved from www.drugabuse.gov/publications/media-guide/science-drug-use-addiction-basics.

11. American Society of Addiction Medicine Board of Directors (2011, August 15). *Public policy statement: Short definition of addiction.* Chevy Chase, MD: American Society of Addiction Medicine Board of Directors.

12. N. D. Volkow & G. Koob (2015, August). Brain disease model of addiction: Why is it so controversial? *The Lancet Psychiatry.* 2(8).

13. U.S. Department of Health and Human Services, Office of the Surgeon General (2016, November). *Facing addiction in America: The Surgeon General's report on alcohol, drugs, and health.* Washington, DC: Health and Human Services.

14. R. B. Huebner & L. Kantor (2011). Advances in alcoholism treatment. *Alcohol Research and Health.* 33(4): 295–299.

15. R. Stinchfield & P. Owen (1998). Hazelden's model of treatment and its outcome. *Addictive Behaviors.* 23(5): 669–683. https://doi.org/10.1016/S0306-4603(98)00015-X.

16. L. R. Seville, A. Schecter & H. Rappleye (2017, June 25). Florida's billion-dollar drug treatment industry is plagued by overdoses, fraud. *NBC News.* https://www.nbcnews.com/feature/megyn-kelly/florida-s-billion-dollar-drug-treatment-industry-plagued-overdoses-fraud-n773376.

17. W. White (1998). *Slaying the dragon: The history of addiction treatment and recovery in America.* Bloomington, IL: Chestnut Health Systems.

18. The American Society of Addiction Medicine (2013). *American Society of Addiction Medicine releases new treatment criteria, modernizing care for addictive disorders* [Press Release]. Retrieved from www.asam.org/docs/default-source/pressreleases/asam-releases-new-treatment-criteria_2013-10-25.

19. D. Mee-Lee, G. D. Schulman, M. J. Fishman, D. R. Gasfriend & M. M. Miller (Eds.) (2013). *The ASAM criteria: Treatment criteria for addictive substance-related, and co-occurring conditions* (3rd ed.). Carson City, NV: The Change Companies.

20. D. Rothschild (2015, February 6). The "third wave" of substance use treatment. *The Fix.* Retrieved from www.thefix.com/content/third-wave-substance-use-treatment.

21. A. Ojehagen & M. Berglund (1989). Changes in drinking goals in a two-year outpatient alcoholic treatment program. *Addictive Behaviors.* 14: 1–9.

22. S. P. Byrne, P. Haber, A. B. Baillie, D. S. J. Costa, V. Fogliati & K. Morley (2019, March). Systematic reviews of mindfulness and acceptance and commitment therapy for alcohol use disorder: Should we be using third wave therapies? *Alcohol and Alcoholism.* 54(2): 159–166. https://doi.org/10.1093/alcalc/agy089.

4 Harm Reduction Models

History of Harm Reduction

Edith Springer is attributed with bringing harm reduction to the United States. A social worker in a methadone clinic in New York, she traveled to Great Britain during the 1980s and observed how differently they were treating their patients.[1] When she returned, she wrote the first article about harm reduction that focused on prevention methods.[2] Springer called it "harm reduction counseling." It takes a preventative approach and respects a person's capacity to change by focusing on their strengths. Harm reduction focuses on health in relation to substance use rather than on morality or legality. The approach establishes safety and educates the substance user. It gives a framework for dealing with substance use and other risky behaviors without requiring abstinence as a goal for treatment or a requirement to receive it.

G. Alan Marlatt called harm reduction "compassionate pragmatism."[3] He believed that it starts with the acceptance that people use substances in ways that negatively affect themselves and those around them. By taking this stance, professionals and alcohol users can collaborate on reducing the risks and effects of alcohol, becoming healthier without having to fight one another on expected outcomes or requirements for abstinence. It is exciting to note that this concept is reaching international levels.[4]

Harm Reduction Psychotherapy

A shift in treatment began in the 1990s when clinicians began to realize that the current approaches for treating those with drug and alcohol problems were not working. A new form of therapy was formed called Harm Reduction Psychotherapy (HRP). It has three main tenets:

1. The clinician should work with the client to develop treatment goals.
2. Treatment should be easy to utilize.
3. Success is any reduction of harm in a substance user's life.[5]

The core values of harm reduction include:

- *Understanding*: The key to changing drinking patterns is to understand why you are using alcohol.
- *Acceptance*: Accept the choices you have made without minimizing the consequences and be open to acceptance from loved ones.
- *Compassion*: Realize that guilt does not help you move forward, so seek forgiveness from yourself and from others you may have harmed.
- *Kindness:* Be kind to yourself and spend time with people who treat you well.
- *Connection*: Your attachment to alcohol can be replaced with connections to healthy people.
- *Freedom to choose*: You have the right to choose the direction of your life.[6]

HRP is a drastic shift from traditional treatment models and programs. The majority of treatment programs require abstinence from all mood-altering substances to enter the program. This is often the biggest barrier of all, preventing the majority who need help from getting any type of help. Traditional therapeutic models generally recommend that clients not be in therapy until they have been "clean and sober" for a period of time. The belief tends to be that individual psychotherapy, family counseling, or couples therapy will be ineffective because therapy will stir things up and potentially cause a relapse. This has never made any sense to me. Why would I withhold help to someone who is struggling—especially when alcohol use may be one of the very reasons the person's mental health, family relationships, and marriage or partnership is stressed? HRP believes, as do I, that if we do not offer help when the person is making lifestyle changes, the changes will not last.

HRP is integrated, meaning that clinicians treat both the mental health and the substance use at the same time. It is ridiculous that for decades, clients have had to go one place for their mental health needs and another for their drug or alcohol issues. Good HRP therapists treat both. Integrated also means that the therapist can switch from one theoretical intervention to another based on what the client is presenting. For example, we may perform a risk assessment when a client speaks about his or her depression. Then we might give psychoeducation on the fight, flight, or freeze response as he or she describes challenges with anxiety. We may also share some grounding and mindfulness techniques for ways to deal with it when it happens. Then as the client shares concerns about how changing drinking patterns might affect relationships, we may draw on family systems ideas. Then the session shifts to their expressing ambivalence about whether they really want to change their drinking habits, so we use Motivational Interviewing techniques. I have always been wary of a clinician who says they practice one type of specialized therapy. I believe a great clinician is one who has a large array of tools in their toolbox.

So who determines what harm is? That is up to the person seeking help, and often the people he or she comes in contact with. An example is this: a husband consumes so many drinks that he stays up late, passes out on the couch, and is unavailable to help with parenting the next morning. He may feel that this is a good way to deal with his work stress, but his wife and kids may disagree. Therefore, the couple and the family have a problem. It is ultimately the family system that determines there is a problem.

Paracelsus, a Swiss chemist from the 16th century, is attributed with the condensed saying: the dose makes the poison.[7] In other words, what is fine for me may be deadly for you. Each individual needs to make this determination. One of our jobs is to help our client figure this out prior to irrevocable harm occurring.

Alcohol Moderation Is Harm Reduction

Alcohol moderation is a form of harm reduction. It challenges the way people have been creating public policy and providing treatment in the United States for over 100 years. The tide is turning, as you read in Chapter 1. In the early 1990s about 93% of treatment was abstinence based and required attendance in a 12-step program, traditionally AA. Thankfully, by 2017 that rate dropped to about 77% of treatment programs.[8] While this is an improvement for those who struggle with the concept of a Higher Power, powerlessness, and the requirement of total abstinence, this still means that the majority of treatment programs are still faith based.

European researchers note that the prevailing treatment for those struggling with an alcohol use disorder is abstinence, despite the reality that alcohol use occurs on a spectrum. They recognize that the majority of people who need treatment for their alcohol use never receive it, mainly because they are expected to be completely alcohol free. Their studies show that "intermediate harm reduction" is a viable, and necessary, treatment option. Intermediate harm reduction focuses on a clinically significant reduction on total alcohol consumption as well as reduction in the number of drinking days. They ultimately concluded that evidence supports reduced drinking approaches—even for those that are alcohol dependent.[9]

Client Examples

Below are several examples of how clients have successfully utilized alcohol moderation. We focused on their incremental changes and looked at the whole person's experience, not just the alcohol use. I find that it is better to pay attention to what is working rather than to focus on what went wrong.

Kaitlyn

Kaitlyn, a middle-aged mom, used wine to take the edge off her day. She worked full-time, then came home to three kids who had homework to complete, practices to get to, and dinner to eat. She felt that a few glasses of wine would make her a better mom because she thought it made her more patient.

Kaitlyn began to recognize that several glasses of wine a night might be a problem when she almost had a car accident coming home from her daughter's dance class. She'd already had three or so glasses when she suddenly realized that she'd mixed up her carpool dates, but she still hopped into the car to fulfill her driving duties. She almost hurt herself, her daughter, and two of her daughter's friends. Kaitlyn scared herself, so she called me.

During the initial evaluation, Kaitlyn said that after scheduling the appointment with me, she reduced her intake from an average of five glasses a night to two or three a night. Rather than launching into a discussion about how bad three drinks could be, I said, "That's amazing! How did you go from five glasses a day to two? That's like a 50 percent improvement! What did you do to manage the stress of the kids and dinner and work?"

In this way, Kaitlyn did not continue to beat herself up. She was able to focus on what was working and develop a plan that focused on building upon her successes rather than punishing her for the mistakes of which she was already keenly aware. Kaitlyn wanted to come back to therapy because we developed an individualized plan for her that did not focus only on her drinking, but why she was drinking and what we could do about it.

Jackie

Jackie was a binge drinker on the weekends when her kids went to their dad's house. As soon as her ex and his new bimbo pulled out of the driveway, she began sipping a cocktail while getting ready to go out and hit the meat market. Her ex had already found someone, so why shouldn't she? In therapy we worked together to help her deal with the implications of the divorce on her life. She began to value herself again and figure out what she wanted in a relationship instead of just finding someone to fill the hours.

One Friday night Jackie ran up quite a bar tab. The next night she decided to practice some of the skills she was learning in therapy. She checked out the singles group at her friend's church. She had nothing to drink that night and actually enjoyed herself. In our next session, my response was to give her a huge smile, share in her excitement, and process what it was like to have sober conversations where the men were not just looking to hook up.

I focused on the night where she had success rather than on the night where she drank more than she had planned. I helped her identify other situations where she could socialize with other people in her situation without alcohol. The next weekend that the kids are with their dad, she is planning to go on a hike with some other single parents.

Mike

Mike walked into my office with a sad, guilty look. His shoulders were hunched over, and he could barely look me in the eye. Prior to seeing me, he had gone to detox to break a physical addiction to alcohol and had been told to go to "90 in 90" (90 Alcoholics Anonymous meetings in 90 days).

Mike hated his job and would often start drinking as soon as he got home from work. In the past, he had often polished off a 12-pack by the end of the night. His wife was happy that he had stopped drinking but was frustrated that he was gone every night at an AA meeting. At least when he was drinking, he had been home and could help with the kids a little bit.

Mike was alcohol-free for two months before he couldn't take the stress anymore and went on a bender. He admitted what happened and talked about the huge fight that had ensued with his wife. Together, they admitted that they both had issues to work through. They came to the agreement that she would begin working part-time so he could finish his degree and get another job.

Mike expected me to admonish him for his use, but I was so excited I could barely contain myself. I congratulated him on working as a team with his wife and coming up with a plan together. I looked at what was important—reconnecting with his life partner, with whom he developed a plan for long-term financial stability and happiness for the whole family—rather than focusing on the one night of drinking that resulted from a poor decision. In fact, this decision opened the line of communication that helped this couple regain intimacy and develop a plan to deal with their stressors.

Promising Models

Over the last several decades, there have been many advances in the field of harm reduction and alcohol moderation. It is encouraging that in November 2016, the U.S. government issued *Facing Addiction in America: The Surgeon General's Report on Alcohol, Drugs, and Health*. The report notes the need for a continuum of care, as there is a spectrum of use. The reports also notes that the more common, but less severe disorders respond well to brief motivational interventions and/or supportive monitoring.[10] Some of the most significant treatments are included next.

The Sinclair Method (TSM)

The Sinclair Method (TSM) was developed by the late Dr. David Sinclair. It involves taking Naltrexone (also known as Nalmefene in other countries) one hour prior to drinking alcohol to create "pharmacological extinction."[11] It is the epitome of alcohol moderation, as the program does not require people to be alcohol free, but its goal is to reduce episodes of heavy drinking.

Sinclair began studying behavioral reinforcement in the 1960s. He theorized that people develop problems with drinking through learned behavior. Each time a person consumes alcohol, the brain releases endorphins, which strengthen synapses in the brain. The more the synapses grow, the more a person thinks about and craves alcohol. Sinclair speculated that an opiate agonist (blocking) medication would weaken the synapses, thus extinguishing the craving by blocking the reinforcing effects of alcohol in the brain. His findings were tested and published in the 1980s. Numerous studies have followed.[12] Its effectiveness for reducing the amount consumed to safer levels is reported to be 78%, while a quarter of users achieve complete abstinence.[13] TSM has been used in other countries for decades. It was popularized in the United States when actress Claudia Christian participated in the documentary *One Little Pill* and formed a nonprofit organization to bring attention to TSM.[14,15]

Behavioral Self-Control Training

Miller, Munoz, Hester, Robertson, Heather, Sanchez-Craig, Sobell, Sobell, and Vogler are attributed with developing Behavioral Self-Control Training (BSCT) and have published widely on their approach.[16,17] It can be used for abstinence or moderation. BSCT incorporates techniques related to alcohol use such as setting goals, self-monitoring, managing consumption, rewarding progress, analyzing drinking situations, and developing coping skills. While a therapist can provide education and homework, the client is ultimately in charge of determining the goals and what they consider success. A well replicated surprise in six clinical trials was that clients working on their own with self-control tools had outcomes at least as good as those for clients working with counselors using the same tools.[18] Research has shown that BSCT is the most empirically validated controlled-drinking intervention.[19,20]

Guided Self-Change Model

Remember the Sobells from Chapter 1? Despite the significant criticism (and eventual exoneration) they faced from the treatment community and general public regarding their studies on controlled drinking, they went on to positively affect the field. In addition to contributing to the development of BSCT, Drs. Mark Sobell and Linda Sobell developed the Guided Self-Change Model of Treatment for Substance Use Disorders in 1984.[21] Guided Self-Change (GSC) includes cognitive-behavioral, Motivational Interviewing, and relapse prevention techniques to help people analyze their substance use and make their own plans for changing. It is best for people who are dealing with less severe substance use disorders. GSC allows the client to set goals regarding their drinking, encourages self-assessment, and emphasizes problem-solving skills.[22]

The Sobells have developed numerous handouts with tips and tools that can be used in session and in real-life situations. GSC helps clients evaluate lifestyle choices, set goals, strengthen commitment to change, identify strengths and resources, guide personal change, and overcome obstacles to change.[23] In 2016 the Surgeon General's Report recognized GSC as an effective treatment for mild substance use disorders.[24] GSC is also included on the American Psychological Association's website of Empirically Supported Treatments.

Motivational Interviewing

Motivational Interviewing (MI) is a counseling theory that was developed by William R. Miller and Stephen Rollnick.[25] MI is a process that I was naturally using early in my career. My traditionally oriented colleagues were wondering what I was doing that was making my clients get better. It wasn't necessary what I was doing. Rather, it was how I was approaching my clients that helped them make changes. MI is one of the most impactful approaches a therapist can use in practicing alcohol moderation.

Miller and Rollnick note that motivation is a flexible state. Thus the therapist's goal is to enhance the client's desire for motivation and ensuing change. We do this by exploring the client's wishes, ambivalence, and resistance for doing something different. The therapist asks many questions. The main goal of treatment is to establish a relationship with the client. The next goal is to build the person's motivation for change. Then we attempt to strengthen the commitment to change. Notice that being alcohol free is neither a requirement nor a goal. The client determines what the objectives are. We may explore the pros and cons of the client's goals. The belief is that the client will come to the decision that works best for him or her.

MI uses OARS. They are the techniques and skills that should be used regularity when meeting with clients. OARS stands for:

O: asks open-ended questions
A: affirms the client's experiences
R: reflects what the client expresses
S: summarizes what the client has shown

Some of the main principles of Motivational Interviewing include the following:

- *Expresses empathy*: We need to let our clients know that we "get it." Instead of berating a client for the consequences of their drinking, I try to understand their "why." I may point out that I understand why they may be drinking every night because it helps them deal with the insomnia related to a trauma they experienced. I let them know that I will not ask them to stop using this coping skill until I have helped them to develop other ways to deal with fears that cause the nightmares and flashbacks. I then offer education on how alcohol negatively affects quality of sleep, relationships, and mood. I am building the relationship by letting my client know that I empathize with their problems and that I can be a resource to them.

- *Develops discrepancy*: The therapist points out how drinking may be negatively affecting their lives. Once we have established a relationship with our clients, we can move to discrepancy. This means that we can point out when a client's behavior is counterproductive to their goals. A good example of this may be with a client who is struggling with depression yet continues drinking on a nightly basis. I might say "Hillary, I understand that a few glasses of wine helps you deal with feelings of loneliness in the evenings. Are you aware that alcohol has depressant qualities that can make your mood worse? Feeling lower prevents you from reaching out to your friends. It also can make your anti-depressant not work as well." This opens up the possibility for discussion. I'm not telling Hillary what to do, but I may make some suggestions. Then we can role-play options that may work for her. This could include trying to go one night without drinking and making plans with a friend. It also might include having a discussion with her psychiatrist about the effects of alcohol on her medication.
- *Rolls with resistance*: MI recognizes that all people struggle with ambivalence (having mixed or contradictory feelings about a person or situation). We need to pace therapy. If we push too hard, our clients may not come back. On the flip side, if we do not challenge enough, they may not feel as if they are getting anything out of the sessions. We may hear: "yes, but" a lot at this stage. Our role again is to point out the discrepancies and help them weigh the pros and cons, offering other perspectives on the situation.
- *Supports self-efficacy*: I often tell my clients that there are times when I will be their biggest cheerleader and will "kick them in the butt" if they need a push. We need to point out our clients' successes. Remember that they are living their lives, so they may not be able to see the changes. We need to point them out, especially the incremental changes. Things I have often said include: "Do you realize that when you first started here, you were having more drinking days than non-drinking days? In the last week, you only drank once. How did you do it?" Or, "That's amazing! You went to that work function even though you were really nervous. How did you manage the open bar?" Or, "Hold on a second. Last month you got drunk three times. This month you stopped at two glasses of wine. How did you make that change?" I am pointing out their success and exploring with them how they did it. This ultimately is instilling self-efficacy by showing them that they have the skill set and, most important, that they can repeat it in the future.

It is only once the client starts engaging in "change talk" that we should begin exploring how to transform. Resist the urge to offer solutions too quickly. Your client probably knows what he or she could be doing differently. We need to first explore what they are doing currently and why they haven't done it yet. A client may say they want to quit drinking yet still has alcohol on most nights of the week. After establishing a relationship with the client, we should explore why they have not made the change they say they want.

In the example that follows, Steven entered treatment because his wife thought he was drinking too much and he no longer seemed happy. He said that he loves his wife and respects her opinion, so he made an appointment with me. I gathered a full biopsychosocial history and determined that Steven is dealing with a mild alcohol use disorder and some symptoms of depression, specifically related to downsizing at his work. He denies other drug use, blackouts, or other mental health symptoms. He, and his wife who joined the last session, agree that his alcohol use has been creeping up as stressors at work increase. When he first started treatment, he was in the Contemplation Stage, admitting that there might be an issue with his drinking, but he was not ready to do anything about it. The first few sessions allowed him a safe space to talk about how much work was affecting him. He is the primary earner, so he did not want to let his wife know how stressed out he was. Session number five might sound something like this:

Steven: I gotta deal with my drinking. I don't like how I feel in the morning or how much money I'm spending on beer. The last few weeks, I've been saying: today is the day. Then on the ride home, I pick up a six-pack. I'm such a failure.

Therapist: Steven, it sounds like you are ready to make some changes. Before we jump into any specific plan, let's look first at what's made it hard to do something different.

Steven: Well, you know how much work sucks these days. I hate my new boss and I never know if I'm the next one to be laid off.

Therapist: That is really stressful, not knowing what's coming. I'm concerned that if you stop drinking right now, you don't have any ways to handle the pressure. Before this ever happened what did you do to deal with stress?

Steven: I used to work out.

Therapist: What made you give it up? Is that something you can fit back into your schedule?

        (We discuss what workout plan would realistically fit into both his schedule and his budget)

Therapist: What else has made it hard to deal with your alcohol use?

Steven: It's just such a habit. I get off work, ride by the store, and my car just seems to stop there.

Therapist: Sounds like you're on autopilot. Is there another way you could go home so that you don't have to pass that gas station?

Steven: That's easy—yeah, I could take the toll road instead.

Therapist: Going a different way is easy to do. But making changes can be hard. Let's also see if we can add some tangible reminders to

	help you. What are some things that you can see, feel, touch, or hold that will remind you to do something different?
Steven:	I'm going to tell my wife that I plan on going to the gym on the way home. If she knows, I'm less likely to pick up beer.
Therapist:	You could also stick my business card in your wallet, next to your credit card so that you have to see it and think about what my face would look like the next time you came in!
Steven:	Oooh, scary! Don't wanna deal with my wife and your Stink Eye!

Traditional therapy might have discharged Steven from treatment for continuing to drink while he was seeing me. While his alcohol use was creating some problems for him, he had no major physical or safety issues related to his alcohol use. His primary issue was not the alcohol, but stress at work. Had I told him that I could not treat him, he likely would not have come back after the session. As a result, his alcohol use could have progressed and caused more problems in his life. I chose to focus on the issues he was willing to talk about—his wife and work. Very quickly, he came to the decision that his drinking was getting out of control and was ready to address it. I helped him explore and waited until he started using change talk ("I gotta deal with my drinking") and explored ambivalence (using alcohol as stress reliever) before I ever introduced a solution.

Rat Park

Author Johann Hari brought the concept of Rat Park into mainstream knowledge. In his TED Talk and bestselling book *Chasing the Scream*,[26,27] Hari presented the work of the late Professor Bruce Alexander and his colleagues at Simon Fraser University in Vancouver, British Columbia. Professor Alexander and his team tested the theory that rats who were given the choice between plain water and water laced with morphine would become addicted to the morphine. The original theory was that addictive drugs caused addiction. The team built "Rat Park," a cage consisting of a large box full of tunnels, toys, and food. The rats could play, have sex, and eat well. The results showed that rats in Rat Park consumed far less morphine than those in traditional cages. Hari best summarized Alexander's studies by saying, "The opposite of addiction is not sobriety, it's human connection." They believe that when rats—and humans—have access to relationships, intimacy, fun, food, and sex, we will chose connection over drugs.

Hari contributed to the harm reduction movement by bringing this concept into the mainstream. His TED Talk has currently been viewed by over 12 million people. He also is demonstrating that we need to focus less on the actual drug or alcohol and more on developing connections. I have always said that people are more successful when we add something (relationships, fun, activities) to our lives than when we take a substance or behavior away.

Box Matter 4.1

DID YOU KNOW? Alcohol is terrible for insomnia. Some think that a few drinks before bed helps them to fall asleep faster. But once they fall asleep, their quality of sleep is poor. Alcohol reduces REM (rapid eye movement), the restorative stage of sleep where dreams occur. This disruption causes daytime drowsiness and poor concentration. Alcohol can also suppress breathing, thus increasing sleep apnea and snoring. Rest is also disturbed, as alcohol is a diuretic that requires trips to the bathroom.[28]

0-0-1-3

A final example of alcohol moderation is from the military in the form of 0-0-1-3.[29] Each of the numbers represents a recommendation.

0: No alcohol for anyone who is underage.
0: No drinking if you are driving.
1: No more than one drink per hour
3: No more than three drinks per event.

The formula stresses the idea that one does not need to consume excessive amounts of alcohol to have a good time and that if you drink, you should have a plan for being safe.

Notes

1. Harm Reduction Coalition (2011). Edith Springer: Goddess of harm reduction. *Interview.* Retrieved from http://harmreduction.org/publication-type/podcast/forty-two/.
2. E. Springer (1991). Effective AIDS prevention with active drug users: The harm reduction model. In M. Shernoff (Ed.), *Counseling chemically dependent people with HIV illness* (pp. 141–158). New York: Harrington Park Press.
3. A. Tatarsky & A. Marlatt (2010). State of the art in harm reduction psychotherapy: An emerging treatment for substance misuse. *Journal of Clinical Psychology: In Session.* 66(2): 117–122. DOI: 10.1002/jclp.20672.
4. S. Suh & M. Ikeda (2015). Compassionate pragmatism on the harm reduction continuum: Expanding the options for drug and alcohol addiction treatment in Japan. *Communication-Design.* 13: 63–72.
5. P. Denning & J. Little (2012). *Practicing harm reduction psychotherapy: An alternative approach to addictions* (2nd ed.). New York: The Guilford Press.
6. P. Denning & J. Little (2017). *Over the influence: The harm reduction guide to controlling your drug and alcohol use* (2nd ed.). New York: The Guilford Press.
7. P. Grandjean (2016). Paracelsus revisited: The dose concept in a complex world. *Basic and Clinical Pharmacology and Toxicology.* 119(2): 126–132. DOI: 10.1111/bcpt.12622.

8. P. Denning & J. Little (2017). *Over the influence: The harm reduction guide to controlling your drug and alcohol use* (2nd ed.). New York: The Guilford Press.

9. K. Mann, H-J. Aubin & K. Witikiewitz (2017, September 22). Reduced drinking in alcohol dependence treatment, what is the evidence? *European Addiction Research*. 23: 219–230 DOI: 10.1159/000481348.

10. U.S. Department of Health and Human Services (HHS), Office of the Surgeon General (2016). *Facing addiction in America: The Surgeon General's report on alcohol, drugs, and health*. Washington, DC: Health and Human Services.

11. J. D. Sinclair (1998). New treatment options for substance abuse from a public health viewpoint. *Annals of Medicine*. 30(4): 406–411.

12. H. R. Kranzler, H. Tennen, S. Armeli, G. Chan, J. Covault, A. Aria & C. Oncken (2009). Targeted naltrexone for problem drinkers. *Journal of Clinical Psychopharmacology*. 29(4): 350–357. DOI: 10.1097/JCP.0b013e3181ac5213.

13. J. D. Sinclair (2001). Evidence about the use of naltrexone and for different ways of using it in the treatment of alcoholism. *Alcohol and Alcoholism*. 36(1): 2–10. https://doi.org/10.1093/alcalc/36.1.2.

14. C. Christian (2016, April 29). [Video file] *How I overcame alcoholism*. Retrieved from https://www.youtube.com/watch?v=6EghiY_s2ts.

15. A. Schomer (2014). Proven entertainment. *One Little Pill*.

16. R. K. Hester & W. R. Miller (2003). *Handbook of alcoholism treatment approaches: Effective alternatives* (pp. 148–159). Needham Heights, MA: Allyn & Bacon.

17. W. R. Miller & R. F. Munoz (2013). *Controlling your drinking: Tools to make moderation work for you* (2nd ed.). New York: The Guilford Press.

18. W. R. Miller (2019, July 7). Personal communication.

19. G. D. Walters (2000). Behavioral self-control training for problem drinkers: A meta-analysis of randomized control studies. *Behavior Therapy*. 31(1): 135–149. https://doi.org/10.1016/S0005-7894(00)80008-8.

20. M. E. Saladin & E. Santa Ana (2004, May). Controlled drinking: More than just a controversy. *Addictive disorders*. 17(3): 175, 187.

21. M. B. Sobell & L. C. Sobell (2005). Guided self-change model of treatment for substance use disorders. *Journal of Cognitive Psychotherapy*. 19(3). DOI: 10.1891/jcop.2005.19.3.199.

22. L. C. Sobell & M. B. Sobell (2011). *Group therapy for substance use disorders: A motivational cognitive-behavioral approach*. New York: The Guilford Press.

23. J-F. G. Morin, M. Harris & P. J. Conrod (2017). A review of CBT treatments for substance use disorders. *Clinical Psychology*. DOI: 10.1093/oxfordhb/97801 99935291.013.57.

24. U.S. Department of Health and Human Services (HHS), Office of the Surgeon General (2016). *Facing addiction in America: The Surgeon General's report on alcohol, drugs, and health*. Washington, DC: Health and Human Services.

25. R. Miller & S. Rollnick (2002). *Motivational interviewing: Preparing people for change* (2nd ed.). New York: The Guilford Press.

26. J. Hari (2015). *Chasing the scream: The first and last days of the war on drugs*. New York: Bloomsbury Publishing.

27. TED (2015, June). *Johann Hari: Everything you think you know about addiction is wrong*. Retrieved from www.ted.com/talks/johann_hari_everything_you_think_you_know_about_addiction_is_wrong.

28. National Institute on Alcohol Abuse and Alcoholism (1998, July). *Alcohol alert no. 41*. Bethesda, MD: National Institute on Alcohol Abuse and Alcoholism.

29. Commander, U.S. 2nd Fleet (2011, March 14). *0-0-1-3 formula keeps alcohol-related incidents at bay*. Story Number: NNS110314-10.

5   Alcohol's Effect on Body, Mind, and Health

I was not going to include the chapter on the effects of alcohol because I thought it would not interest people. However, it turned out to be one of the most impactful chapters in my first book *Can I Keep Drinking? How You Can Decide When Enough is Enough*. People who read it said that the information about how drinking was affecting their brain, body, and mood was one of the factors that influenced them in changing their drinking patterns. People who had been ambivalent about making changes to their drinking patterns read it and said that this was the chapter that got their attention and pushed them further along the change process to alter their drinking habits. Many felt that the consequences outweighed the benefits of drinking and chose abstinence or significantly cut back on their use. Thus, I am including an expanded version of the effects of alcohol in this work.

One of the challenges with alcohol is that many of its effects are not immediate. A number of these conditions take years to develop. This makes it harder to see the potential seriousness of frequent alcohol use. My hope is that with education and information, people can make more informed decisions before any permanent damage occurs.

No Safe Level

I know this may not be a good way to start, but we have new research. A 2016 groundbreaking study that reviewed the impact of alcohol use in 195 countries over a 25-year period has significant implications.[1] They found that alcohol use is a leading factor in the global disease burden and causes substantial health loss. They reported alcohol use increases the risk of all-cause mortality and is especially true for all cancers. This study was the first one to conclude that there is no safe level of alcohol use. This is significant as the medical community was reporting that a glass or two of wine a day was healthy.

While there is no safe level, it does not mean that alcohol is evil or always dangerous. It means that consumption comes with risks. Just as science shows us that sugar and trans fats are not healthy for us does not mean that people do not still enjoy consuming them. Drinking can be a pleasurable experience and accompaniment to many types of celebrations. Our job is to educate people so they can make an informed choice about what they put into their bodies. Recall my description of the majority of drinkers as "donuts." About 37% of the drinking population is consuming alcohol at an amount and frequency that is not causing significant problems. I have said that drinking alcohol is like eating donuts: having one or two occasionally will not cause much damage if you do not have other health issues, but having multiple donuts every day is eventually going to lead to serious consequences.

Alcohol affects every organ in the body, including the brain. The life expectancy of someone who drinks heavily is shorter than that of others who drink less. It is the third main contributor to disease in the world, with one-third of the deaths related to alcohol being the result of suicides, accidents, and drowning.[2] The World Health Organization reports that over three million people die each year from an alcohol-related incident.[3] To put this in perspective, approximately 8,200 lives are lost every day of the year.

The effects of chronic alcohol use get progressive, while binge drinking causes many accidents. Generally, the more and the longer one drinks, the more damage that occurs to the brain and body. In my practice, the clients who develop cancer, have cirrhosis, need a liver transplant, and suffer from alcohol-induced dementia tend to be chronic, heavy drinkers. However, there are exceptions where I have seen these problems in people as young as in their 20s and 30s.

I believe that all of us are entitled to unbiased information about what we put into our bodies and the impact it has on us. In this chapter I have compiled some of the main negative effects of alcohol. The impact that drinking has on you individually depends on many factors, including your age, weight, other co-occurring mental or physical health disorders, how much and how often you drink, your gender, the presence of other foods or drugs in your system, and the time period in which the alcohol is consumed. Just Say Know—know the effects of alcohol to make informed choices.

Central Nervous System Depressant

Alcohol is a central nervous system depressant. Depressants are a class of drugs that slow down the functioning of the brain by depressing the central nervous system (CNS). The CNS includes the brain and the spinal cord. It controls most of our main functions like taking in information, controlling motor function, thinking, understanding, reasoning, and emoting. The CNS also deals with neurons that form a network that carries information to and from our extremities, muscles, and organs.[4]

Alcohol is one of the most popular depressants. People use it to unwind and relax. The calming effects of depressants can be pleasurable. Initially, one may feel more energized as the alcohol reduces inhibitions and increases socialization. This is why alcohol is often called a "social lubricant." Alcohol can temporarily make people forget their problems. This all sounds like a wonder drug, but what happens to the brain and body when people drink too much or too often?

Brain

The effects of alcohol on the brain are significant. Alcohol interferes with the brain's communication pathways. Drinking alcohol can cause changes in mood and behavior as well as make it difficult to process information and think clearly. It also affects coordination. Functional MRIs show that the regions of the brain most affected by alcohol are the cerebellum, limbic system, and cerebral cortex.[5]

The cerebellum, located in the back of the brain, is the area that controls motor coordination. In the short term, damage to the cerebellum includes a loss of balance and resultant stumbling, which increases the risks of accidents and injury. People under the influence also tend to have lapses in judgment and slowed reaction time. These are the main reasons why alcohol impairs the ability to operate a motor vehicle.

The limbic system is responsible for memory and emotions. People may do or say things that are out of character because inhibitions are lowered and may not remember doing or saying them. Some people fight when they are intoxicated or become more emotional. This is the alcohol affecting their emotions. Individuals loosen up with one or two drinks, but an excess of alcohol alters feelings and perceptions of the enjoinment.

The cerebral cortex regulates our ability to think, plan, and behave intelligently, and it connects to the rest of the nervous system. Damage to it affects the ability to solve problems, remember, and learn. People may identify with these experiences: having the most amazing idea, story, or plan, then the next day wondering what was so great only a few hours ago or seeing a video or hearing about what one thought were professional-style dance moves or song lines.

Alcohol affects the neurotransmitters in the brain. These include serotonin, endorphins, and glutamine. You may have heard of serotonin in connection with antidepressants. A certain class of medication prescribed to help with depression is called SSRIs (selective serotonin reuptake inhibitors). Serotonin helps regulate mood. People who suffer from depression are thought to have problems with the levels of serotonin in their brains. Alcohol is believed to interrupt normal transmission of serotonin; thus, people who are regular drinkers may suffer from higher rates of depression than those who do not partake.[6]

Endorphins are another type of neurotransmitter that alcohol interferes with. Endorphins are natural substances that increase feelings of relaxation and euphoria. When individuals begin drinking, they feel good initially; but over time these important chemicals are damaged. It makes it harder for natural events and experiences to bring genuine happiness and feelings of pleasure.

The third main neurotransmitter that alcohol damages is glutamine. It is believed that glutamine is responsible for memory. Even moderate drinking can cause people to have fuzzy memories. Damage to glutamine production may also contribute to why people who drink heavily black out.

A neuropsychologist with whom I consult describes alcohol as a neurotoxin. Alcohol literally causes brain damage, while long-term drinking actually shrinks the brain. Alcohol alters neurons, which reduces the size of brain cells. The brain mass shrinks and the inner cavity grows larger. These changes affect a variety of abilities, including motor coordination, sleep, mood, learning, and memory.

Cardiovascular System

Another significant area that alcohol impacts is the cardiovascular system, which consists of the heart, blood vessels, and blood. The cardiovascular system is working every second of the day, delivering oxygen and nutrients to the cells and carrying away unnecessary materials.

The heart is the center of the cardiovascular system. Chronic drinking causes the heart to experience a number of complications.[7] The heart may develop cardiomyopathy, a stretching and drooping of the heart muscle, which weakens the heart and prevents it from pumping enough blood to nourish the organs. Another complication of the heart is atrial fibrillation, an arrhythmia in which the upper and lower chambers of the heart are out of rhythm. This can lead to a blood clot or stroke. Alcohol use also exacerbates the various problems that lead to strokes, hypertension, arrhythmias, and cardiomyopathy.

Additionally, the lifestyle of regular alcohol users contributes to health problems. Drinkers often have irregular sleeping patterns, smoke cigarettes, use other drugs, and may not eat healthfully or exercise regularly.

Liver and Pancreas

One organ we may not think a lot about is the liver. The liver's job is to detoxify, synthesize protein, and produce chemicals necessary for digestion. Heavy drinking can cause inflammation, which leads to stenosis (a fatty liver); alcoholic hepatitis (inflammation); fibrosis, a change in the liver caused by inflammation; and cirrhosis, a complication of liver disease which involves loss of liver cells and irreversible scarring of the liver. All of these can be fatal. When the liver is damaged, it can no longer function well and allows toxic substances to travel to the brain. Long-term alcohol use is the most common cause of liver failure.[8]

Liver damage occurs in three stages. The first phase is a fatty liver. In this stage the liver cells have stopped breaking down fat and begun to use alcohol as fuel. The unprocessed cells accumulate. The second stage is called alcoholic hepatitis. During this stage the liver cells have begun dying as a result of the fat and the direct toxic effects of the alcohol. The body's defense is to cause inflammation. At this stage the liver is swollen, sore, and tender to the touch. The person may start to experience nausea, vomiting, gray stool, and jaundice (yellow-appearing eyes and skin). The third stage is called cirrhosis. Many of the liver cells have died and been replaced by fibrous scar tissue. If alcohol consumption does not cease, the individual will need a new liver. In order to be on most transplant lists, the person must have shown complete abstinence from alcohol for a year.

If a person stops or reduces their alcohol consumption in the first and second phases, the damage can often be reversed. This is why I recommend to all of my clients who have consumed alcohol on a regular basis that they get their liver enzymes checked so that we know the extent of the damage.

The pancreas is another organ that does not get a lot of attention until it is too late. Alcohol causes the pancreas to produce toxic substances that can lead to pancreatitis, a dangerous inflammation and swelling of the blood vessels that prevents proper digestion. An attack of pancreatitis is very painful. Research shows that the combination of heavy drinking and cigarette smoking exacerbates the condition.[9]

Immune System

Drinking too much or too often can increase the risk of developing certain cancers, including mouth, esophageal, throat, liver, and breast cancer. Alcohol weakens the immune system, making us more susceptible to diseases and sicknesses. Drinking slows the body's ability to fight off infections for 24 hours after consumption.[10] I also remind my clients how often they need to use the bathroom when drinking and how aware of sanitation they are at that point.

Pregnancy

Alcohol can affect a developing fetus. If a woman consumes alcohol while pregnant, she exposes her baby to Fetal Alcohol Spectrum Disorders (FASD).[11] Symptoms include abnormal facial features and severe reductions in brain function, coordination, emotional control, academic and vocational ability, and socialization. The child's brain will be smaller than normal and have fewer brain cells. They will have lifelong learning and behavioral problems that will likely decrease his or her quality of life.

Driving

Alcohol affects the ability to drive or operate heavy machinery in multiple ways.[12] It impairs judgment, reaction time, depth perception, coordination, vision, and reflexes. All of these affect our ability to react to the changing situations that occur when driving. The National Highway Traffic Safety Administration reports show that about a third of the people who die in car crashes each year are the result of drunk driving.[13] Mothers Against Drunk Driving (MADD) reports that every two minutes, someone in the United States is injured in an alcohol-related accident and that drunk driving costs the United States $130 billion a year.[14]

These are preventable statistics. I recommend that if an individual has had more than one drink, he or she should not operate a motor vehicle. Plan ahead for a designated driver, and if one has too many drinks, pay for transportation. With the accessibility of ride services, there should be no excuse for getting home safely.

Accidents and Injuries

The most common health risk from alcohol consumption comes in the form of accidents and injuries. One study showed that drinking was involved in 38.1% of serious arguments, 56.6% of threats, and 67.9% of incidents of physical aggression.[15] It is significant to note that physical violence was associated with intoxication, not moderate alcohol use.

Traumatic Brain Injury

Alcohol use and traumatic brain injury (TBI) are closely related.[16] Up to two-thirds of people who have a TBI have a history of risky drinking. Between 30% and 50% of people with TBI were injured while they were intoxicated. People who have TBI and continue to drink heavily increase their risk of having poor outcomes for overall health and wellness. After TBI, many people notice their brains are more sensitive to alcohol. Drinking increases the chances of getting injured again, makes cognitive problems worse, and increases emotional problems such as depression. Staying away from alcohol is strongly recommended to avoid further injury to the brain and to promote as much healing as possible.

Sleep

The National Sleep Foundation estimates that 20% of Americans use alcohol to help them fall asleep.[17] While it may increase drowsiness, the reality is that it actually worsens the quality of sleep. Drinking decreases the time spent in the most restful and restorative stage: REM. This is where we experience rapid eye movement and is where we dream. Dreaming is necessary to store and encode memories.

Drinking alcohol before bed is linked with more slow-wave sleep patterns known as delta activity. This is where we experience deep sleep that allows for memory formation and learning. However, alcohol turns on alpha activity, which should occur when we are sitting quietly, not during the night.

While individuals may fall asleep quickly after drinking, it is also common to wake up in the middle of the night. Alcohol affects the normal production of chemicals in the body that trigger sleepiness and subside once enough sleep has occurred. After drinking, production of adenosine (a sleep-inducing chemical in the brain) is increased, allowing for a fast onset of sleep. But it subsides as quickly as it came, making one more likely to wake up before adequate rest has occurred. Drinking alcohol also impacts the ability to stay asleep as it is a diuretic, requiring trips to the bathroom

Alcohol also interrupts our circadian rhythms. These rhythms help our bodies stay in sync with a 24-hour day like an internal clock that sends signals for things like digestion, hormones, and temperature regulation. Additionally, alcohol relaxes the entire body. This sounds great, but it also relaxes the muscles in our throats. This makes people more prone to snoring and the potentially life-threatening sleep apnea.

The National Health Service in the United Kingdom notes that a lack of sleep can impact us in numerous ways.[18] Missing just an hour and a half decreases our alertness, putting us at risk of accidents and injuries. It impairs our ability to think and encode. Encoding allows us to transfer information that we saw, heard, and learned throughout the day into our long-term memory so that we can recall it in the future. Lack of sleep impairs our mood, which can affect our relationships with the people around us. This also makes us less likely to participate in healthy activities like eating well, socializing, or exercising.

Chronic sleep deprivation adds up and becomes more serious. These impacts include high blood pressure, heart attack, stroke, obesity, and decreased sex drive. Long-term lack of sleep also affects our appearance. Over time, it leads to premature wrinkles and undereye circles. Research also shows that impaired sleep increases cortisol, a stress hormone. Cortisol is known to break down collagen, the protein that keeps our skin looking young and smooth.[19]

Weight

While alcohol is fat-free, it is terrible for weight management.[20] Most alcohol has double the amount of sugar as most carbohydrates. It is also calorie dense, with almost twice as many calories as in protein or carbohydrates. Alcohol also slows the body's ability to burn fat. Once it gets into the body, it gets converted into acetaldehyde, then acetate, and finally acetyl-CoA. These are inefficient fuel sources. The body cannot store these metabolites. Your body has to burn these off first, and other fuel sources like fat and sugar must wait. Ultimately, alcohol puts the body in a fat-storing mode. Whatever you are eating while drinking will be stored while the effects of the alcohol are being processed. The body absorbs alcohol faster than it can metabolize it.

Not only does alcohol lower inhibitions, making us more susceptible to making poor food choices, but it also activates an area of the brain that regulates food intake.[21] Nerve cells make what are called agouti-related proteins, which stimulate food intake. So we are getting a triple whammy of impulsive eating, lowered metabolism, and increased appetite.[22]

Box Matter 5.1

DID YOU KNOW? Heavy alcohol users may consume more calories in their drinks than in their food, causing weight gain and nutritional deficiencies. Light beers have about 100 calories per serving, the average glass of wine has about 120, and an ounce of liquor is around 100. Add in mixers and the calorie and sugar count goes up. For example, a 12-ounce margarita can have 680 calories. If someone drinks three, they have reached their recommended daily caloric intake.[23]

Abstainer Bias

In the mid-1990s, doctors believed that moderate alcohol consumption (fewer than 21 drinks for men and fewer than 14 drinkers per week for women) had positive effects on cardiovascular health.[24] Having a glass or two of wine was believed to increase a number of mechanisms that are associated with blood clotting, which could reduce the likelihood of a heart attack. Moderate drinkers were reported to have a 50% reduction for ischemic stroke because of these mechanisms. They also thought that moderate alcohol consumption also offered protection against gallstones and increased bone density by 10–20% which can reduce the risk of osteoporosis. It was also reported that alcohol use increased levels of HDL cholesterol ("good cholesterol"), which lowers the HDL/LDL ratio that inhibits the formulation of coronary artery atheroma. Even though many studies were showing that light-to-moderate alcohol consumption lowered risk of mortality from cardiovascular disease, they pointed out that heavy drinking significantly increases the risk of death from all causes, including cancer, cardiovascular disease, and accidents.[25]

Again, new research is changing what we thought about the health benefits of alcohol use. In 2016 researchers analyzed 87 studies that supported the idea that moderate alcohol consumption leads to a longer life.[26] These studies included data from over four million people. They found an effect called the "abstainer bias." Previous data that was being used to show that moderate drinkers were healthier than those who did not drink was due to the abstainer bias. The abstainer bias is when low-volume drinkers (fewer than 21 drinks a week) appear healthy when they are compared against people who abstained from alcohol. This is because alcohol abstainers often have worse health, possibly because the abstainers once had a problem with alcohol or were not drinking because they had serious health issues.

The researchers found that when they took out the data from those who did not drink, moderate drinkers no longer had a lower-than-usual risk of mortality. They also ultimately concluded that there is no safe level of drinking.

Question the Source

When I was studying for my undergraduate degree in psychology, my research and statistics professor taught me to always question your source. This has served me well in my career as well as my personal life. Just because someone wrote it does not make it true. A study often gives authority to the message. Many never question who funded the researchers who completed the study. Those who pay may abuse their power and skew the results.

For decades the health benefits of alcohol use have been encouraged. The reality is that much of the research has been funded by alcohol companies.[27] A 2015 Gallup Poll found that one out of five people believe that moderate alcohol use is good for your health. These numbers are higher for people who do drink.[28]

Other research shows that studies that are funded by the food industry are four to eight times more likely to conclude that something that financially benefits its sponsor.[29] If you're wondering, it is the companies who benefit from the sale of alcohol that have been funding studies that say alcohol is good for our health.[30] This can be confusing when the researchers are legitimate medical doctors. Always question your source before you believe the results.

Many argue that the United States has a conservative view on alcohol and that countries who have a lower drinking age view consumption differently. While it is true that people in European countries tend to drink at earlier ages, they tend to see alcohol as an accompaniment to a meal, while many young Americans are binge drinking for effect, not taste. Remember that the World Health Organization says that even if there are some slight benefits to alcohol, the risks far outweigh them. Other recent studies have come to the same conclusions.[31]

Risk Analysis

As part of therapy I perform a risk analysis. I ask my clients to explore if the benefits of ongoing alcohol use are worth the potential structural, chemical, emotional, and physical damage that regular drinking can do. This information is not provided as a scare tactic, but as a way for your clients to make informed decisions. This is what harm reduction strategies do: Just Say Know.

Notes

1. M. G. Griswold, N. Fullman, C. Hawley, N. Arian, S. Zimsen, H. D. Tymeson, V. Venkateswaran, A. D. Tapp, M. Forouzanfar, J. S. Salama, K. Abate, D. Abate, S. Abay, C. Abbafati, R. Suliankatchi, A. Zegeye, V. Aboyans, M. M. Abrar & P. Acharya (2018). Alcohol use and burden for 195 countries and territories, 1990–2016: A systematic analysis for the global burden of disease study 2016. *Lancet.* 392: 1015–1035.

2. M. Shahre, J. Roeber, D. Kanny, R. D. Brewer & X. Zhang (2014). Contribution of excessive alcohol consumption to deaths and years of potential life lost in the United States. *Preventing Chronic Disease.* 11(13): 130293. http://dx.doi.org/10.5888/pcd11.130293.

3. World Health Organization (2108). *Global status report on alcohol and health 2018.* Geneva: World Health Organization. License: CC BY-NC-SA 3.0 IGO.

4. T. Newman (2017, December 22). All about the central nervous system. *Medical News Today.* Retrieved from https://www.medicalnewstoday.com/articles/307076.php.

5. E. V. Sullivan, A. Harris & A. Pfefferbaum (2010). Alcohol's effects on brain and behavior. *Alcohol Research & Health.* 33(1–2): 127–143.

6. N. Banerjee (2014). Neurotransmitters in alcoholism: A review of neurobiological and genetic studies. *Indian Journal of Human Genetics.* 20(1): 20–31. DOI: 10.4103/0971-6866.132750.

7. M. R. Piano (2017). Alcohol's effects on the cardiovascular system. *Alcohol Research.* 38(2): 219–241.

8. C. Nordqvist (2018, February 6). What's to know about liver disease? *Medical News Today.* Retrieved from www.medicalnewstoday.com/articles/215638.php.

9. P. Chowdhury & P. Gupta (2006). Pathology of alcoholic pancreatitis: An overview. *World Journal of Gastroenterology.* 12(46): 7421–7427. DOI: 10.3748/wjg.v12.i46.7421.

10. D. Sarkar, M. K. Jung & H. J. Wang (2015). Alcohol and the immune system. *Alcohol Research.* 37(2): 153–155.

11. P. A. May & J. P. Gossage (2011). Fetal alcohol spectrum disorders. *Alcohol Research and Health.* 34(1): 16–23.

12. National Highway Traffic Safety Administration (2018). *Traffic safety facts 2016 data: Alcohol-impaired driving.* Washington, DC: U.S. Department of Transportation. Retrieved from https://crashstats.nhtsa.dot.gov/Api/Public/ViewPublication/812450External.

13. X. Zhao, X. Zhang & J. Rong (2014). Study of the effects of alcohol on drivers and driving performance on straight road. *Mathematical Problems in Engineering.* Article ID 607652. https://doi.org/10.1155/2014/607652.

14. MADD (2019, May 3). *Statistics.* Retrieved from www.madd.org/statistics/.

15. S. Wells, K. Graham & P. J. West (2000). Alcohol-related aggression in the general population. *Journal of Studies on Alcohol.* 61(4): 626–632.

16. C. H. Bombardier & A. Turner (2009). Alcohol and traumatic disability. In R. Frank & T. Elliott (Eds.), *The handbook of rehabilitation psychology* (2nd ed., pp. 241–258). Washington, DC: American Psychological Association Press.

17. National Sleep Foundation (2019, May 5). *How alcohol affects the quality—and quantity of sleep.* Retrieved from www.sleepfoundation.org/articles/how-alcohol-affects-quality-and-quantity-sleep.

18. National Health Service (2018, May 30). *Sleep and tiredness: Why lack of sleep is bad for your health.* Retrieved from www.nhs.uk/live-well/sleep-and-tiredness/why-lack-of-sleep-is-bad-for-your-health/.

19. B. Bush & T. Hudson (2010). The role of cortisol in sleep. *Natural Medicine Journal.* 2(6).

20. M. Usman (2109, February 2). *How does alcohol consumption affect your weight and shape?* Retrieved from www.weightlossresources.co.uk/body_weight/alcohol-effect.htm.

21. C. Winter (2017, January 11). Why does alcohol make you hungry? Biological link between drinking and binge eating discovered. *ABC.net.AU News*. Retrieved from www. abc.net.au/news/2017-01-11/why-does-alcohol-make-you-hungry/8176220.

22. S. Cains et al. (2017). Agrp neuron activity is required for alcohol-induced overeating. *Nature Communications*. 8: 14014. DOI: 10.1038/ncomms14014.

23. National Institute on Alcohol Abuse and Alcoholism (2019, March 11). *Alcohol calorie calculator*. Retrieved from www.rethinkingdrinking.niaaa.nih.gov/Tools/Cal culators/Calorie-Calculator.aspx.

24. Royal College of Physicians, Royal College of Psychiatrists, Royal College of General Practitioners (1995, June). *Alcohol and the heart in perspective—Sensible limits reaffirmed. Report of a joint working group.* ISBN 1 86016 019 0.

25. S. Roth (2017, April 17). *Light-to-moderate alcohol consumption can reduce risk of death, while heavy alcohol consumption can have opposite effect.* Retrieved from www.acc. org/about-acc/press-releases/2017/08/14/14/04/light-to-moderate-alcohol-con sumption-may-have-protective-health-effects.

26. T. Stockwell, J. Zhao, S. Panwar, A. Roemer, T. Naimi & T. Chikrizhs (2016). Do "moderate" drinkers have reduced mortality risk? A systemic review and meta-analysis of alcohol consumption and all-cause mortality. *Journal of Studies on Alcohol and Drugs*. 77(2): 185–198.

27. A. Almendrai (2018, April 14). Alcohol companies are funding research to convince you drinking is healthy. *Huffington Post*. Retrieved from www.huffpost.com/ entry/alcohol-companies-want-you-to-drink-more-and-theyre-funding-research-to-make-it-happen_n_5ad123bce4b077c89ce8a835.

28. R. Rifkin (2015, July 28). One in five Americans say alcohol use is healthy. *Gallup News*. Retrieved from https://news.gallup.com/poll/184382/one-five-americans-say-moderate-drinking-healthy.aspx.

29. L. I. Lesser, C. B. Ebbeling, M. Goozner, D. Wypij & D. S. Ludwig (2007). Relationship between funding source and conclusion among nutrition-related scientific articles. *PLoS Medicine*. 4(1): e5. https://doi.org/10.1371/journal.pmed.0040005.

30. R. C. Rabin (2018, March 17). Federal agency courted alcohol industry to fund study on benefits of moderate drinking. *New York Times*. Retrieved from https:// www.nytimes.com/2018/03/17/health/nih-alcohol-study-liquor-industry.html.

31. S. Andréasson, T. Chikritzhs, F. Dangardt, H. Holder, T. Naimi & T. Stockwell (2014). Evidence about health effects of "moderate" alcohol consumption: Reasons for skepticism and public health implications. In *Alcohol and society*. Stockholm: IOGT-NTO & Swedish Society of Medicine.

6   Evaluation, Diagnosis, and Self-Assessment

The first several chapters gave a history of harm reduction, identified the different types of drinkers, and described the harms from alcohol use. The next several chapters will focus on clinical skills. This will describe the steps of performing an evaluation, forming a diagnosis, and helping your clients self-assess.

Evaluation

Before you can assist your client in self-assessment, you must first complete an evaluation. The most important thing you can do when practicing alcohol moderation is to develop a relationship with your client. If your client does not feel comfortable with you, he or she will not tell you anything. Before asking any questions, I explain the process to them. "Today I'm going to be asking you a lot of questions. I want to get to know you, what you've struggled with. I want to know what's worked and what has not." Here I'm letting them know that they are in charge, not me. I am their guide. I will respect the things that have not helped and not try them again.

When I meet with my clients for the first time, I also let them know that there is a Spectrum of Substance Use (described in Chapter 2). I hold up my hands to demonstrate. With one hand, I show the more than 30% of the population that uses no substances at all. With the other hand, I show addiction (severe alcohol use disorder), which accounts for only a small percentage (6%) of the population. I pinch my fingers to show them that this is actually a small number. Studies have shown that one of the reasons people do not enter treatment is because they are concerned about the stigma of being labeled an "alcoholic" or "addict."[1]

Box Matter 6.1

DID YOU KNOW? The words *alcoholic* and *alcoholism* were coined in 1848 by a Swedish physician named Magnus Huss. By the end of the 20th century, it had become the accepted way of describing alcohol problems, particularly in the United States where people experiencing problems with drinking were previously called drunkards or inebriates.[2]

I continue that my job is to figure out where they fit on the spectrum and what their goals are. It's helpful to state that just because one uses alcohol or other drugs does not mean they are an "alcoholic" or "addict." I choose those words on purpose because they are rife with stigma. I make it clear that I don't like those words and won't use them, unless that is what they chose. They determine what alcohol means in their life. By doing this I have conveyed the message that I don't make any judgments. I also tell them that what I care most about is *why*. I want to understand why they are using alcohol and what it does for them so that we can personalize a plan for their unique situation.

Before meeting the client in person, my first contact will most likely be with the client via telephone. Even if they may have emailed or left a message, I want to talk with them first so I can offer a human connection. I want the person to know that many people who have worked with me have gotten better, but that each person's path is their own. I share that there are many tips and tools I can offer, but we will figure, together, the right ones for them. Prior to meeting me in person, they have completed online forms so that it does not take time away from the intake session. I briefly review them and ask if they have any questions.

I find that it is very important to go over what confidentiality means. Many people who are using alcohol have engaged in behaviors that they are embarrassed about and hide from their loved ones, and that can be against the law. They may have done things that are illegal, such as drinking and driving, other substance use, or stealing. It is my job to help them feel safe to share what is really going on for them and make sure that they know that I am not going to tell anyone about what they are doing. I may phrase it as follows:

What we talk about is confidential. I can't ethically or legally tell anyone one about what we talk about. You may tell me about some things that you are not proud of or actions that may be illegal. I cannot tell anyone about things that happened in the past. The only times I can break confidentiality is if there is a serious, imminent, foreseeable risk to yourself or someone else or if there is suspected child, elder, or sexual abuse, or if you give me permission to talk to other people who might be helpful in your care. These may include family members, previous or current treatment providers, your lawyer, or your psychiatrist. Before I ever talk with any of them, you and I will review what we may discuss.

To increase their comfort in disclosing information, I go a step further to describe 42 CFR Part 2, which has to do with substance use disorders treatment confidentiality regulations.[3] I explain that federal laws protect their information, prohibiting unauthorized disclosures and thus preventing information revealed in treatment from being used to prosecute them. I wait to sign any releases of information until the end of the evaluation so they get a chance to become comfortable with me. I state that we will figure who we think should be involved in their treatment. I let them know that I will still work with them even if they do not want me to talk with anyone else, but I inform them of how it may affect our treatment if they refuse to sign any releases.

Confidentiality can be challenging when clients are court involved for pending legal charges, probation/parole, and divorce and custody proceedings. Typically, all I share is a letter with a treatment update. These usually describe attendance and progress in treatment. I make them as brief as possible, without revealing the content of the work we are doing. Each situation is unique, and some require more oversight. There are some situations where complete abstinence is required, such as for probation/parole, court orders, Child Protective Services, or conditions for employment such as the Department of Transportation and the Federal Aviation Administration. The therapist needs to learn what is required and to inform the client of what will be shared at the onset of treatment.

After I have gone over what to expect, confidentiality, 42 CFR Part 2, and my treatment philosophy, I ask them if they have any questions for me. This puts me on an even playing field. While I am the expert, this shows that I am open, and the person is invited to ask about my background. Sometimes it is about my education or experience, which I am happy to answer. I believe that this is more about ensuring the person that I am knowledgeable and safe than their challenging me. When you go to a doctor, you want to know that he or she knows what he is doing. The same should be true for substance use disorders treatment and therapy. Sometimes people ask about my substance use. If they do, I put the focus back on them and ask something like: "What is the question behind your question?" Usually they want to know if I will "get" them and if I can help them.

In case you are wondering, I never reveal my background with alcohol or drugs. If I did, then the session becomes about me. If I say that I have had a problem, the person wonders what my recovery was like, if I am going to push my beliefs and experiences on them, or if I am healthy enough to help them. If I say that I did not have a problem, I run the danger of their thinking I will judge them or could not understand their experience. The therapy is about them, not me.

Prior to beginning to take down information, I want to know how they feel about seeing me. Was it their choice? Has a loved one set an ultimatum? Is it court or job ordered? All of this guides me in how to proceed and helps me assess what stage of change they are in. Will I need to go slowly?

Educate more? Jump in because they have had a lot of treatment? Pace them? Acknowledge that they may have had treatment that did more harm than good?

The first formal question I ask is what made them contact me. There is usually some type of precipitating event. It may be: "I got a DUI," "my spouse thinks I drink too much," "I'm drinking more and more," "my depression is bad," "I keep having panic attacks," "I can't sleep," "my boyfriend/girlfriend broke up with me," or "I think I have a drinking problem, but I don't want to stop."

Once I get a general idea of what brought them in, I thank them for sharing that with me. Your clinical skills should inform you of whether it is appropriate to empathize, validate, reassure, offer hope, or educate. They may have had to say the same thing repeatedly if they have been in multiple treatment programs, or they might have been a crisis that they are still processing. If you want to jump in and give advice or a recommendation—stop! You know nothing about this person. You need to get more information and get to know them better.

The next area that I focus on is getting a general background. I've been doing this for almost three decades, so I have a system. It does not mean that mine is right. You will develop one, too. I also work in private practice, so I am not limited by government or agency practices. Make sure you know what your employer/agency/funding source/insurance company requires.

I transition and will say something like: "Now we will go backwards to move forwards. I want to get some information about you, if it's okay. I want to know about things that are significant to you, things that shaped you, good or bad. I'll take you through a chronology so that we stay organized because life can be messy! I may ask you about school, work, relationships, moves, treatment. Are you ready?"

In this way, I have let the person know that I have a purpose and prepared the person for the way in which I will be soliciting information as well as some of the things I may be asking about. I am using casual language on purpose. We don't need to use clinical jargon or psychobabble. This person is likely going through one of the toughest periods in their lives. We don't need to make them feel dumb just so we can sound smart. Your clinical skills should guide you to determine if this is a person who needs you to act and sound like an authority. For example, if I have a male executive, lawyer, or technology professional, I may focus more on outcomes, goals, and proper terminology. If I am evaluating a teenager, I keep it simple; no bullshit. For a female who has experienced trauma, I am softer and slower paced. You should adapt your language and demeanor to the client, not the other way around. Finally, I ask them if they are ready to start. This shares the power even if I am the one leading it.

"Tell me, where were you born? Were there any complications with your mother's pregnancy or delivery?" As a clinical supervisor, I recommend that you get good at typing or writing in phrases and spellchecking later. Remember that your goal is to build rapport with your potential client, not just gather information.

"From birth to age 5, do you recall anything that stands out? Any medical issues, moves, deaths, changes in the family?" If I have a family member in the room, I joke that this is the reason they are here, but I keep my main focus on the identified client even if it is a younger or less verbal person.

"What about ages 5 to 10? This is usually the start of elementary school." Some people have not thought about these times for decades, so be aware that you can be triggering some difficult times or they may truly not remember. Many people who have had trauma or unhappy childhoods cannot recall much detail. How they are telling their history is as important as the actual details.

"How about 10 to 15, this is usually middle school (or whatever it is called in your area)?"

"What about high school?" This is typically where I start to get a lot more information. You may need to control the flow. Your clinical skills should guide you as to how you deal with sensitive information such as sexual abuse, loss of a loved one, suicidal thoughts, etc. Connect with the person, but do not do therapy. I may say something like; "I'm sorry that you experienced that. How is it affecting you today? Is that something that you would like to focus on in treatment? I have worked with other people who have dealt with that and we've worked on ways to feel better."

"Tell me about your 20s." Notice that I am taking them through time periods. I am likely organically getting information about trauma, treatment, family of origin, mental health, spirituality, education, work, etc. I find that it flows better for me and feels more natural than my filling in the blanks and checking the boxes. I go back later to cut and paste, rather than have my client fit my evaluation form.

Notice anything that's missing yet? The substance use disorders evaluation. Even if people begin to bring up drug or alcohol use, I wait until the end because I want to have formed some type of connection with them. I use humor, when appropriate, to diffuse the tension. And I connect when it makes sense over smaller details like sports or activities they did, places they lived, hobbies they have. "You're from New Jersey. I grew up there." "You swam in high school. Me too. What was your event?" "You spent time in Europe. I hope to visit there sometime." You are a person, too, and can connect on lighter subjects. We have been asking them about difficult topics, but we can pace them to have a moment of respite from the gory details. Therapy does not have to be all about the bad.

Once I have completed a general biopsychosocial spiritual assessment and mental health evaluation, I let them know that I am now going to do the substance use disorders and addictive behaviors evaluation. While this book is about alcohol moderation, it is important to gather information about processes addictions that involve food, gaming, self-harm, internet, pornography, spending, sexual behaviors, etc. Here, I remind them again that there is a spectrum of use and that while they may admit to using a drug or drinking, I do not think they are an "addict" or "alcoholic" (remember, I purposely use those words because of their pejorative meaning). I also state that "Over a lifetime people use different amounts with different impact. So I want to get information about your first use, last use, heaviest use, and recent use of a number of different substances." In addition to pattern, quantity, frequency, route of administration, etc., I also ask what they liked about each substance. This helps me learn their "why" so that we can begin developing treatment goals. I also ask what their family's (and employer's, school, legal) goals are.

The final questions that I ask are: "Is there anything else that I have not asked that you think I should know?" "What questions do you have for me?" and "What are your goals?" The first question may reveal something that is important to them. It shows that I couldn't possibly have all the information about them and that I respect that they have goals. I have gotten answers like: "My pet is sick," "My girlfriend is pregnant," and "I'm worried about my friend." Some may also reveal a secret that they have been holding onto that is affecting their mental health, like: "I want to leave my spouse," "I'm having an affair," or "I think I'm gay." All of these areas may be important to address in treatment.

The second question elicits their buy-in to the process and legitimately answers any logistical or anxiety-related questions about what they can expect. The final question about their goals helps me to see what is important to them. The best outcomes for treatment occur when we take a collaborative approach with the client who selects the goals for treatment and the therapist offering education, support, and perspective.[4]

My evaluations often take about two hours. In addition to the clinical interview, I may administer a measurement tool like a Substance Abuse Subtle Screening Inventory to confirm my diagnosis.[5] I might also do a Breathalyzer or administer a urine drug screen. Giving these screens is dependent upon many factors, including whether I need to do one for a court order or if I am trying to get a baseline number for their substance use. It is less about catching them in a lie. I prefer to offer drug and alcohol screening as a refusal skill and accountability tool than as a way to police my clients. An experienced clinician can usually tell when a client is still actively using substances based on their presentation in treatment.

It is important to pace the evaluation process. Some people are verbal and go on tangents. It is okay to rein them in with a statement like: "That sounds like something you want to discuss, maybe we can go into more depth in a session," "We are getting a little off track, I want us to focus more on . . .," or "The therapist in me wants to go more into that, but would you be willing to stick with me and move on to learning more about . . ." While the person is the expert on their life, you are the expert who needs to gather enough information to make a recommendation.

Before the client leaves, I give them an idea of what I think might be helpful for them. I ask for their consent before we start any form of treatment. They leave with a general plan and an appointment scheduled. The next session will be in days, not weeks. They have initiated services because they either want to or they have to. Part of successful harm reduction treatment is that there are no barriers to services. Availability of services should be immediate. If there is a gap in time between the initial call and the evaluation or between the evaluation and the onset of treatment, the client may not return for help. You will have lost an opportunity to help someone who is suffering.

Diagnosis

The word *alcoholic* is not actually a clinical or diagnostic term. It's a name that people have used since the mid-1800s to describe an alcohol drinker who is experiencing problems. The way that professionals make a clinical diagnosis is with the *Diagnostic and Statistical Manual of Mental Disorders*, 5th edition (DSM-5). This is the book that clinicians, including doctors, psychiatrists, social workers, therapists, and psychologists, use to diagnose emotional and behavioral problems. Insurance companies require a DSM diagnosis to provide reimbursement for behavioral health services.

The DSM-5, the latest edition of the DSM, came out in May 2013. One of its major changes is in the way clinicians diagnose substance-use disorders. Formerly, only two categories for alcohol misuse existed: abuse or dependence. A simple explanation for each was:

Alcohol abuse: If alcohol use causes a problem, it is a problem.
Alcohol dependence: This term describes a person needing to drink to avoid physical withdrawal symptoms and needing more and more of it to achieve the same effect.

Many people incorrectly interchanged the two definitions. This was dangerous because the two categories were very different and required drastically different treatments. It is important to note that someone who is physically dependent on alcohol may not ever be able to safely drink again; but the much larger group of alcohol abusers, with the right tools and supports, often can consume alcohol at safer levels.

The DSM-5 eliminated the category of dependence to help distinguish between the compulsive drug-seeking behavior of addiction and the normal tolerance and withdrawal that patients who are legally prescribed medication may experience when stopping their prescriptions. The diagnoses were also recategorized on a continuum to include mild, moderate, and severe substance-use disorders. The information that follows is taken directly from the DSM-5.[6]

Alcohol Use Disorder

Alcohol use disorder is a problematic pattern of alcohol use leading to clinically significant impairment or distress, as manifested by at least two of the following, occurring within a 12-month period:

1. Alcohol is often taken in larger amounts or over a longer period than was intended.
2. There is a persistent desire or unsuccessful efforts to cut down or control alcohol use.
3. A great deal of time is spent on activities necessary to obtain alcohol, use alcohol, or recover from its effects.
4. Craving, or a strong desire or urge to use alcohol.
5. Recurrent alcohol use resulting in a failure to fulfill major role obligations at work, school, or home.
6. Continued alcohol use despite having persistent or recurrent social or interpersonal problems caused or exacerbated by the effect of alcohol.
7. Important social, occupational, or recreational activities are given up or reduced because of alcohol use.
8. Recurrent alcohol use in situations in which it is physically hazardous.
9. Alcohol use is continued despite knowledge of having a persistent or recurrent physical problem that is likely to be exacerbated by alcohol.
10. Tolerance, as defined by either of the following:
    a. A need for markedly increased amounts of alcohol to achieve intoxication or desired effect.
    b. A markedly diminished effect with continued use of the same amount of alcohol.
11. Withdrawal, as manifested by either of the following:
    a. The characteristic withdrawal syndrome for alcohol (see the next subsection).
    b. Alcohol (or a closely related substance, such as a benzodiazepine) is taken to relieve or avoid withdrawal symptoms.

The DSM-5 now looks at chemical use on a continuum similar to the Spectrum of Alcohol Use:

Mild Alcohol Use Disorder: presence of two to three symptoms
Moderate Alcohol Use Disorder: presence of four to five symptoms
Severe Alcohol Use Disorder: presence of six or more symptoms

Alcohol Withdrawal

Because I believe it is important for people to have accurate information, I have also included the criteria for alcohol withdrawal.[7] Many people are confused about the difference between a hangover—which may include gastric distress, grogginess, nausea, vomiting, and headache—and true alcohol withdrawal. Since experiencing actual alcohol withdrawal can be potentially life-threatening, it is important to determine if your client is experiencing a dangerous medical condition.

A. Cessation of (or reduction in) alcohol use that has been heavy and prolonged.
B. Two (or more) of the following, developing within several hours to a few days after the cessation of (or reduction in) alcohol use as described in criterion A:

1. Autonomic hyperactivity (e.g. sweating or pulse rate greater than 100 bpm).
2. Increased hand tremor.
3. Insomnia.
4. Nausea or vomiting.
5. Transient, visual, tactile, or auditory hallucinations or illusions.
6. Psychomotor agitation.
7. Anxiety.
8. Generalized tonic-clonic seizures (formerly known as grand mal seizures).

C. The signs or symptoms in Criterion B cause clinically significant distress or impairment in social, occupational, or other important areas of functioning.
D. The signs or symptoms are not attributable to another medical condition and are not better explained by another mental disorder, including intoxication or withdrawal from another substance.

How many of these symptoms has your client experienced? Please realize that if he or she has experienced any of them, it is unlikely that they will be able to safely drink again. They are likely in the 6%, the "pickles," not the 22% who are "cucumbers." If your client has seizures, fever, hallucinations, or delirium tremens ("the shakes"), that person needs to go to the nearest emergency room or call 911 and get into a detoxification program.

Experiencing delirium tremens is potentially life-threatening. Alcohol often initially enhances the effect of GABA (gamma-aminobutyric acid), a neurotransmitter that produces feelings of relaxation and calm and can also induce sleep. However, heavy use of alcohol suppresses GABA so that the body requires more and more of it to achieve the same effect, a condition otherwise known as tolerance. Heavy alcohol use also suppresses glutamate, the neurotransmitter that produces excitability. When regular users stop drinking, the chemicals rebound and can cause dangerous consequences such as seizures.

I have seen both men and women go through withdrawal from drinking all types of alcohol, including beer, wine, and liquor. This medical condition does not distinguish between users. Potentially life-threatening withdrawal symptoms can begin as early as two hours after the last drink, but the dangerous symptoms often begin to peak around 48 to 72 hours after alcohol cessation. Delirium tremens, however, may not peak until five days after stopping drinking. A person with the shakes needs to get medical attention immediately because it can progress to life-threateningly high blood pressure.

If a client is unsure of the role alcohol is playing in their life or they are not seeing how damaging it can be, I will often pull out the DSM-5 and go over the symptoms with them. It can be powerful for them to check off these boxes from an authority more than just my clinical opinion.

AUDIT

A tool that I may use in helping my clients self-assess is the AUDIT, developed by the World Health Organization in 1987.[8] AUDIT stands for Alcohol Use Disorders Identification Test. It is a self-assessment questionnaire about alcohol consumption that is commonly used to assess alcohol consumption, drinking behaviors, and alcohol-related consequences. The AUDIT consists of ten questions about alcohol use. The responses can easily be tallied to determine the degree to which a person may experience consequences from alcohol use. It can be used to give feedback to the individual and open up a dialogue about the potential consequences of alcohol use. It is designed to be used by health practitioners in a variety of settings but also can be self-administered. The AUDIT is used worldwide and has been translated into 37 languages. The questions asked appear in Figure 6.2:

AUDIT

QUESTIONNAIRE

PLEASE CIRCLE THE ANSWER THAT IS CORRECT FOR YOU

Questions	0	1	2	3	4
1. How often do you have a drink containing alcohol?	Never	Monthly or less	2–4 times a month	2–3 times a week	4 or more times a week
2. How many standard drinks containing alcohol do you have on a typical day when drinking?	1 or 2	3 or 4	5 or 6	7 to 9	10 or more

Figure 6.2 AUDIT Questionnaire

Questions	0	1	2	3	4
3. How often do you have six or more drinks on one occasion?	Never	Less than monthly	Monthly	Weekly	Daily or almost daily
4. During the past year, how often have you found that you were not able to stop drinking once you had started?	Never	Less than monthly	Monthly	Weekly	Daily or almost daily
5. During the past year, how often have you failed to do what was normally expected of you because of drinking?	Never	Less than monthly	Monthly	Weekly	Daily or almost daily
6. During the past year, how often have you needed a drink in the morning to get yourself going after a heavy drinking session?	Never	Less than monthly	Monthly	Weekly	Daily or almost daily
7. During the past year, how often have you had a feeling of guilt or remorse after drinking?	Never	Less than monthly	Monthly	Weekly	Daily or almost daily
8. During the past year, have you been unable to remember what happened the night before because you had been drinking?	Never	Less than monthly	Monthly	Weekly	Daily or almost daily
9. Have you or someone else been injured as a result of your drinking?	No	Yes, but not in the past year	Yes, during the past year		
10. Has a relative or friend, doctor or other health worker been concerned about your drinking or suggested you cut down?	No	Yes, but not in the past year	Yes, during the past year		
					Total

Figure 6.2 (Continued)

AUDIT

QUESTIONNAIRE

SCORING THE AUDIT

Scores for each question range from 0 to 4, with the first response for each question (e.g., never) scoring 0, the second (e.g., less than monthly) scoring 1, the third (e.g., monthly) scoring 2, the fourth (e.g., weekly) scoring 3, and the last response (e.g., daily or almost daily) scoring 4. For questions 9 and 10, which only have three responses, the scoring is 0, 2, and 4 (from left to right).

A score of 8 or more is associated with harmful or hazardous drinking. A score of 13 or more in women, and 15 or more in men, is likely to indicate alcohol dependence.

Source: Reproduced, with the permission of the publisher, from The Alcohol Use Disorders Identification Test: guidelines for use in primary care, AUDIT, second edition. Geneva, World Health Organization, 2000 (The AUDIT test: interview version Page 17 http://whqlibdoc.who.int/hq/2001/WHO_MSD_MSB_01.6a.pdf, accessed 30 April 2013)

Figure 6.2 (Continued)

Dominant Drinking Patterns

Another way I help clients self-assess is in examining how they consume alcohol. There are typically four types of drinking patterns:

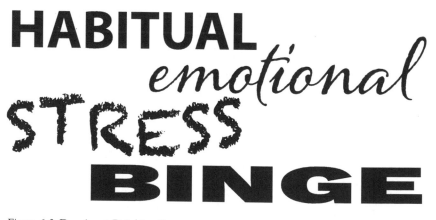

Figure 6.3 Dominant Drinking Patterns

Habitual: drinks at the same time, place, or situation. Some examples include: as soon as the game starts, he cracks open a beer; she has a glass of wine while cooking dinner; or the family that celebrates events with drinking. By changing the time, place, or situation, this drinker may be able to get out of the habit and develop ones that are less damaging.

Emotional: consumes alcohol as a way to change mood. This has also been called self-medicating. One has a drink to loosen up in a social situation. It may be a way to deal with anxiety, depression, insomnia, or relationship issues. This is one of the reasons it is important to do a thorough assessment and explore why a person drinks. Once we know the "why," we can go about identifying different coping strategies.

Stress: drinks as a way to deal with the fluctuations in life. This drinker has a fight, then has a drink to relax. Problems at work? They hit the bar to unwind. We need to help our clients understand the patterns that they are in and explore ways to either cope with the situation or develop a plan to change the stressful situation.

Binge: has four alcoholic drinks for women/five drinks for men in a period of less than two hours. There is intent to feel the effect of alcohol. This drinker may not drink on a regular basis, but when they do, it may be hard to stop until the alcohol is gone, everyone has gone home, or they throw up or pass out. Identifying the triggers that lead up to a binge can be helpful in doing something different. It also may require a change in the people they spend time with or the places they go, like a bar, club, or party.

People may notice that they fit into one or more dominant drinking styles at different times in their lives. Your job as a therapist is to assist your client in recognizing which one they are in and develop a plan for other ways to manage patterns, emotions, stressors, and limits.

Spectrum of Decreasing Alcohol Use

Clinicians often tell me that one of the areas that they struggle with in practicing alcohol moderation is feeling like they are teaching their clients to drink. Studies find that when given a combination of education and counseling, many clients will actually choose abstinence.[9] The people who enter your office have typically been experiencing problems related to their alcohol use for a period of time, even if they are not willing to admit it. If we label them something that they are not ready to acknowledge, they may not come back. We want to be able to engage them in a discussion about their drinking and potentially be able to offer them education and tools about how to lead a more balanced life.

Below is a process that occurs when we practice alcohol moderation. There is a lot of information about the process of alcohol developing into a problem, but little on how moderation can happen. The Spectrum of Alcohol Use actually has another side: Decreasing Alcohol Use. Alcohol moderation is about decreasing the harms from drinking.

Figure 6.4 Spectrum of Decreasing Alcohol Use

On the continuum of the Spectrum of Alcohol Use is decreasing alcohol use. With alcohol moderation, people can transition down from heavy use to safer use. This might mean making the decision not to change the amount of alcohol use, but the situation in which it is consumed. This could include drinking only on weekends, when a parent does not have his or her kids, or not drinking and driving. Safer use can mean decreasing the amount and frequency of alcohol use. While drinking six beers still falls into the heavy alcohol use category, it is better than drinking a 12-pack of beer.

The next step down would be going to controlled use. Again, the amount and frequency might not be at moderation levels, but they are improving. For example, an individual may drink at a level where he or she no longer experiences a blackout. Or they keep to the limit they decided, even if it is more than 14 a week for women or 21 a week for men. They may reduce their alcohol use to a level where their BAC is lower so that they do not have a hangover the next morning. Or they do not become so intoxicated that they make poor decisions such as engaging in risky sexual behaviors, eating poorly, or damaging loved ones' trust.

The next transition on the spectrum is moderation. This is where a person has explored their drinking amount, frequency, intent, and impact. The amount falls within moderation guidelines for their gender. They do not drink every day, or if they do, it is no more than one a day for women or two for men. They are not drinking to the point of intoxication. They have a plan and they stick to it.

The other end on the Spectrum of Alcohol Use is abstinence. As is noted in other areas, about one-third of people who attempt alcohol moderation eventually choose to stop drinking. Some have determined that they do have a problem with alcohol and decide that complete abstinence is necessary. Others decide that not drinking is preferable to drinking. Some find that it takes too much work to plan ahead and constantly be on guard. One client described it as "petting the dragon." It was too hard for him to have to make a plan each time, and it was easier just to make the commitment that alcohol was no longer a part of his life. Another client stated that there was no longer anything she missed about drinking more than she enjoyed being alcohol-free.

Notes

1. C. Probst, J. Manthey, A. Martinez & J. Rehm (2015). Alcohol use disorder severity and reported reasons not to seek treatment: A cross-sectional study in European primary care practices. *Substance Abuse Treatment Prevention Policy*. 10(32). DOI: 10.1186/s13011-015-0028-z.
2. M. Keller & G. E. Valliant (2019, April 24). Alcoholism. *Encyclopedia Britannica*. Retrieved from www.britannica.com/science/alcoholism.
3. Department of Health and Human Services (2017, January 18). Rules and regulations. *Federal Registrar*. 82(11).
4. A. Tatarsky (2007). *Harm reduction psychotherapy: A new treatment for drug and alcohol problems*. Lanham, MD: Rowman & Littlefield Publishers.
5. The SASSI Institute (2019, May 10). Retrieved from https://sassi.com.
6. American Psychiatric Association (2013). *Diagnostic and statistical manual of mental disorders* (5th ed.). Washington, DC: American Psychiatric Association.
7. *Ibid.*
8. J. B. Saunders & O. G. Aasland (1987). *WHO collaborative project on identification and treatment of persons with harmful alcohol consumption*. Report on phase I. Development of a Screening Instrument. Geneva: World Health Organization.
9. A. Ojehagen & M. Berglund (1989). Changes of drinking goals in a two-year outpatient alcoholic treatment program. *Addictive Behaviors*. 14(1): 1–9. https://doi.org/10.1016/0306-4603(89)90011-7.

7 Engaging Your Client

Stages of Change

The following Stages of Change model can be helpful with engaging your client in the treatment process. James Prochaska and Carlo DiClemente developed the Stages of Change also known as the Transtheoretical Model in the late 1970s.[1] They were actually studying how smokers were able to give up their habit, but it applies just as well to the evaluation of alcohol use. They noted that change occurs through an individualized process of stages.[2] Determining where your client is in the change process can help in how you intervene and develop goals with them.

Precontemplation

When someone is in the Precontemplation Stage, they may not consider their alcohol use a problem. They may not yet have experienced any negative consequences, or they may not be ready to acknowledge the severity of consequences that have already occurred. They are not ready to acknowledge that there is a problem behavior that needs to change.

Mark was a 22-year-old college senior who was treasurer of his fraternity. For him, this meant that he kept track of the keg money and ordered the beer for the weekend parties. Mark was proud that he could drink more than all of his fraternity brothers. He often went out during the week too, because he was a senior and wanted to have fun before joining the real world.

One night Mark was pulled over and given a DUI citation. He spent the night in jail, lost his driver's license, and was ordered to complete 16 weeks of substance-use education. Mark was furious. He thought that he was just like his frat brothers, and after four years of hard work, he felt he had the right to have a little fun. Mark compared himself with his friends and did not think he was any worse than they were. He had only wanted to get home from the bar that night, and he felt that the cops in his area were just out to make money on the fines. They should be arresting the real criminals, he thought. Mark was not yet ready to make any changes.

Working with someone in the Precontemplation Stage can be challenging. In our example here, Mark is not thinking of making any changes in his life at this time. He does not acknowledge that there could be a problem.

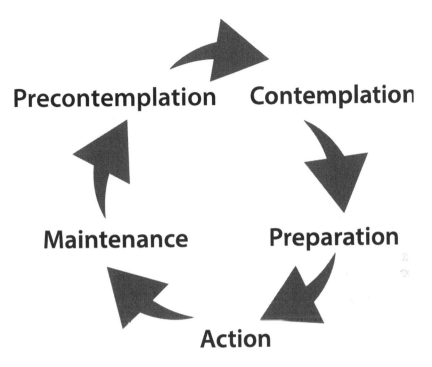

Figure 7.1 Stages of Change

Up until the DUI, his drinking had been fun and he had experienced few consequences, most likely because he was responsible only for himself.

For Mark to get the most out of the court-ordered education, his therapist must validate that he is not yet ready to make a change. Trust must be established, because Mark is an unwilling participant. Friends or family members who are concerned about him can also express concern and point out how they have been affected by his drinking; however, they all should clarify that any decision to change is his. The goal in the Precontemplation Stage is to explore the impact of Mark's alcohol use, not to force him to make changes to his drinking. Emphasis should be on what the people in his life say about his use, the way his choices might affect his job search, and whether his ability to be independent is compromised by his drinking.

At this stage, forcing people to do something against their will often backfires because they may not acknowledge that they have a problem. They will often fight back and become more entrenched in their belief that they are just like everyone else. In my work, I try to make the exploration nonjudgmental yet personal. I often include examples of people with whom they can identify and share how these people dealt with their issues.

Sometimes more negative consequences occur, and the expanded thought process can push a person into the next stage.

Box Matter 7.2

DID YOU KNOW? Many DUIs occur in the morning hours. The average body processes alcohol at a rate of .016 BAC per hour. This is why it is generally safe to have one drink per hour and still be able to drive. However, one must consider the amount and the number of hours they have been drinking. Many people try to be responsible after a night of heavy drinking and choose to stay where they are rather than drive. However, when they wake up in the morning, their body is still processing the alcohol. They may not feel impaired, but the alcohol is still in their system. If they drive and are pulled over, they may register a high Breathalyzer reading.[3]

Contemplation

If your client is in the Contemplation Stage, they are beginning to acknowledge a problem with their drinking, and may be thinking about taking steps to make a change. Although they might have tried to cut down or modify drinking patterns, they are not yet be ready to make substantial changes.

Lauren was a 30-year-old single professional. As part of her job, she attended quite a few marketing events, which were often held in bars or restaurants. Initially, Lauren was very nervous with the social aspect of her job and uncomfortable with the idea of trying to sell herself to get new business. When she first started, she would have a glass of wine or two to help her loosen up and feel more comfortable. Recently she noticed that her two glasses of wine had turned into three or more, and she went home with some of her male colleagues on more occasions than she would like to admit.

After a binge, Lauren would feel so embarrassed and guilty that she would go to the store for a bottle of wine to drink away her feelings regarding the night before. She was late to work a few times because of a hangover and avoided certain work functions for fear that she would run into one of her one-night stands.

Lauren wanted to get married and began to wonder whether the guys she kept picking up were marriage material. A few of her friends expressed concern about how much she was drinking and the choices she was making. She wondered if perhaps it was time to talk to a therapist. But she would always get too busy and decide to wait until after the holidays or some other event.

Lauren was ambivalent about making changes. She was on the fence and not ready to do something anytime soon. A good friend or therapist should validate that Lauren is not sure whether she should make some lifestyle changes and let her know that any decisions she makes will be hers. The therapist should weigh the pros and cons of any changes with her and come up with a plan on how to deal with each. I would have her consider an answer to these questions: "If you were to make a change to your drinking, what would it look like?" and "What are you most concerned about if you decide to change how you drink?"

Giving Lauren unbiased education and information could also be helpful in assisting her to make a decision. If people are too harsh and confrontational, she may revert to denial, or she may feel bad and continue her drinking patterns secretly to deal with those negative feelings.

A person moves out of the stage of contemplation when making a conscious decision to change their alcohol behaviors.

Preparation

When your client is in the Preparation Stage, they are ready to alter their drinking patterns. They have likely begun planning how to make the changes and are prepared to take action. Some consider this person the ideal client because they are motivated and want help. The therapist's job is to assist in developing the goals and kinds of changes they plan to make. I always ask: "What is your goal for drinking?" Never assume that someone wants complete abstinence. Sometimes they want to keep drinking or try to drink in less harmful ways. We can explore the pros and cons of all choices with them. Their initial goal may change as they start to have different actions. Many of my clients say that they want to try moderation. Sometimes they find that it takes too much thought and willpower to monitor their drinking. And many times people who say that they will never give up alcohol actually chose abstinence once they go without drinking for a period of time. The goals should be fluid based on their changing needs and experiences.

In this stage, we assist our clients in obtaining the necessary resources. Some of them may include ongoing sessions with you, attending a support group, learning about moderation, talking with a doctor about medications, inviting the family into treatment, and developing a support and accountability network. In the next several chapters, we will review specific tools for assisting your clients in achieving their goals.

Dave was a middle-aged computer programmer with two children. He worked long hours in the city and just wanted to unwind in the evenings with a few beers while he watched sports. Dave often fell asleep in front of the television and woke up hung over, not able to help with the kids or household chores. Last week his son woke up early, found him passed out on the couch, and began building a fort with his father's empty beer cans.

Dave's wife often complained that he was not available to help with parenting, and they had not had sex in several months because she was angry and resentful toward him. He had attempted to cut down on his drinking and even made it a few days without any beer. Later that week, Dave's wife sat him down and said that if he did not address his alcohol use, she was going to ask him for a separation. Dave believed she was serious this time, so the next morning he began looking up local therapists.

Dave recognized that he had a drinking problem. He did not want to admit it, but the threat of losing his family finally pushed him into action. He was motivated to make changes.

The goal here would be to help Dave identify obstacles to the change process and help him problem solve. He should identify his supports. When he makes positive steps, like going several days without drinking or following through with attending meetings, he and his therapist should explore how he was able to do it. If the focus is on his successes, he can build upon that rather than only lament his failures. If he goes from daily drinking to drinking only three times that week, or from drinking a 12-pack to drinking only two beers, those are successes. I would say things like: "How were you able to cut back?" "What did you gain?" and "What is your next step?"

Action

In the Action stage, clients make changes to their drinking patterns. Treatment can be used to assist clients in making the changes, explore how well the modifications worked, and identify if those changes are maintainable in the long run. I often say things like: "How is that working for you? Your family?" "Is that something you think you can keep doing?" and "What is coming up that might get in the way?"

Tamika was a 45-year-old stay-at-home mother. She had been drinking since her teens. Her childhood was not a happy one. It was filled with all the challenges that come from living with a father who drank too much and then being parented by an angry and depressed mother after their divorce.

As an adult, Tamika struggled with her own bouts of depression. She felt she had no identity and always had her guard up with her husband, fearing that he too would leave. She drank to help numb her feelings. She chose vodka because it gave her more bang for the buck, and she'd heard somewhere that the smell was less detectable.

Her two teenaged children began finding her hidden bottles around the house, and while her husband assured her that he loved her, he couldn't stand to see her in so much pain. During the past year, Tamika completed a five-day inpatient detox program, saw a therapist for her depression and unresolved issues from her childhood, and attended a weekly dual-diagnosis group with other adults dealing with addiction and its impact on their lives. For the first time in over 20 years, she began to like herself. Though she sometimes still sneaked a few drinks, she gave her family permission to let her therapist know so they could deal with it in treatment.

Over a lifetime, clients may cycle through many of these stages. The coping skills that worked in the past may cease to help as new life challenges arise. Sometimes people have the best intentions yet still struggle with maintaining the changes to drinking patterns. The maintenance phase focuses on how to keep the changes going.

Maintenance

The Maintenance Stage occurs after individuals have changed their drinking patterns. The goal now is to keep the healthy behavior going to prevent a relapse to the old behavior. Many of my most successful clients schedule regular check-in appointments with me. These people have worked long and hard to get to where they are in their recovery process and do not want to go back to where they were. Some of them have chosen complete abstinence, and some are working on drinking in moderation.

Joe was a 65-year-old who had just retired from a long career in the military and then the private sector. He was married and had three kids who had finished college and moved out to begin their own lives. He and his wife were finally living "the life." They had retired to a warm climate, and Joe spent his days golfing and nights playing cards or shooting the breeze with friends.

Joe was a Scotch drinker. Throughout his life, he'd had periods where his drinking was too much. In his 30s he had attended an intensive outpatient program and some AA meetings. In the last few years, he had been seeing a therapist who was helping him develop a moderation plan. The plan included drinking only one night of the week, not before 5 p.m., and never consuming more than three drinks at a time.

Joe had begun noticing that he was having a few beers on the golf course and that his neighbor was providing bourbon during their weekly poker games. He realized that both the amount and frequency of his drinking were creeping up again, and his wife was complaining that he was becoming moody and irritable. He made an appointment with his therapist and began reworking the moderation plan.

Joe's alcohol use and consequences varied over the years. His drinking was not as bad as it had been at other times in his life, but he did not like the person he was becoming as his recent drinking increased. He and his wife had saved for a lifetime to be able to travel in their later years. If his alcohol intake continued to escalate, he worried that his health would begin to suffer, and he would not be able to enjoy his grandkids or take that European vacation.

Joe made the decision to check in with his therapist to rework his plan. He decided on a period of complete abstinence again. Once his system had been clean for a few months, he was able to have his weekly Scotch but eliminated beer on the golf course and the liquor during poker night. Both games improved as a result.

It is important to note that the stages described in this section can be looked at as a cycle that people often move through sequentially. However, Prochaska and DiClemente realized that although people often go through these stages in the described order, they also can skip a stage or move forward and backward through them. I have found that people cycle through the stages over a lifetime. We may resolve an issue, but then a crisis or a life change happens, and we need to readjust to the stages.

Cost-Benefit Analysis

One of the steps that I recommend early in treatment is for clients to perform a cost-benefit analysis of their alcohol use. I do this the opposite way from what most expect. By admitting that there are benefits to alcohol use, I can have an honest discussion about what my clients are experiencing. They have become accustomed to being berated about the negatives without anyone understanding why they continue to drink despite consequences.

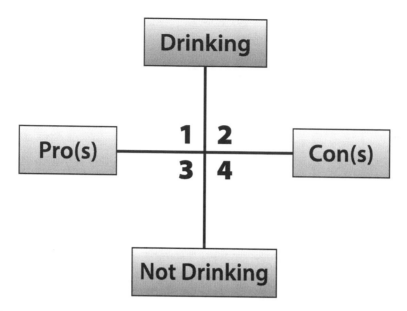

Figure 7.3 Cost-Benefit Analysis

Much of traditional therapy focuses on quadrants 2 and 3, the consequences of drinking and the benefits of not drinking. In fact, many traditional 30-day rehabilitation programs, hours of an IOP (intensive outpatient program), and court-ordered groups focus on the impact of alcohol use. The information is provided in a "scared straight" manner. However, studies have shown that this type of education does not yield an effective long-term impact.[4]

Quadrant 2 explores the cons of drinking. Almost everyone has some idea of the negative impacts of drinking. Most can list numerous legal, health, relational, and mood problems. I have found that although people can usually identify these negative consequences, it is often in a general, impersonal way. If time in treatment is dedicated to education, it should be personalized to what the client is actually or potentially experiencing. All too often, professionals and family members focus on threats. Extreme messages cause most to tune it out, feeling like "that could never happen to me."

Quadrant 3 is very similar to the second quadrant in that it is very logical. Most people can identify why it would be good to stop drinking. I have found that the most effective therapy occurs and real change takes place when we explore the first and fourth quadrants. This should be personalized and individualized to the problems that are affecting the one struggling with drinking. Hearing about major consequences of alcohol use or drinking and driving accidents makes people manage their fear about the possibility rather than change the behavior, as well as rationalize the behavior because nothing bad happened to them, so they continue it.[5] These tactics can also trigger people who do not have adequate coping skills. Do not waste time in therapy on "what ifs," but on what has already happened to them and developing an action plan for what they can do about it.

Additionally, the popular belief is that if people knew how bad alcohol was for them, they would stop. In fact, studies show that substance users generally know more about the chemicals they are using than those who do not.[6]

It is crucial for those trying to help drinkers experiencing problems to identify and acknowledge the benefits of their alcohol use. Obviously, they would not have continued to drink if it were all bad. The severe consequences often do not begin until years into the established drinking patterns. Exploring the benefits of drinking accomplishes several things for drinkers experiencing problems. It puts them at ease, reducing defensiveness and validating that they are not crazy or being judged for engaging in the drinking behavior. Second, helping identify why someone drinks allows you both to devise a plan of action. Third, it begins the process of grieving the death of old drinking patterns and establishing a healthier relationship with alcohol.

Donna was a 45-year-old mother of three kids. From the outside, she looked like the ideal stay-at-home mom. She made the kids' lunches every day, volunteered in their classrooms, drove the carpools, and could be counted on if anyone needed a favor. Her alcohol use was helping her get through the day and covering up her mental health issues.

What none of the people who admired her knew was that Donna suffered from low self-esteem, depression, and anxiety. She believed that if she could make everything look fine, it would be fine. No one knew that once she dropped off the kids, she began sipping alcohol throughout the day to get rid of her fears and negative emotions. By the time her husband and kids got home, she was quite buzzed but forced herself to make a dinner from scratch, do crafts for the Girl Scout and Boy Scout troops, and bake for the church fundraiser.

One morning her husband took out the recycling and was shocked to see the empty bottles in the bin. His first thought was that his wife must have been having an affair with a man who drank a lot. There was no way his perfect wife could have a drinking problem. Her husband confronted her, and she tearfully admitted how stressed out, sad, and anxious she really was.

Donna began treatment. While she was away in the rehabilitation center, the family had to figure out ways to manage all of the responsibilities that Donna had taken on and overachieved in. In treatment, Donna learned that she had value for who she was, not what she did. She practiced setting limits, using positive self-talk, and implementing more effective coping skills.

Donna and her family are much happier these days. The family now spends time doing the activities that they enjoy, and Donna finds fulfillment in these, rather than by checking off items she thought were expected of her. The kids had always wondered why Mommy's smile did not reach her eyes, but now they play games, talk, and joke instead of running to the next activity.

The fourth quadrant offers another perspective in exploring the benefits derived from drinking. In preparing to make a change, all involved have to look at what happens if a person does decide to stop drinking or attempts to moderate drinking.

Pat and Bill were high school sweethearts. They had been married for over 20 years. Drinking was a part of the way they socialized, relaxed, celebrated, and vacationed. They enjoyed going to wine tastings and beer festivals. The couple also enjoyed cooking and figuring out which wines paired best with their meals. If they were stressed out or angry with each other, they just had a drink. In this way, they were able to avoid many fights. But they eventually discovered that more and more resentments were not getting addressed because they were ignoring the problems and just getting buzzed.

One night on the way home from a get-together with friends, Bill was pulled over for a DUI. Both he and Pat had consumed a number of drinks, but neither felt intoxicated. After years of drinking, their tolerance level had become quite high.

Bill hired an attorney for court but still had to serve ten days in jail for a high Breathalyzer reading. Additionally, he was required to have an interlock system installed on his car (an apparatus that he had to blow into and be alcohol free to start his car) and complete 16 weeks of an education class while remaining alcohol free. During this time, Pat and Bill were forced to examine how much drinking had become a part of their relationship and to come up with better communication strategies, because life was not always a party.

Pat realized that she could not blame Bill for the DUI because she'd had just as much to drink as he did. Deep down, she knew she had to change, too.

Despite their poor method of communication, they loved each other very much and decided to reevaluate the ways they could spend their free time together and resolve problems. They signed up for a dance class, started hiking, and focused more time on activities than on alcohol. Pat and Bill participated in a couples' retreat with their church and learned how to communicate with each other directly rather than trying to drink issues away.

Even though the restrictions that the court imposed on Bill have now been satisfied, the couple no longer makes alcohol a priority. By having drinks only on special occasions rather than every night, they have both lost weight, enjoy more energy, and deal with issues as they arise. Instead of sipping mixed drinks on the beach for their next vacation, they are planning a high adventure trip where they will kayak, rock climb, and zip line. People who know them say they look and act ten years younger.

Motivational Interviewing Scaling

One of the tenets of Motivational Interviewing (described more in depth in Chapter 5) is assessing readiness for change. Steven Rollnick developed the Readiness Ruler, which has been shown to be an effective tool to assess if a person is ready to make changes.[7] An easy way to do this is to ask scaling questions:

"On a scale of one to ten, with one being not at all and ten being 'let's start now,' how ready are you to make a change to your drinking patterns?"

READINESS SCALE

Figure 7.4 Readiness Scale

I find that the Readiness Scale is useful for several reasons. First, it engages them in the process. It is on their terms, not mine. This is important because many people enter treatment under duress. An incident may have happened, a loved one may have threatened to end a relationship, or they came to satisfy a legal or a job requirement. Second, it helps us both determine their motivation to do something different. As noted in the Stages of Change Model, we need to intervene differently if someone does not see there is a problem versus their wanting to make changes. We can ask questions like "What would it take for you to go from a one to a three?" or "How would your family respond if you went from a three to a five?" Lastly, we can use the scales as a way to measure change over time. As therapists, we see people at intervals, so we will notice change while the client may become frustrated thinking that things are the same. We can say: "When you first started you were a two, now you are at a five. Look at how much progress you have made."

IMPORTANCE SCALE

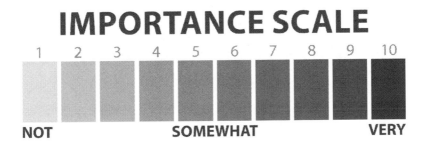

Figure 7.5 Importance Scale

The next question would be: "On a scale of one to ten, with one being not important at all to ten being the most important thing to me now, how important is it for you to change your drinking patterns?"

The Importance Scale can be helpful as well. The popular belief is that in order for people to make changes, they have to want to make changes.

I disagree. As noted earlier, most people enter treatment under duress. It is because something negative happened or someone is forcing them to do so. The people who come to me are usually for external reasons, not because they want help. I find that it can take weeks, if not months, for the desired change to become internally motivated. I agree that change occurs best when people want it, but my job is to explore the process. That's why the Importance Scale is helpful. A person can be very low on the Readiness Scale but high on the Importance Scale. Therapy can be used to point out these discrepancies and help our clients determine how life could be if they made changes and what might happen if they chose not to do so.

Notes

1. J. O. Prochaska, C. C. DiClemente & J. C. Norcross (1992). In search of how people change: Applications to the addictive behaviors. *American Psychologist*. 47: 1102–1114. PMID: 1329589.
2. J. O. Prochaska, J. C. Norcross & C. C. DiClemente (1994). *Changing for good*. New York: Morrow. ISBN: 0-380-72572-X.
3. S. Zakhari (2019, March 9). *Overview: How is alcohol metabolized by the body?* National Institutes on Alcohol Abuse and Alcoholism. Retrieved from https://pubs.niaaa.nih.gov/publications/arh294/245-255.htm.
4. K. Witte & M. Allen (2000). A meta-analysis of fear appeals: Implications for effective public health programs. *Health Education and Behavior*. 27(5): 591–615.
5. G. Hastings, M. Stead & J. Webb (2004). Fear appeals in social marketing: Strategic and ethical reasons for concern. *Psychology and Marketing*. 21(11): 961–986.
6. P. Dermota, J. Wang, M. Dey, G. Gmel, J. Studer & M. Mohler-Kuo (2013). Health literacy and substance use in young swiss men. *International Journal of Public Health*. 58(6): 939–948.
7. M. Hesse (2006). The readiness ruler as a measure of readiness to change poly-drug use in drug abusers. *Harm Reduction Journal*. (3)3. DOI: 10.1186/1477-7517-3-3.

8 *Alcohol Moderation Assessment*

This chapter is the essence of this book—taking the *Alcohol Moderation Assessment*. The original version was called the *How Do I Know if I Can Keep Drinking Quiz.*[1] It included open-ended as well as yes/no questions. I found that a limitation was that it was best completed with a clinician in order to understand the results. While it was an effective tool for the clinicians I had been able to train over the last five years, I wanted to be able to reach a broader number of people.

Based on feedback, I have updated the quiz with newer research and additional predictors. The new title is the *Alcohol Moderation Assessment*. The current version has all yes/no questions for which the answers are tallied. That number then falls on a range that gives a prediction for the likelihood of being able to successfully practice alcohol moderation. An individual can now take the test on his or her own and have a direction for making lifestyle changes, or the assessment can be used as part of a treatment program.

Interpreting the Assessment

Answers to the *Alcohol Moderation Assessment* predicts the likelihood that an individual will be successful in practicing alcohol moderation. Checking "yes" on the first 17 questions are negative predictors for successful moderation. You will notice that some of them are not specifically related to alcohol consumption but are environmental risk factors. Answering "yes" on any of questions 14 to 17 usually mean that a person is unlikely to be able to practice alcohol moderation. These questions have to do with how the body has been affected by alcohol and are often signs of severe alcohol dependence. The last three questions are protective factors. They are attributes that help individuals deal with stress and decrease the chance of a negative outcome. While several of the questions are about childhood and adolescence, the person filling it out should be thinking about the last six months of functioning. Please see the following interpretations for each of the questions.

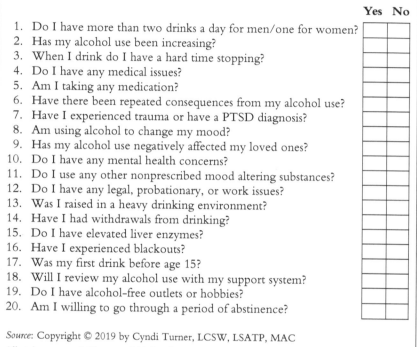

Figure 8.1a Alcohol Moderation Assessment

1. Do I have more than two drinks a day for men/one for women? As noted in previous chapters, women who have no more than one drink a day and men who have no more than two are considered to be drinking in moderation. The larger the amount and the more frequently one drinks, the harder it is to change this pattern. Drinking every day is a negative predictor. If an individual associates drinking with specific events, it may be more challenging to moderate drinking. If nights and weekends signal drinking time, it will be very important to develop new associations.

ALCOHOL MODERATION

ASSESSMENT

SCORING THE ALCOHOL MODERATION ASSESSMENT

- For questions one through thirteen, give yourself one point for any "yes" answers.
  POINTS:_____

- For questions fourteen to seventeen, give yourself two points for any "yes" answers.
  POINTS:_____

- For questions eighteen to twenty, subtract a point for any "yes" answers.
  POINTS:_____

Total your points. The amount reflects your likelihood of being able to successfully practice alcohol moderation.

TOTAL POINTS:_____

< 0 Points	Good
1–5 Points	Fair
6–10 Points	Poor
> 11 Points	Unlikely

Figure 8.1b Scoring the Alcohol Moderation Assessment

Julia was in her 50s, worked full-time, and was now helping raise her single daughter's six-year-old son. On top of that, her father's health was declining, and he had to be moved into a nursing home. Julia was at the end of her rope. She found that martinis were a great way to deal with her stress. However, she noticed that she was going to the liquor store so often that the clerks there greeted her by name. In addition, her daughter told her that her grandson had begun asking why Grandma acted funny at night.

Julia decided that she couldn't eliminate any of her responsibilities, so she needed to find other ways to deal with her stress. She joined her local gym and discovered yoga, as well as two other women who were dealing with similar life struggles. Together they picked at least one weekend day a month for a girls' day, took turns babysitting each other's grandkids, and went to lunch after visiting their parents so they could vent about their stressors.

Julia was not a lifelong drinker. Although she had begun drinking every day, it was due to situational stressors. Once she found other ways to manage the stress, she realized that she did not need the outlet of alcohol every day. Julia cut down her drinking to having martinis only when she went out for dinner. She is now enjoying more energy in the morning, no heartburn at night, and feeling more joy in her relationships.

2. Has my alcohol use been increasing? Refer back to Chapter 5, where we reviewed how to diagnose substance use disorders according to the *Diagnostic and Statistical Manual of Mental Disorders*, 5th edition (DSM-5). The first criterion noted was, "Alcohol is often taken in larger amounts or over a longer period than was intended."[2] For many, this process creeps up over time. No one starts out by polishing off a bottle by themselves or drinking the entire 12-pack. The amount and frequency of alcohol use can increase over a period of years. A typical process is this: An individual may have a glass or two of wine a couple of times at social events. They find that they like the effect, so they bring a bottle home and start having one with dinner. A waiter is not pouring it, so the standard pour of five ounces becomes eight or nine ounces at home. One glass becomes two servings. Over time the individual does not get the same effect from one glass, so they begin having two or three, which is actually three to four servings, putting them in the category of heavy alcohol use. This process is called tolerance.

Tolerance refers to criterion number ten: Tolerance, as defined by either of the following:

a.   A need for markedly increased amounts of alcohol to achieve intoxication or desired effect.
b.   A markedly diminished effect with continued use of the same amount of alcohol.[3]

Tolerance is especially dangerous when it reaches the point of physical addiction—when the body will go through a withdrawal process if it does not get the substance.

3. When I drink, do I have a hard time stopping? You may have heard the term "One is too many and ten is not enough." This refers to the person for whom once they start drinking, it is very hard to stop. Some individuals do not stop drinking until the alcohol is finished, they pass out, or everyone goes home. Some individuals cannot fathom how people can leave some of their alcoholic beverage unfinished. This type of drinker often consumes all liquids, including nonalcoholic beverages, quickly. They don't sip; they swallow in quick succession.

Other drinkers seem to "reach a point of no return" or "flip a switch." This typically has to do with the physiological effect of alcohol. When most individuals reach a blood alcohol content of 0.04–0.06, they become relaxed, have lowered inhibitions, become more talkative, and have impaired judgment. This often takes only two to three drinks for most people.[4] This is another reason why it is important to stay within moderate drinking guidelines. People around this type of drinker will often say, "One moment you were fine and the next it was like there was a different person."

Some individuals recognize this point of no return and can decide not to cross that line. They stop drinking. Others may be consuming alcohol so quickly that the psychological effects also hit quickly, and they lose their ability to make good judgments because the alcohol has impaired them.

Answers to this question also relate to the second DSM-5 criterion: "There is a persistent desire or unsuccessful efforts to cut down or control alcohol use."[5] Some individuals may realize that they are losing control over their ability to control their intake. Some may not yet be ready to admit it. This is why it is important to review the assessment with a trained professional, a trusted loved one, or someone whose feedback can be heard.

4. Do I have any medical issues? This and the next question have to do with the ninth DSM-5 criterion: "Alcohol use is continued despite knowledge of having a persistent or recurrent physical problem that is likely to be exacerbated by alcohol."[6]

There are some obvious all-or-nothing predictors related to medical conditions. The most common include pregnancy, cirrhosis, elevated liver enzymes, diabetes, or cancer. There are many others that should be discussed with your doctor. Additionally, if they have high blood pressure, high cholesterol, or a weakened immune system, they probably are not a candidate for moderate drinking.

Chapter 5 reviewed how alcohol affects every organ in the body. Although the health risks associated with heavy drinking can take years to develop, they also can make current conditions worse. I recommend an open conversation with their doctor so that they can make an educated decision on the amount of alcohol, if any, that is acceptable for their health.

5. Am I taking any medications? There are contraindications for drinking with many medicines and supplements. Some medications, when taken with alcohol, can intensify drowsiness and put you at risk for accidents, falls, and even death. These may include medications for heart disease, insomnia, pain relief, and colds, as well as medications for psychiatric conditions like depression, anxiety, bipolar disorder, ADHD, and schizophrenia. Alcohol interactions can also occur with over-the-counter medicines like antihistamines, pain relievers, cough medicines, and some herbal preparations. Alcohol is known to affect antibiotics, antidepressants, antiseizure medications, benzodiazepines (for anxiety), opiates (for pain), and beta-blockers (for heart or high blood pressure).[7]

This medication list is by no means exhaustive. I recommend that individuals check with their doctor, psychiatrist, or pharmacist to determine the impact of alcohol on any medications they are taking. Many psychiatrists report that alcohol mixed with antidepressants reduces their effectiveness. Each person should make an educated decision on whether it is safe to drink and take certain drugs. Be aware that a combination of alcohol and some drugs, such as sleeping medications, benzodiazepines, and certain medications for depression, can have lethal consequences. I always recommend taking prescribed medications instead of taking a drink.

6. Have there been repeated consequences from my alcohol use? This question refers to DSM criteria five, six, and seven:

- Recurrent alcohol use resulting in a failure to fulfill major role obligations at work, school, or home.
- Continued alcohol use despite having persistent or recurrent social or interpersonal problems caused or exacerbated by the effect of alcohol.
- Important social, occupational, or recreational activities are given up or reduced because of alcohol use.[8]

Some consequences are hard to deny, such as a legal charge, loss of a job, or the end of a relationship. However, some of the consequences can be more subtle. Denial causes people to minimize what happens when inebriated. If they always seem to end up in a physical fight, engaged in a debate that leads to screaming, passed out snoring on the couch, or if someone else always seems to end up crying, it may be a good idea to look at alcohol's contribution to the problem. Only the drinker and the people closest to them can determine if their drinking is a problem. As I said previously, if it causes a problem, it is a problem.

This is where self-assessment is really important. I recommend that the drinker seek the observations and opinions of the people closest to them. If they heard the same concern from someone more than once, it may be valid. If an individual had the same complaint from a number of people, it is likely true. It may be hard to hear, but feedback from others can let them know what it is like to be on the receiving end of their actions, especially when they are not themselves or have been denying the effects of drinking on themself and those around them.

William and his partner James had been together for over ten years. He and James would often go out to the clubs and imbibe in the nightly specials. After several years of working hard, they were able to purchase a house that they turned into their home. William still preferred to go out, but James liked to stay in.

The couple often hosted monthly dinner parties. William was the social butterfly, always with a drink in his hand and a story to tell. However, William and James had begun fighting more, especially about William's going out. James was concerned about the money he was spending, how late nights were affecting his health, and the risks of driving home. His trust in his partner was decreasing, and their sex life took a turn for the worse. Not as many friends were attending their parties. William would often get loud and rude after a few drinks, James was then left making apologies and cleaning up after everyone.

Problem drinking is not always as obvious as a DUI, a loved one ending a relationship, or health issues. Drinking can affect the quality of our relationships. Intimacy may decrease, fights may occur, and ongoing tension can damage a couple's happiness.

7. *Have I experienced trauma or have a PTSD diagnosis?* Experiencing trauma is one of the main predictors for having a substance use disorder. In one survey of adolescents receiving treatment for substance use, more than 70% had a history of trauma exposure.[9] Teens who experienced physical or sexual abuse were three times as likely to use substances than those who have not.[10] And 59% of young people with post-traumatic stress disorder (PTSD) develop substance use disorders. Another study found that 60% to 80% of Vietnam veterans seeking PTSD treatment have alcohol use problems. They tend to binge drink in response to memories of trauma.[11] Another study reports that approximately 8% of the population will develop PTSD during their lifetime. There is a strong correlation between experiencing trauma and developing a substance use disorder.[12]

8. *Am I using alcohol to change my mood?* It is very important to understand why one drinks. There are many possible reasons. If it is to escape from feelings or an unpleasant situation, this is a negative predictor. It will be important to develop coping skills to deal with any underlying psychiatric issues like depression, anxiety, obsessive-compulsive disorder, or insomnia. If one is drinking to avoid problems in a relationship, job, or living situation, it is time to evaluate the environment. See if acceptable changes can be made to the situation, or examine whether it is time to leave a job or a relationship. Therapy can be very helpful in working through these issues.

Lee was a 51-year-old entrepreneur. He was intelligent, successful, and had all the trappings of success that a man could want: beautiful wife, three healthy kids, and enough money to take several vacations a year. But he could not seem to get a handle on his depression. He would use alcohol to deal with feelings of sadness and worthlessness.

Lee scared himself the night he drove home after a business meeting and could not remember how he got there the next morning. He spent the next several months in individual therapy, addressing issues that had haunted him from childhood. Because he was still struggling with symptoms, he also sought the help of a psychiatrist to find the right antidepressant that significantly reduced his symptoms without causing serious side effects.

Lee chose to go through a period of abstinence from alcohol. During this time he developed better coping and communication skills, but he really missed wine. He *was one of the rare people who could tell the difference between a $10 bottle and a $100 bottle. He developed an Alcohol Moderation Plan that allowed him to drink his favorite wines only in social situations and never more than two glasses at a time.*

If Lee noticed the frequency of his drinking increasing, or if his depression symptoms began affecting his day-to-day life, he first talked it over with his wife. Lee trusted her opinion, and she was able to give support without criticism. If he did not feel better in two weeks, he would schedule an appointment with me to come up with strategies to help him feel better again.

Again, if one drinks to change their mood, it is a negative predictor. If an individual drinks as part of a holiday or social gathering and are not trying to change mood or emotions, it is a more positive predictor. Even better is if individuals can appreciate a fine wine that brings out the flavor in food, enjoy a cold beer on a summer day, savor the flavor of an aged liquor, or relish making a toast with champagne. Successful alcohol moderators see alcohol as part of the event, not the main event.

9. Has my alcohol use negatively impacted my loved ones? If drinking is causing problems in primary relationships, that person may have to decide which is more important to them. Parents also need to be aware of messages about alcohol that they are sending to their children. I ask if they want their children to have the same relationship with alcohol that they do. Realize that kids are sponges. Parents set the example for what is normal because they are the primary adults in their children's lives; what their children see them do is imprinted on their brains as normal. All other experiences will be compared to these early first observations and impressions.

If a client's children are adolescents, they may begin to experiment with alcohol. I warn them about the trap of "Do as I say, not as I do" and how they will lose all credibility. The teenagers I see in my adolescent dual-diagnosis program report little respect for parents who yell at them for going to a party and drinking, while they are holding their own glass of alcohol and slurring their speech from one too many.

Sid was a 74-year-old father of two and grandfather of five who was looking forward to celebrating his golden anniversary with his wife. He admitted that when he was in his 30s, he had a problem with alcohol. As a result, he became a regular AA participant and even sponsored new members. After several years, he stopped attending meetings, believing he had heard and said it all.

After almost 20 years of sobriety, Sid wondered if he finally had this thing licked and could be "normal" again. To Sid, "normal" meant that he could drink like most people, without consequences and able to stop with one or two glasses. However, when Sid drank, it was in secret. One of his favorite places to drink was in the car. It gave him a double adrenaline rush. After a few months and too many close calls, he realized how dangerous this was for him and confessed to his wife. He decided to stop drinking liquor but still had the occasional glass of wine.

Sid never became intoxicated again, but every time his wife saw him with alcohol or smelled it on his breath, she reverted right back to the misery of the earlier years of his heavy drinking. Sid decided that his wife's happiness and well-being were more important to him than drinking. They just celebrated their 50th anniversary, and they toasted each other with sparkling cider.

10. Do I have any mental health concerns? The likelihood of having both an alcohol use disorder and a mental health disorder is very high. The 2014 National Survey on Drug Use and Health found that about eight million people in the United States have an alcohol use disorder as well as a mental health disorder.[13] If someone struggles with depression, bipolar disorder, anxiety, schizophrenia, post-traumatic stress disorder, or obsessive-compulsive disorder, and that person drinks, this is a negative predictor. However, once these issues are stabilized, one may be better able to explore whether moderate drinking is an option.

The National Alliance of Mental Illness (NAMI) notes that drinking can be a way of self-medication—that is, people seek the effects of alcohol as a way to make their symptoms less painful.[14] However, alcohol can actually worsen underlying mental illness while the person is under the influence or during withdrawal from alcohol. Drinking can make the symptoms of depression worse and increase panic attacks, not only from the actual chemical use, but also from the consequences of drinking. Additionally, alcohol use can trigger the onset of psychosis.

As noted earlier, it is critical to address any mental health issues before trying to drink moderately. This can be done in a variety of ways. It may be by developing better coping skills, getting out of a bad relationship or situation, seeking appropriate medication, resolving issues with a therapist, developing meaning in some form of spirituality, or learning new ways to relax and have fun. There is no quick fix and no one answer. One will likely need to address many areas, but any investment should result in a healthier, happier version of life.

11. Do I use any nonprescribed mood altering substances? The use of any other nonprescribed mood altering substances (drugs) is a negative predictor. As noted previously, if an individual uses a substance in order to change his or her mood, he or she is likely to remain in that pattern.

John was a single 33-year-old alcohol and marijuana user. He had decided that his drinking was causing him a lot of problems. He had developed quite a beer belly, suffered from high cholesterol and high blood pressure, and had to take medications for them. He wanted to be in a relationship but had no motivation to meet anyone new.

When John realized that most of his paychecks were going to beer and weed, he decided to get some help. He began therapy. His group members offered him great support and accountability, but he was reluctant to address his marijuana use. He said it was a natural substance and smoking it did not have any negative effects on him.

Six months later, John was abstinent from alcohol but still smoked pot several times a week. He held the same hourly-paying job, played video games for fun, and had no significant other. He couldn't figure out why nothing had changed. Had he stopped smoking marijuana, he might have had a better chance to evaluate his life and been more proactive in his life goals. Because he was still using a mood-altering substance, he was unable to gain enough clarity to fully evaluate his life.

12. Do I have any legal, probationary, or work issues? These are obvious negative predictors. If one's freedom, driver's license, or job is on the line, they should not keep drinking. Once the probationary period has passed, developing an alcohol moderation plan can be explored.

13. Was I raised in a heavy drinking environment? No one specific gene determines if you will have a problem with drinking. There are hundreds of genes in a person's DNA that can influence the likelihood of developing an alcohol-related problem. Genetics appear to be responsible for about 50% of our risk of developing an issue.[15] People will be about four times more likely to have an alcohol use disorder if they have a direct family member such as a parent or sibling who has an issue.[16]

While our genes are responsible for half of our likelihood of developing an alcohol use disorder, the other 50% is due to our environment. As noted previously, the people who raise us and the atmosphere we live in shapes our sense of what we think is normal. If an individual was raised in a family where alcohol was a part of daily living, their outlook will be impacted by this. When alcohol is seen as the way to celebrate, socialize, deal with stress, or end the day, people develop skewed perceptions. Adult children of alcoholics (ACOA) are three to four times more likely to develop an alcohol use disorder. This is often due to the chaotic environment, neglect of physical and emotional needs, and poor boundaries.[17]

Negative Predictors

The next four questions are negative predictors for alcohol moderation. This is why the assessment assigns two points for every affirmative answer. If individuals experience these, they are most likely dealing with a severe alcohol use disorder with a physical addiction. It is unlikely that they will be able to successfully practice alcohol moderation. When the body becomes physically addicted to alcohol, willpower and behavior modification are ineffective.

14. Have I had withdrawals from drinking? The final DSM-5 criteria address withdrawal:

Withdrawal, as manifested by either of the following:

a.   The characteristic withdrawal syndrome for alcohol.
b.   Alcohol (or a closely related substance, such as a benzodiazepine) is taken to relieve or avoid withdrawal symptoms.[18]

If someone has experienced delirium tremens ("the shakes") or a seizure, they are unlikely to be able to safely drink again. If an individual has had hallucinations or delusions (seeing or hearing things that are not there), these are serious symptoms that are negative predictors for being able to moderate drinking.

Remember that tolerance to and suffering withdrawal from alcohol indicates a severe drinking issue. There is consequently much less of a chance that one can keep drinking safely or moderately. It is possible but comes with very high risk. Individuals should evaluate why continuing to drink is so important to them. I recommend speaking with a therapist trained in addiction treatment and moderation to help make this critical life decision.

15. Do I have elevated liver enzymes? As described in Chapter 4, alcohol can destroy the liver. Heavy drinking causes inflammation, fatty deposits, and scarring.[19] When the liver is damaged, it can no longer perform its metabolizing jobs, thus allowing toxic substances to travel to the brain.

One way to tell if the liver has been damaged by alcohol use is through a liver enzyme test, also known as a liver function panel. I recommend that anyone who has consumed alcohol on a regular basis and wants to attempt alcohol moderation get their liver enzymes checked. It is a simple blood test that can be ordered by any doctor. There are even at-home test kits that involve a finger prick.

The test shows the number of enzymes that are flowing out of your bloodstream due to cell damage.[20] If these are elevated, I caution people against trying moderation. If someone still wants to try, I suggest they go for compete abstinence for six months and then repeat the test.

I warn people about starting and stopping heavy drinking. The liver is one of the only organs that can regenerate. This sounds great. However, if one consumes alcohol on a repairing liver, it is extremely dangerous. The new cells are very sensitive and are more likely to become damaged at a faster rate.[21]

16. Have I experienced blackouts? If a person has had more than one blackout, this is a negative predictor for continued use of alcohol. There are two kinds of alcohol-related blackouts.

The first is associated with binge drinking. Binge drinking is defined as drinking several drinks (four for women, five for men) within a two-hour period that elevates the blood alcohol level to 0.08 or higher. This type of blackout may occur once or twice before the individual learns his or her limits and decides not to make the same mistake again. This is often seen in the teenage or college-aged drinker who consumes a large quantity of alcohol in a short period of time. Blackouts occur when they play drinking games that involve taking shots, participate in butt chugging or eyeballing, play beer pong, or consume a specific amount of alcohol as the loser of a drinking game. In addition to injury, fighting, and sexual assault, this type of blackout can seriously impair learning and memorization—typically a major role function for young adults in college or learning a trade.[22]

The other type of blackout, which is more concerning, occurs on a more regular basis typically in the heavy drinker.[23] The large amount of alcohol consumed prevents the brain from forming long-term memories, and the drinker loses a period of time. This is not forgetting a few things one said last night, but losing a few hours, not remembering things one did or how one got home. This is extremely dangerous because people may take risks that they normally would not, such as taking other drugs, going home with a stranger, or driving a car while impaired.

A blackout indicates brain damage. Alcohol is preventing the brain from encoding experiences and turning them into long-term memories.[24] If an individual has had repeated blackouts, it is a negative predictor for the ability to moderate drinking; the body may have developed a tolerance to drinking. For most people, a safety valve will turn on, and they will do one of several things when they drink excessively. They will consciously decide to stop consuming drinks, pass out (fall asleep), or throw up. Most people do not and are not able to drink to the point of having a blackout.

17. Was my first drink prior to age 15? Beginning to drink before the age of 15 is a strong negative predictor. One study of over 40,000 adults found that nearly half of the people who began drinking before the age of 15 met the criteria for a severe alcohol-use disorder. That percentage dropped to less than 10 percent if they waited until age 21.[25]

Researchers at the National Institute on Alcohol Abuse and Alcoholism (NIAAA) believe that alcohol more negatively affects younger teens' brains because they are not yet fully developed. Alcohol can lead them to make choices that focus more on immediate pleasure versus making choices that avoid the long-term impact that heavy drinking can bring.

In addition to the legal reasons, there are very real biological reasons to delay drinking until the age of 21. Current research tells us that the brain is not fully developed until, on the average, age 26. This is significant because of a process called *cell adaptation*.[26] Cell adaptation refers to the changes made by a cell in response to adverse environmental changes. In other words, if a substance is introduced into a developing brain, the brain cells believe they need this substance to continue developing. If an underdeveloped brain is given alcohol, it will adjust and continue to need more and more of it to grow. This is what we call *tolerance*. Tolerance to alcohol is a negative predictor for the ability to moderately consume it.

The Centers for Disease Control (CDC) report that most drinking under the age of 20 is in the form of binge drinking.[27] The intent is to get drunk, not to enjoy the taste. Younger people are usually chasing the physical and social effects of alcohol and are not likely to consume only a moderate amount; thus, the earlier alcohol is introduced, the higher the rate of addiction.[28]

Jorge was a shy young man. In accordance with his cultural upbringing, he lived at home until he was in his late 20s. He had saved up enough money and now wanted to see what it was like to live independently.

Jorge moved to a new area, but he was very shy and struggled to make new friends. He found that going to happy hour at bars was a good way to meet people. He learned that after five or six drinks, his social anxiety disappeared and he could openly talk with anyone. This worked great until he got pulled over for a DUI.

While Jorge's drinking pattern classified him as a heavy drinker (having several binges a month, drinking more than five drinks at a time, and drinking multiple nights a month), he had not yet developed a tolerance to alcohol. This was likely due to the fact that he had delayed drinking until he was 28, when his brain was fully developed. Because his prefrontal cortex—the area of the brain that is last to develop and is responsible for thinking, memory, and judgment—was mature, he eventually realized that there were other, healthier ways to meet friends, and he found better ways to deal with his social anxiety.

One day Jorge took a risk and struck up a sober conversation with a neighbor. Together they participated in other nondrinking activities that allowed him to develop better social skills, which reduced his fear of talking to new people. He still goes to the occasional happy hour but no longer feels the need for the social lubrication. His new girlfriend and wallet are happy that he no longer is a regular at the local bar.

Protective Factors

The next three areas have to do with protective factors. This is why the scoring for the assessment subtracts a point for each affirmative answer. They are behaviors that increase the potential for successful alcohol moderation.[29]

18. *Will I review my alcohol use with my support system?* Research shows that one of the most positive predictors of success for a person's ability to moderate his or her drinking is having a good support system.[30] There are many reasons for this. One is that people with a good support system tend to be happier and have lower rates of mental health issues. A support system also helps people stay accountable. When you look in the eyes of someone you love, they can often feel your guilt, and you want to be a better person for them.

This is why the best weight-loss programs include some form of accountability, which in turn leads to more goals achieved. If you have to share a food journal with a nutritionist, you are more likely to think about what you put into your body. And the scale does not lie—it knows when you have had too many chips or cookies. The same can be true with keeping a drinking diary that you share with your support system. Writing how often, how many, and the impact of your drinks can be very telling.

I ask my clients: Who in your life has what you want? Identify those qualities and figure out how to emulate them. Find a mentor who helps with honesty, tracking goals, and finding solutions. This may be a friend, loved one, parent, online support group, therapist, spiritual leader, or fellow moderator.

Honesty is crucial. The support system should have a copy of the Alcohol Moderation Plan, which will be developed in the next chapter. I suggest giving loved ones permission to challenge and confront as well as celebrate successes. The support people should be strong enough to handle any resistance and give guidance.

19. *Do I have alcohol-free outlets or hobbies?* Alcohol often becomes a way to relax and have fun. It is important to develop activities that do not involve drinking. I let all of my clients know that they will have more success if they add something that they enjoy rather than just focus on avoiding alcohol. We do better when we have an enjoyable outlet rather than a deficit.

20. *Am I willing to go through a period of abstinence?* As discussed more in the next chapter, before trying moderation, I recommend being alcohol-free for

a period of four months. Studies have shown that those who go through a period of abstinence were more likely to reach their alcohol-related goals.[31]

One of the main reasons is to handle a wide variety of situations without alcohol. During this time, some experience discomfort. The goal is to identify triggers and learn other coping skills. Being chemically free helps bring emotions to the surface, thus giving you an opportunity to manage life in a different way.

When thinking about being alcohol-free, some focus only on negative emotions such as anxiety, stress, depression, boredom, and anger. Most are pleasantly surprised at the emergence of positive feelings that perhaps had been numbed by alcohol: joy, awe, love, compassion, and empathy.

Additionally, people fall into unhealthy patterns. This period of abstinence allows time to break them. Drinking or not drinking becomes less of an issue when your attention, time, and activities are on other opportunities. I recommend saying "I choose not to drink" rather than "I can't drink." The former implies empowerment rather than deprivation.

Notes

1. C. Turner & C. James (2013). *How do I know if I can keep drinking quiz* (Author).
2. American Psychiatric Association (2013). *Diagnostic and statistical manual of mental disorders* (5th ed.). Washington, DC: American Psychiatric Association.
3. American Psychiatric Association (2013). *Diagnostic and statistical manual of mental disorders* (5th ed.). Washington, DC: American Psychiatric Association.
4. National Institute on Alcohol Abuse and Alcoholism (2018, October). *Understanding the dangers of alcohol overdose.* Retrieved from https://pubs.niaaa.nih.gov/publica tions/AlcoholOverdoseFactsheet/Overdosefact.htm.
5. American Psychiatric Association (2013). *Diagnostic and statistical manual of mental disorders* (5th ed.). Washington, DC: American Psychiatric Association.
6. American Psychiatric Association (2013). *Diagnostic and statistical manual of mental disorders* (5th ed.). Washington, DC: American Psychiatric Association.
7. R. Weathermon & D. W. Crabb (1999, November 1). Alcohol and medication interactions. *Alcohol Research and Health.* 23(1): 40–54.
8. American Psychiatric Association (2013). *Diagnostic and statistical manual of mental disorders* (5th ed.). Washington, DC: American Psychiatric Association.
9. L. Khooury, Y. L. Tang, B. Bradley, J. F. Cubells & K. J. Ressler (2010, December). Substance use, childhood traumatic experience, and post traumatic stress disorder in an urban civilian population. *Depression and Anxiety.* 27(12): 1077–1086.
10. National Child Traumatic Stress Network (2008). *Understanding links between adolescent trauma and substance abuse: A toolkit for providers* (2nd ed.). Washington, DC: American Psychiatric Publishing, Inc.
11. J. Volpicelli, G. Balaraman, J. Hahn, H. Wallace & D. Bux (1999). The role of uncontrollable trauma in the development of PTSD and alcohol addiction. *Alcohol Research and Health.* 23(4): 256–262.
12. C. H. Bombardier & A. Turner (2009). Alcohol and traumatic disability. In R. Frank & T. Elliott (Eds.), *The handbook of rehabilitation psychology* (2nd ed., pp. 241–258). Washington, DC: American Psychological Association Press.
13. Center for Behavioral Health Statistics and Quality (2015). *Behavioral health trends in the United States: Results from the 2014 national survey on drug use and health* (HHS Publication No. SMA 15-4927, NSDUH Series H-50). Retrieved from www. samhsa.gov/ data/.

14. National Alliance on Mental Illness (2019, May 14). Retrieved from www.nami.org/Find-Support/Living-with-a-Mental-Health-Condition/Taking-Care-of-Your-Body/Drugs-Alcohol-Smoking.

15. American Society of Addiction Medicine (2011, August 15). *Public policy statement: Definition of addiction.* Retrieved from www.asam.org/resources/definition-of-addiction.

16. Edenberg, H. J. (2003, June). *The collaborative study on the genetics of alcoholism: An update.* Bethesda, MD: National Institute on Alcohol Abuse and Alcoholism.

17. C. W. Hall & R. E. Webster (2007). Risk factors among adult children of alcoholics. *International Journal of Behavioral Consultation and Therapy.* 3(4): 494–511. http://dx.doi.org/10.

18. American Psychiatric Association (2013). *Diagnostic and statistical manual of mental disorders* (5th ed.). Washington, DC: American Psychiatric Association.

19. S. K. Herrine (2018, January). *Liver structure and function: Merck manual professional version.* Retrieved from www.merckmanuals.com/professional/hepatic-and-biliary-disorders/approach-to-the-patient-with-liver-disease/liver-structure-and-function/?msclkid=2382e46601c815879deeb8e4bc76ef56&utm_source=bing&utm_medium=cpc&utm_campaign=EDL_MERCKUSA_Hepatic%20and%20Biliary%20Disorders-C-S_SE_SEM_N_MIX_NTL_US_EN_M&utm_term=what%20is%20liver%20function%20test&utm_content=Liver%20Structure%20and%20Function%20(Exact).

20. C. P. Davis & W. C. Shiel Jr. (2019, March 7). Liver blood tests (normal, low, and high ranges & results). *MedicineNet.* Retrieved from www.medicinenet.com/liver_blood_tests/article.htm#what_are_the_basic_functions_of_the_liver.

21. T. Newman (2018, March 2). What does the liver do? *Medical News Today.* Retrieved from www.medicalnewstoday.com/articles/305075.php.

22. J. Smolen (2018, September 19). Binge drinking and blackouts: The sobering truth about lost learning in students. *The Conversation.* Retrieved from https://theconversation.com/us/search?utf8=✓&q=%29.+Binge+drinking+and+blackouts%3A+The+sobering+truth+about+lost+learning+in+students.+

23. A. M. White (2003). What happened? Alcohol, memory, blackouts, and the brain. *Alcohol Research and Health.* 27(2): 186–196.

24. D. F. Sweeney (2011). Take blackouts seriously. *Addiction Professional.* 9(4): 54–57.

25. B. F. Grant & D. A. Dawson (1997). Age of onset of alcohol use and its association with DSM-IV alcohol use and dependence. Results from the national longitudinal alcohol epidemiological survey. *Journal of Substance Abuse.* 9: 103–110.

26. P. C. Clapp, S. V. Bhave & P. L. Hoffman (2009). *How adaptation of the brain to alcohol leads to dependence: A pharmacological perspective.* National Institute of Alcohol Abuse and Alcoholism. Retrieved from https://pubs.niaaa.nih.gov/publications/arh314/310-339.htm.

27. Centers for Disease Control and Prevention (2018, October 24). *Fact sheet: Binge drinking.* Retrieved from www.cdc.gov/alcohol/fact-sheets/binge-drinking.htm.

28. J. Allen, G. V. Mohatt, C. C. T. Fok, D. Henry & R. Burkett (2014, June 21). A protective factors model for alcohol abuse and suicide prevention among Alaska native youth. *American Journal of Community Psychology.* 54: 125–139. DOI: 10.1007/s10464-014-9661-3.

29. E. B. Robertson, S. L. David & S. A. Rao (2003). *Preventing drug use among children and adolescents (In brief).* National Institute on Drug Abuse: Rockville, MD.

30. L. D. Johnston, P. M. O'Malley, J. G. Bachman & J. E. Schulenberg (2007). *Monitoring the future: National results on adolescent drug use: Overview of key findings, 2006.* Bethesda, MD: National Institute on Drug Abuse.

31. M. Sanchez-Craig, H. M. Annis, A. R. Bronet & K. R. MacDonald (1984). Random assignment to abstinence and controlled drinking: Evaluation of a cognitive-behavioral program for problem drinkers. *Journal of Consulting and Clinical Psychology.* 52(3): 390–403. http://dx.doi.org/10.1037/0022-006X.52.3.390.

9   Period of Abstinence

This chapter may seem out of place with my message about alcohol moderation. I recommend to all of my clients that before they try to moderate their drinking, they actually stop drinking for a period of time. I have found that my clients achieve the best results when they remain totally abstinent from alcohol for four months. Other research concurs that individuals who go through a period of abstinence are more likely to reach their alcohol-related goals.[1] This chapter will explain the rationale and review tools for obtaining alcohol-free time.

Why Four Months?

Some moderation programs recommend being alcohol-free for 30 days. I find this is often not long enough. Most of us can make a change for a short period of time but struggle to maintain it long-term. Of the many New Year's resolutions you have made, how many have actually become part of your day-to-day life? I am a regular gym user. In my gym, the classes fill up during the month of January and I often must wait to use the elliptical, or I have to search for the weights I want to use for a particular workout. However, by March I have my pick of all the equipment. That's because most people's good intentions fizzle out after a few weeks.

Have you ever tried to diet? I know I have. I give up my happy food—chocolate—and count my calories. I have successfully lost the pounds, only to eventually gain them back again. Why do so many of us struggle to make lasting change? We often give up behaviors that are not good for us, but we may not identify *why* we were making poor choices and *how* to maintain the positive changes. Pop culture has us believe that it takes 21 days to make a change. It actually takes much longer when it comes to changing drinking habits.

Box Matter 9.1

DID YOU KNOW? The idea that it takes three weeks to form a habit is attributed to Dr. Maxwell Martz, a cosmetic surgeon. He reported in his book that it took patients an average of 21 days to get used to a new image after surgery. Over the years, this was misquoted so many times that people began to believe this was actually data from a study.[2]

You may be familiar with the term *white knuckling*. Some say it originated with nervous flyers who gripped the armrests of their seats so tightly that their knuckles turned white. I believe many drinkers metaphorically do this. They hold on for a while and muscle through some alcohol-free time. Sometimes this is to prove to themselves or someone else that they don't really have a problem and can stop at any time. The concern is that during this time they may not be dealing with the internal reasons for their drinking and therefore are not developing necessary coping skills.

In my practice, I actually want my clients to feel some discomfort during this period of abstinence. This gives us the opportunity to identify why they have been turning to alcohol.[3] Once we know this, we can develop a reasonable plan of action.

Some people try to justify their drinking by saying they drink out of habit, not because of negative emotions like sadness or anger or to avoid something painful or uncomfortable. Even so, I still recommend four months of not drinking. This will enable people to cycle through an entire season of events without alcohol in order to create new traditions. If a person goes four months without drinking, they will likely have to come up with a plan for handling holidays, birthdays, anniversaries, parties, sporting events, annual get-togethers, and other such events without relying on alcohol.

Ed was an intelligent, independent 39-year-old IT guy who was responsible for a large government department. The stress and long hours were killing him. He discovered that one or two beers helped him relax and fall asleep, but these soon turned into four or five beers and sometimes some bourbon as well. Ed was a runner and did not like the gut he was developing from his excessive drinking.

Ed came to me looking for help for his insomnia and stress. When I suggested that he might want to be alcohol-free before we addressed those issues, he looked at me in horror, saying, "But how will I function? I can't sleep without it." I assured him that I wasn't asking him to start that night. My job was to give him some tools to manage life better. I don't take away a client's primary coping skill of drinking (unless they need to be medically detoxed) before helping them to develop new ones. As Ed implemented new coping skills, he found he could fall asleep faster and actually had a better quality of sleep without alcohol.

People often fight me about going through this period of abstinence. They argue that they are not "alcoholics." I agree. Most of them are not. But they came to me because alcohol was causing some type of problem in their lives, whether it was a legal consequence, health related, a partner's complaint, or a friend's concern.

I encourage abstinence from alcohol for four months. Most know what it feels like to be a regular drinker but don't know what life is like without alcohol anymore. Therapy at this stage should be about addressing fears of not drinking, planning for risky situations, and developing alternative ways to relax, socialize, cope, etc. Going through a temporary period of absence is more manageable than thinking one can never drink again. Most are surprised at the new perspectives they gain about themselves and the people around them.

One of the main reasons I recommend four months of alcohol-free time is for people to see how they handle a wide variety of situations without alcohol. During this time, your clients will experience discomfort. The goal is to learn other coping skills besides using alcohol. Being chemically free also helps bring emotions to the surface, thus giving an opportunity to manage life in a different way.

Faced with the concept of abstinence, most focus only on negative emotions such as anxiety, stress, depression, boredom, and anger. We need to let them know that positive feelings that perhaps had been numbed by alcohol—joy, awe, love, compassion, and empathy—will begin to emerge. The range of emotions that people experience when they are chemically free often surprises them. Therapy should focus on the benefits. Many of my clients also enjoy feeling more stable. When they are drinking, life can feel like sharp, jagged ups and downs while abstinence feels more like manageable, rolling waves.

Additionally, sometimes people fall into unhealthy patterns. This period of abstinence should give individuals enough time to break these patterns and determine to what degree—if any—they want alcohol to be part of the next stage of life. Most don't want to go back to the way their drinking was. The distance allows them to see patterns. By stepping away, they can get a different perspective. I have found that about half of my clients who go through a period of sobriety chose complete abstinence even when this was not their goal at the outset of treatment. Once people experience life without alcohol, they often find that it is better than what they imagined, as they were only focused on what they would lose, not what they could gain. Drinking or not drinking becomes less of a focus when one shifts their attention, time, and activities to other opportunities. I recommend that people say "I choose not to drink" rather than "I can't drink." The former implies empowerment rather than deprivation.

People who seek therapy for their alcohol use generally know that it has become a problem. Many hope for an easy way to cut down on drinking without having to totally quit drinking. Nonetheless, I do recommend being alcohol-free for a period of time. However, I will not refuse to work with someone if they are not alcohol-free. Going through a period of abstinence offers the following benefits:

- The safest known level of alcohol is no alcohol. If you do not drink, you do not face any further health, legal, social, or family problems.

- Being clean offers perspective. It is an opportunity to see how one thinks, feels, and acts in a variety of situations without the effects of alcohol.
- Abstinence allows people to more naturally feel emotions. It offers an opportunity to learn other ways to deal with them more effectively and without distraction.
- Not drinking gives a chance to break habits, experience a change, and build confidence to live without alcohol.
- Being alcohol-free can help identify triggers related to use.
- Being clean helps people clearly see the problems they were trying to avoid through their use of alcohol.
- Not drinking may allow the medications to work more effectively, thus reducing the need to drink in order to deal with symptoms.

Sal, a self-employed mechanic in his 40s, stared at me in shock. I had just recommended that he try four months of abstinence. I said that the purpose was to feel the discomfort that he had been drinking away and see what new feelings emerged. He didn't jump up and leave the room, so I let him know that during the four months of abstinence we would observe together what he was experiencing and that I would help him develop coping skills as well as identify how and when positive ones surfaced so that he would repeat those.

I let him know that I would be his biggest cheerleader when he experienced success and would teach him how to build upon the wins. I also told him that I would challenge him if he continued to make poor decisions. In this way, I offered him not only support and encouragement, but also the necessary accountability for when he felt hopeless or his willpower wavered.

Getting SOBER

This section discusses some helpful skills to successfully abstain from alcohol for four months. AA has a great acronym for sober:

Son
Of a
Bitch
Everything is
Real

This is exactly we want to have happen for our clients. Deal with life on life's terms. Regular alcohol use takes the edge off so that life feels out of focus. Abstinence allows people to gain clarity to see reality and identify changes they want to make. Maybe their relationship is stressed because of their partner's anger concerning drinking. During the alcohol-free time they can learn better communication skills that will lead to greater intimacy. I point out to my clients that when they stop drinking, they have a more even playing field. Trust can be regained, and they have more of a voice when they take drinking as an issue off the table.

Additionally, without the salve of drinking, people realize that it has been affecting their motivation to make beneficial lifestyle changes. Many of my clients are frustrated with themselves when they realize that their alcohol use was covering up a problem rather than helping them cope. Without alcohol, they have their full faculties to make changes. Most are happier without alcohol because they can more fully enjoy, rather than tolerate, their lives.

Therapy is for dealing with any issues from the past that are still affecting people. In the early weeks of abstinence, many feel emotionally raw. We can offer perspective, tools, insights, and support during this period.

For many, alcohol was their primary way to relax, socialize, and have fun. I ask my clients what they used to enjoy prior to their regular alcohol use. I remind them that nothing that is healthy in the long run will work as quickly as alcohol did. But I also let them know that other activities will likely not have the same physical, emotional, relational, and financial consequences that regular alcohol use had on them.

Boredom is one of the main causes of relapse.[4] We all need something to look forward to each day, whether it is enjoying a good cup of coffee, working out, chatting with a coworker, snuggling with our mate, or watching our favorite show or sporting event. On a weekly basis, we need something that gets us excited. Maybe it's having dinner with friends, going to a movie, participating in a community event, or seeing a show. We also should have bigger things to look forward to, like planning a getaway, crossing something off our bucket list, or taking a road trip.

One of my best friends has a great idea to help him experience life. He gets his local recreation guide and picks a number from one to whatever the number of pages in that quarter's issue. Then he opens the guide and picks an activity from that page. As a result, he has done some interesting activities, met some fun people, and has funny stories from the activities that were flops. The idea is to get out and do something. People may not like nine out of ten things they try, but the tenth one may become a new hobby or passion, and they may make some great friends in the process. As a therapist, one of the few times I give homework is to have fun. I require my clients to pick an activity and report back. Many struggle with this, but once they do something, their happiness is priceless.

Mindfulness-Based Relapse Prevention

Here's another way to get SOBER. I like the play on words because people tend to remember acronyms better. Below is a mindfulness-based relapse-prevention technique that breaks down the word *sober* and recommends steps for each of the letters:[5,6]

Stop
Observe

Breathe
Expand
React

S—STOP: get out of autopilot mode. By this I mean stop doing things automatically without even being fully aware of what you are doing. For example, you get into your car to go run errands, and a few minutes later you somehow end up at the first store on your list. You did not consciously tell yourself to turn here, speed up, stop, go left, or park. Your brain just ran with the thought and got you there. This works well in neutral situations, but think of the times when you run on autopilot regarding unhealthy behavior. You get in the car and automatically light up a cigarette. Maybe you sit on the couch, turn on the television, and unconsciously finish a whole bag of chips. Many people do this with their drinking, too.

Michelle's goal was to remain abstinent from alcohol. She wasn't alcohol dependent but did not like the consequences that her drinking caused to her health and her family. She had made it nine months without a drink. Then she attended a large family gathering in a restaurant. The table was set beautifully to include both water glasses and wine glasses. The server promptly filled both glasses for all adult guests.

Michelle was happily chatting with her favorite cousins. She was so involved in the conversation that she did not notice that she drank the entire glass of house white, which the waiter dutifully refilled. It was not until she got up to use the ladies' room that she realized she was a little tipsy. She was angry with herself, and her husband stared at her accusingly later that night.

Michelle was drinking on autopilot. Though she had no intention to consume alcohol at this event, she had also made no active effort not to drink. If she had been more mindful, she may have been more successful in maintaining her sobriety. She could have had a conversation with her husband beforehand, asking for his support; asked the waiter to remove her wine glass; and ordered her favorite nonalcoholic beverage before she got swept up in the emotion of the event.

O—OBSERVE: observe emotions, urges, physical sensations, and thoughts. In other words, know your triggers. Many drinkers spend a lot of time in an artificial emotional state—either thinking about drinking, being under the influence, or recovering from the impact of drinking. As they go into early abstinence, I prepare them by noting that they may experience a heightened sensitivity to their environment, but this is not a permanent state. I share this because this is why many people give up abstinence in the early days. They think, "If this is what being alcohol-free feels like, I don't want it."

I recommend people be aware of how they feel as they go into a drinking situation. They notice certain reactions in their body before they actually become conscious thoughts. These may be signals that require their attention and action. The more awareness they have of what is going on internally, the better they can deal with the external enjoinment. I remind them that giving in to a momentary urge may not yield the best outcome for the long term.

I ask the following questions when a client describes a craving:

- How does your body feel physically?
- What do you feel emotionally?
- What do you want to do?
- What can you do?

B—BREATHE: pay attention to breathing. I ask them the following questions: Are you breathing in and out slowly and evenly? Are both your chest and your stomach rising and falling with each intake and exhale, or do you sometimes gulp for air? Do you sometimes hold your breath? Is your breathing rapid and shallow? Focus on your respiration; it can tell you a lot about how you are feeling.

Breathing is something we do unconsciously thousands of times a day. A change in normal breathing can signify that we are experiencing negative emotions. When we get upset, angry, scared, or nervous, we tend to go into fight-or-flight mode. In this reaction, the body either prepares to fight perceived danger or gears up to run away from it. The heart rate increases, stomach production shuts down, hormones are secreted, pupils dilate, and breathing rate speeds up.

A simple way to recognize when one is struggling emotionally is to check breathing. If they are experiencing negative emotions, they will tend to breathe more quickly and shallowly, in the upper half of your chest. The simplest way to calm down this fight-or-flight reaction is to practice deep breathing. It is so simple, yet it unleashes a powerful calming response.

I take my clients through this exercise and say the following: Ideally, sit in a comfortable place without crossing arms or legs. Place one hand on the chest and one hand on the stomach. The goal is to take in full, deep breaths, making sure that your stomach rises.

If you are alone, you might want to close your eyes. Breathe in slowly for a count of five, hold for five seconds, and then release slowly on a count of five. Try to go through the cycle five times. Don't be surprised if the first time you try this, you feel a little dizzy and uncomfortable. This is just your body readjusting. The more you practice this technique before you get stressed, the lower your stress level will be, and the less likely it will be for your emotions to escalate quickly.

If you were ever to catch me in traffic with my kids arguing in the back seat, you would see that I had one hand on the wheel and one on my stomach. I would be practicing deep breathing so I wouldn't crash into the idiot in front of me or get involved in the sibling fight behind me.

E—EXPAND: expand awareness to the entire body and the surrounding area. I ask my clients to pay attention to their surroundings and how they make them feel. They should identify any triggers that they are facing. Think through what would happen if they remained in this environment and what would happen in if they took a drink.

This process is called a body scan. It is an easy mindfulness exercise where individuals focus on what they are feeling in their body. I find it helps to go through several cycles of deep breathing, then do a body scan.

I teach individuals to notice what thoughts are running through their mind. I tell them that they don't have to do anything about them; just observe them as if they were words floating by. I ask them: Do you feel any stress or tension in your head or face, your neck, or shoulders? What is going on in your stomach? How does your back feel? Are you clenching your teeth, hands, or jaw?

Mindfulness is about noticing, not necessarily reacting in the moment. When we learn to be present in the moment, we can manage our emotions better. Once they have expanded their awareness, this often kicks in the parasympathetic nervous system, the one that relaxes the body and calms down the fight-or-flight response. Next, they can evaluate with their logical, not emotional brain.

If they are experiencing negative physical symptoms, take a moment to determine whether they can could take action to address them. If they are feeling excitement, happiness, or relaxation, celebrate the feeling and figure out how they can repeat and increase it in a healthy way!

R—RESPOND: the goal is to respond, not to react. A reaction tends to be emotional, while a response is more intentional. To respond mindfully means you are aware of both your internal and external experiences and are making a conscious choice of what to do about them. Once people know what is going on in their mind and body, they can take the appropriate steps. Realize that sometimes they may not know what they are feeling or what to do. I tell them that is a great time to call a friend or partner or to post on a moderation forum and get some perspective. We often make things worse in our own heads, but people who know and love us can offer a different perspective, bring us back to reality, help us make decisions, and provide support.

Help your client identify who they would be willing to call. Explore who is able to give support and perspective. I encourage them not only to reach out when there is a problem but to keep regular contact. Often, these contacts can pick up on shifts in mood and behavior, warding off a problem and preventing it from being a full-blown crisis. People often make the mistake of waiting until there is an issue, not wanting to "burden" anyone.

Reducing Risky Situations

Traditional treatment says that people experiencing problems from alcohol must give up all people, places, and things associated with drinking. I have a different approach. I focus more on *levels of risk* because sometimes we are unable to avoid them completely. Sometimes the people are our family, and the places are our homes or places where we must go in our day-to-day lives. When we look at life in terms of black and white, we often give up because an all-or-nothing approach is unrealistic and too hard to maintain. I prefer to explore the shades of gray. I recommend that my clients identify risky people, places, and things and consider their levels of risk associated with them.

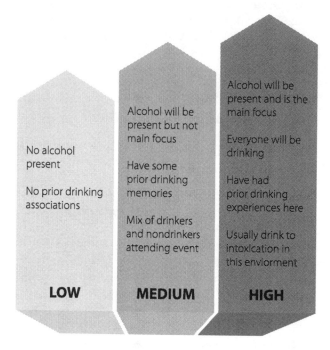

Figure 9.2 Levels of Risk

LOW RISK: Alcohol is unlikely to be at this event, the people in attendance are not regular drinkers, and they have no past associations of alcohol here. I encourage my clients to stay in low-risk situations as they are going through a period of abstinence and when they begin practicing moderation. I recommend they have a plan before attending the event or location. Then make sure the people they are going with know their current drinking goals and either bring a nonalcoholic beverage or have a nonalcoholic drink choice in mind before getting the question: Can I get you a drink?

MEDIUM RISK: Alcohol may be present at this event, but it is not the main focus. They may have consumed alcohol at this place in the past, but also have nonalcohol-related memories of it and know people there who will not be drinking. This is a situation that they could attend, but they should have a plan and go with a support person who is aware of their goals and challenges.

HIGH RISK: If they go to this bar, house, party, concert, casino, club, or sporting event, drinking will be taking place. They drank in these situations and with these people in the past. They have never participated in this event without consuming alcohol. As individuals are readjusting drinking patterns, high-risk situations may be places to avoid until they are more confident and comfortable with their new plan.

Dan's friends had one of the funniest ways of dealing with risky situations. He was a self-admitted pickle who drank to excess, had received several DUIs, blacked out frequently, and had lost things that were important to him, including his marriage and ability to drive a car. Dan participated in a recovery program that included detox, individual therapy, dual-diagnosis group therapy, and regular support group attendance.

One of Dan's closest childhood friends was getting married. The best man planned to have the bachelor party in Las Vegas. Dan's friends did not have an issue with alcohol; binge drinking was the main agenda. Dan's friends wanted him to go on the trip so badly that they offered to pay for a prostitute to stay with him to make sure he did not drink when they were out!

Dan realized that this trip was too high of a risk for him, and he decided not to go. He skipped the bachelor bacchanal but happily attended the weekend events for the wedding. He recently celebrated five years of sobriety.

Urge Surfing

Another goal in the early months of alcohol abstinence is developing self-regulation skills through mindfulness techniques. This is learning how to tolerate negative emotions and delay rewards. G. Alan Marlatt is credited with the concept of "urge surfing."[7] The idea is that cravings are like waves, and breathing is like a surfboard that carries you through the wave. We can use deep breathing to ride out the wave (craving).[8] I find this is helpful because it acknowledges that the desire to drink can be powerful, but that there is a simple technique a person can use anywhere, anytime (breathing). Because urge surfing can be visualized, people can also see that an urge is not permanent. It may peak but will eventually dissipate, as waves do.

I remind people that just because we have a thought or feeling does not mean we have to indulge it. Distraction is another healthy way to manage cravings. I recommend developing a list of healthy distractions to have in place prior to needing it. Knowing what to do in a crisis helps individuals feel more prepared for what to do when they are having a craving. Remember all those fire drills you participated in as a kid?

I find that individuals are more likely to follow through with activities that they come up with, but sometimes they need help developing ideas. For many, alcohol has been a part of their lives since they were teenagers. Here are some of the most common that can be done alone and do not require transportation or significant amounts of money:

_____ Listen to a podcast
_____ Read a magazine
_____ Call a friend
_____ Play a computer game
_____ Watch a television show
_____ Listen to music

_____ Journal
_____ Pray
_____ Meditate
_____ Take a walk
_____ Do your nails
_____ Take a bath
_____ Organize something
_____ Lift weights
_____ Tune into a sports event
_____ Do housework
_____ Reach out to your support person
_____ Play with your kids
_____ Surf the internet
_____ Attend a self-help meeting
_____ Read recovery literature
_____ Review online moderation tools
_____ Post on a moderation forum
_____ Watch a yoga video on YouTube
_____ Look up funny animal videos
_____ Say the Serenity Prayer
_____ Watch a TED Talk
_____ Prepare a meal
_____ Leave a message for your therapist

When discussing cravings, I ask my clients to think about the following questions:

1.   *What am I feeling physically?*

   Pay special attention to your head, neck, and stomach. These are the places where you will often experience the physical outlet of emotions. Explore what happened right before the urge. What does the urge want? If it could speak, what would it say to you right now? Is it trying to tell you something about yourself?

2.   *What am I thinking?*

   Oftentimes you will experience a rush of many different thoughts. Pay attention to any self-defeating patterns. Take several deep breaths and imagine any negative thoughts being placed into the cargo hold of an airplane. Imagine the negative thoughts and patterns flying away so that you can focus on healthy, positive thoughts and patterns. The more senses you engage in a positive thought or image, the less able you are to think about the negative one.

3.   *Where do you feel most happy, safe, and comfortable?*

   Recall what you see, hear, feel, and smell. It helps to bring up a location where you have been. When you recall this place, your brain remembers the positive feelings and elicits the positive emotions associated with it.

4.   *What are my go-to healthy distractions?*

Practice healthy distractions. Review the list of activities presented earlier. When you experience a craving, do something different. Sometimes just getting up and moving to a different space can help reduce an urge to drink.

5.   *If my distractions do not work, what action can I take?*

Sometimes you just need to acknowledge a craving and then focus on something else. It can be uncomfortable, but the pain is not permanent. Occasionally cravings are intense. Reaching out to someone may be important to help you reality test, stay busy, and be accountable.

Dealing With Triggers

A trigger often increases an urge to drink. I recommend not judging it as "good" or "bad." Experiencing a trigger is a point at which we can intervene. I view it as an opportunity for change. I help my clients identify what was leading up to the craving. This is where we can identify triggers, practice tools for how to reduce the possible stressor, and develop tools for how to handle similar situations in the future. Sometimes just having a plan is enough to empower people that they can influence what happens to them.

There are several types of triggers. Identify which ones affect your client. Then develop a plan for how to reduce their occurrence as well as plan for when they will face them. A therapist's job is to offer perspective and help people see different angles and solutions.

Emotional: this is how you feel. Most people acknowledge only negative emotions like sadness, loneliness, depression, and anger. However, positive ones like confidence, satisfaction, and excitement can also cause a relapse.

Physical: this refers to what your body feels like. Sometimes people reach for a drink to alter their physical state. It may be to help them relax, manage stress, or feel numb. Regular drinkers are often used to having a quick fix that alters their mood and physical state quickly. Sometimes we need to remind them that very little will work as quickly as alcohol did, but that a benefit to using other tools is that there may be fewer consequences to them.

People: it sounds cliché, but there are people who make one want to drink. It may be because others around them are all drinking and they feel like they are missing out. Or individuals have a negative history with that person, so they drink to deal with hurt, anger, or resentment.

Availability: there will be alcohol present. Sometimes it is obvious, like at a bar, sports event, wedding, or party. These events may need to be avoided for a period of time because adequate willpower and coping skills have not yet been developed. AA has great sayings when it comes to being around alcohol: "If you stand by the buffet table long enough, you're going to eat." "Hang around a barbershop a while and you're going to get a haircut." Or, "Wait in line at the hot dog stand, you're going to eat a hot dog."

Social pressure: if I am around these people or this situation, I will feel like I am expected to drink and will be an outcast if I do not. This trigger is like a combination of people and availability.

Memories: I have strong, positive recollections of drinking in these situations, and it is hard to remember any consequences. This is where I teach the concept of "play it through."

Play It Through 24

One way to deal with the triggers and cravings is to "play it through 24." The idea is to identify what would happen if one took a drink. I ask people to think through the following:

> What will happen in the next 24 seconds?
> What would happen in the next 24 minutes?
> What can occur in the next 24 hours?
> What about the next 24 days?

It is important to recognize that the chemical effects of alcohol are powerful. The first drink may feel good. People may experience an initial relief, soothing, or relaxation. When I get people thinking about the next 24 minutes, some recognize that they may not stop at just one drink. However, when some think about the next 24 minutes, they recognize that they may not stop at one or two and stop caring about the consequences. Playing it through the next 24 hours, or even 24 days, can help to identify what their alcohol goals are. They may realize that the consequences outweigh their pleasure. The trick is to know how many this is for your client. For some, one is too many, and the end of the bottle is not enough. For others, having several occasionally keeps them in a healthy zone.

Figure 9.3 Play It Through 24

At this point, it may still seem like I am advocating for complete absti- nence. I recommend only going through a period of time. Based on each individual's experience, we can then determine the next steps. While the tools listed in this chapter are more appropriate for achieving sobriety, they can still be used to monitor the effectiveness of moderation. The next sev- eral chapters will explore tools for alcohol moderation.

Notes

1. M. Sanchez-Craig (2013). *Saying when: How to quit drinking or cut down.* Toronto, Canada: Center for Addiction and Mental Health.
2. J. Selk (2013, April 15). Habit formation: The 21-day myth. *Forbes.com.* Retrieved from www.forbes.com/sites/jasonselk/2013/04/15/habit-formation-the-21-day- myth/#48ee9dcddebc.
3. E. Fouquereau, A. Fernandez, E. Mullet & P. C. Sorum (2003, June). Stress and the urge to drink. *Addictive Behaviors.* 28(4): 669–685. https://doi.org/10.1016/ S0306-4603(01)00276-3.
4. M. Kadam, A. Sinha, S. Nimkar, Y. Matcheswalla & A. De Sousa (2017). A compara- tive study of factors associated with relapse in alcohol dependence and opioid depend- ence. *Indian Journal of Psychological Medicine.* 39(5): 627–633. DOI: 10.4103/IJPSYM. IJPSYM_356_17.
5. S. Bowen, N. Chawla & G. A. Marlatt (2011). *Mindfulness-based relapse prevention for addictive behaviors: A clinician's guide.* New York: The Guilford Press.
6. K. Witikiewitz, S. Bowen, E. N. Harropt, H. Douglas, M. Enkema & C. Sedgwick (2014). Mindfulness-based treatment to prevent addictive behavior relapse: Theo- retical models and hypothesized mechanisms of change. *Substance Use Misuse.* 49(5): 513–524. DOI: 10.3109/10826084.2014.891845.
7. B. D. Ostafin & G. A. Marlatt (2008). Surfing the urge: Experiential acceptance moderates the relation between automatic alcohol motivation and hazardous drink- ing. *Journal of Social and Clinical Psychology.* 27(4): 404–418. https://doi.org/10.1521/ jscp.2008.27.4.404.
8. K. Griffin (2010). Interview with G. Alan Marlatt: Surfing the urge. *Inquiring Mind.* 26(2).

10 Alcohol Moderation Tools

This chapter will describe some of the most common alcohol moderation tools and how clients can put them into practice. Below are some of the behaviors a person can practice to help make alcohol moderation more successful. They are grouped in topics that include: blood alcohol concentration, physical, emotional, environmental, tracking, and motivational.

Blood Alcohol Concentration

Know Your BAC

Successful moderators know the effects of their blood alcohol concentration (BAC). It is the percentage of alcohol in the bloodstream. Alcohol is classified as a sedative or depressant substance because it impairs or "slows down" mental and physical functioning. The long- and short-term effects of alcohol use have been well studied. For the average person who does not have a physical dependence on alcohol, these are the most common effects of a rising blood alcohol level:[1]

> 0.02%–0.039%: Most drinkers begin to feel the effects of alcohol. People experience slight euphoria, loss of shyness, and relaxation.
> 0.04%–0.059%: There is a feeling of well-being, relaxation, low inhibitions, and warm sensations. People start to have some impairment of judgment and memory. Feelings of euphoria emerge. People tend to get more talkative and confident.
> 0.06%–0.99%: Balance, speech, vision, reaction time, and hearing is slightly impaired. There is reduced judgment and self-control. Reasoning and memory are impaired.
> 0.10%–0.129%: There is a significant impairment of motor coordination and judgment. Speech is slurred. Balance, peripheral vision, reaction time, and hearing are all impaired.
> 0.130%–0.159%: People have gross motor impairment and lack of physical control. Vision is blurred and there is a loss of balance. Euphoria is decreasing, and people being to feel unwell.
> 0.160%–0.199%: People feel nauseous and act sloppily.

0.200%–0.249%: The individual needs assistance walking. They are mentally confused. They may be vomiting and experiencing a blackout.

0.250%–0.399%: Alcohol poisoning is occurring. The person may lose consciousness, have a seizure, irregular and slow breathing, blue-tinged or pale skin, low body temperature, and an inability to be awakened. This is a medical emergency that can lead to brain damage or death.

0.40%: Onset of coma and potential death due to respiratory arrest.

While there are increasingly depressant effects on the body, most people experience an initial stimulating effect. In lower doses, alcohol increases arousal, but with ongoing consumption, alcohol reduces energy and awareness. People feel good initially with the first drink or two, but the effects become more impaired and dangerous over time. This is why most moderation programs recommend keeping your BAC below 0.06.[2]

A person's BAC will range based on a number of factors. The more they weigh, the more fluid they have in their body, the more the amount of alcohol gets diluted, thus having less of an effect. Therefore, the less a person weighs, the more quickly alcohol will affect them. Women tend to have higher BACs for the same amount of alcohol as a man consumes. Women also generally have higher percentages of fat and therefore less water in their bodies to dilute the alcohol.

Dilute Your Drink

Another way to prevent the BAC from rising as rapidly is to dilute the alcoholic beverage. Simply adding extra ice, including more nonalcoholic mixers like soda, or reducing the amount of liquor in a mixed drink can all help. Instead of drinking straight liquor, have it on the rocks. Or people can make a spritzer out of wine. I caution moderators about drinks that are more flavorful, as they can wind up consuming more.

Pace and Space

The idea behind "Pace and Space" is to have no more than one drink per hour and to space drinks out over a period of time. Individuals should have a plan for how many drinks they are going to have in a given time frame. Simply putting the beverage down in between sips can help people pace themselves. If a drink is in your hand, you are more likely to drink it. Pacing and spacing also refers to having a nonalcoholic beverage in between alcoholic drinks. I encourage having a glass of water for every alcoholic drink, although other people may prefer soda, juice, or tea.

Rotate Nonalcoholic and Alcoholic Beverages

Rotating between a nonalcoholic beverage and one containing alcohol helps in several ways. It helps people pace themselves and prevents the BAC from rising too quickly. Rotating beverages also prevents the dehydration that alcoholic beverages can cause, which may lead to hangovers.

Sip Slowly and Mindfully

When drinking, sip slowly and mindfully. Some people eat and drink quickly, causing digestion problems, overeating, and overdrinking. If one drinks quickly, the effects hit faster, making it harder to pace oneself. This is why drinking straight liquor and doing shots can be risky because the alcohol goes into the bloodstream rapidly. If they sip slowly, they can savor their drink. One may find that they don't actually like how their alcohol tastes and realize they were only drinking for effect. Alcohol is a high-calorie beverage. I ask my clients to make sure they are enjoying it.

Know Your Point of No Return

Some also call this the "F**k-It point" when they appear to have no off switch. Most people reach this point around a BAC level of 0.06%. They are unable to determine if they have had enough. For most people, this is two to three drinks.

Box Matter 10.1

DID YOU KNOW? Drinking coffee, going for a walk, or taking a cold shower will not help you sober up. On average, it takes two to three hours for a single drink to leave the body. Nothing can speed up this biological process.[3]

Physical

Satisfy Physical Needs First

Alcohol cravings may be a sign that biological needs are being unmet. Prior to taking a drink, people should first satisfy their physical needs. I ask clients to assess if they are hungry. When we experience low blood sugar, we become irritable, impatient, anxious, and shaky. All of those can mimic a craving. Then I have them identify if they are thirsty. Early signs of dehydration can include hunger pangs, fatigue, and headache. Many people consume beverages loaded with caffeine, like soda, coffee, and tea, which have a diuretic effect. They also should look at if they are tired. This too makes people irritable and reduces willpower and judgment. People should never take a drink if any of these three areas are not addressed first.

Eat Before You Drink

Alcohol is absorbed into the bloodstream from the stomach and the small intestine.[4] If an individual does not have any food in his or her stomach, the alcohol will go directly into the bloodstream, causing the BAC to rise faster and the person to feel the effects more rapidly. It also helps to drink nonalcoholic beverages to dilute the alcohol in the stomach and slow absorption.

Emotional

Pay Attention to Urges

An urge is the desire to start or continue drinking to the point of intoxication. People, places, situations, events, and emotions all can be triggers. Once they identify the urges, they can develop a plan of how to cope. Sometimes it may be to best to avoid the situation that leads to urges, and sometimes people need a plan to manage an urge when it occurs. This can include leaving the situation, calling a friend, reviewing a list of why one chose to change their drinking patterns, etc.

Do Not Drink When Upset

Alcohol is a depressant. While one may initially experience feelings of relaxation, warm sensations, and lowered inhibitions, in larger doses it affects judgment, reasoning, memory, and self-control. Alcohol will typically magnify the emotions. For example, if a person drinks when he or she is angry, the alcohol will reduce that person's inhibitions and he or she is more likely to get into a physical altercation. If that person is upset about a breakup, a few drinks will alter his or her judgment and that person may have causal sex with a stranger, only to regret it in the morning.

Alcohol is also known to reduce the effectiveness of many medications. Regular alcohol use interrupts neurotransmitters that are needed for regulating our mood.[5] It also narrows perceptions so that people do not respond to cues around them. If someone is prone to anxiety, they will be on higher alert. Those who struggle with depression will interpret the world around them even more negatively.

My clients report that when they use alcohol to change their mood, they often feel worse for several days afterward. Keep in mind that when a substance gives an emotional lift, there will be a converse reaction with an even worse mood as a result. In the long run, people are on a never-ending cycle where they are trying to recover from the last emotional dip. Their baseline mood lowers every time they drink until depression is their baseline state.

Unpairing

In the initial small doses, alcohol releases the feel-good chemicals of opioids and dopamine. However, the "placebo effect" also occurs. We believe alcohol is doing something so we feel something. Clients have reported an instant feeling of gratification as soon as they grab the cold beer or being relaxed as soon as they take the first sip—long before any alcohol has reached the bloodstream to cause any effect. Therefore, I talk with my clients about what I call "unpairing."

People associate the pleasurable effects of alcohol with the action of drinking. It becomes their way to relax, celebrate, have fun, end the day, reward oneself, etc. An exercise I do with my clients is to identify what drinking equals for them. This is like understanding their "why." We can help them unpair alcohol with each of these things. Just as the pairing can be developed, it can be undone. Once people recognize this association, we can look at other ways to achieve their desired effect. Some common pairings include:

Beer = the end of a day
Wine = my reward
Champagne = celebration
Cocktail = party

Remember that over a third of the population does not drink alcohol at all, and the majority can take it or leave it. I remind my clients of this because they cannot image situations or events in which people do not drink. Many of my clients notice that when they go through the period of abstinence, they were the one who was encouraging alcohol to be present. Sometimes they also realize that most of their friends and situations involved alcohol and may need to change some of their people or places.

Environmental

Never Drink Alone

Drinking alone often indicates that a person is trying to change their mood, which is a negative predictor for moderation. While people certainly can get out of control when around others, being around people can be a type of check. If practiced mindfully, one can see their behavior reflected in the people around them. A person can notice if they are drinking more or less than others. I encourage drinkers to pay attention to whether others are sipping their drinks or doing shots. Then they should notice if others are becoming intoxicated and determine a plan to safely get home. A successful Alcohol Moderation Plan (discussed in the next chapter) identifies in greater depth what a safer drinking plan will look like.

Don't Keep Alcohol in the House

We tend to eat or drink what we have easy access to. If there is no alcohol in the house, it creates a small speed bump where you have to get dressed, leave the house, and go to a store, bar, or restaurant to get a drink. Having to make a trip to the store, restaurant, or bar gives them a few minutes to think about whether they really want a drink or if something else will satisfy your craving. If it is in the house, people are less likely to think it through. Some say that they keep alcohol in the house for guests. If they are having people over they can buy just enough and then send any leftovers home with guests.

Drink Only in Social Situations

My most successful alcohol moderators drink only when there are other people around, as part of a social event. They do not make drinking the main focus.

Only Consume Alcohol During the Event

Don't drink before or after the event, only during. Some people consume alcohol prior to the event to calm their nerves before entering the social situation. I work with my clients to explore why this anxiety is occurring, to see if this is a signal that they should not attend, and role-play ways to manage small talk. I remind my adults that they are not a young adult anymore and don't need to "pre-game." Younger individuals tend to do this to feel alcohol's effects faster, drink at home because they were underage, or because the alcohol was less expensive than at a bar or restaurant.

Pick a Nonalcoholic Drink

I make sure that all of my clients know what nonalcoholic beverages they enjoy on a regular basis as well as when they want to be more festive. Some find they manage fine at home but then feel like they are missing out when they attend a celebration where others are drinking. Many alcoholic beverages can come in the form of a "mocktail." These are what some call beach or boat drinks but do not have any alcohol in them. They can order a virgin margarita, piña colada, mojito, etc., and still feel like they are on vacation or celebrating. Mocktails can be quite elaborate and include exotic fruits and other mixers with fewer calories and consequences.

Craig worked in the restaurant industry for most of his life, so drinking was a big part of special occasions for him. One day in a therapy session, he was lamenting that he would be celebrating his birthday during his period of abstinence. He had always looked forward to hanging out with the regulars and having them buy him a drink rather than making one for them. Given that he had bartended for years, I suggested he create a "mocktail," a nonalcoholic mixed drink. I could see the wheels turning in his mind as we ended the session.

The next week, he came in proudly for two reasons. One was that he had celebrated his birthday alcohol-free, finally sticking to his commitment after many failed attempts. And two, he had created a new mocktail that was going to be added to the restaurant's menu and named after him!

Rehearse a Response

Many people who are regular drinkers associate "drink" with an alcoholic beverage. They don't view water, soda, tea, juice, or coffee as a drink. Many times regular drinkers who become abstinent or change their drinking patterns are worried about how other people will react to their decision or how to answer the question of what to drink. I ask my clients to think back to the last social gathering they attended. Then I question: how much did your best friend drink, your significant other, your coworker, neighbor, etc.? This reality testing process can help them to realize that they are putting more attention on what they are consuming than others likely are. It may feel like there is a spotlight on them, but I help them see that there usually is not. And if there are those that may question them, we role-play how to deal with the situation.

I help them prepare a short response for how to handle the question: Would you like a drink? It may be helpful for moderators to tell a close friend or family member that they have changed their drinking patterns so that they can run interference. If someone's in-laws are big drinkers, they can ask their spouse to talk to them to make sure there are no uncomfortable moments, or bring their own drink and have it in their hand so they avoid altogether the question of what to drink.

Below are some statements that others have found helpful:

- "No, thank you."
- "I'm doing a cleanse."
- "No, I'm not pregnant; I just feel like having water."
- "I'm saving my calories for dinner."
- "Alcohol and I no longer mix."
- "I'm trying to lose this belly."
- "Not drinking is my New Year's resolution."
- "I'm giving up alcohol for Lent."
- "Oh, I've already got something."
- "I'm the designated driver."
- "I'm doing a challenge."
- "My doctor wants me to lose a few pounds."
- "I'm on probation."
- "I'm watching my sugar level."
- "My doctor is monitoring my A1C levels."

- "It makes me sick."
- "I've had my share."
- "I don't drink anymore."

Humor works well to put everyone at ease. Additionally, people can always speak the simple truth or order a mocktail. They should use the one-liner they are most comfortable with. In sessions we practice saying it out loud before they arrive at your destination. In this way, they will feel more prepared when they are confronted with a drinking situation, thus avoiding an awkward moment for their as well as their host. When individuals set the tone of being relaxed and comfortable, the people around them will respond positively. Individuals may also want to devise a signal with the person they are with to let them know when it is time to go. I also suggest this for friends and couples who just want to go home early!

Avoid High-Risk Situations

If one has always consumed alcohol in that situation, at that place, or with those people, they should be avoided. I focus my clients not on what they will lose but on what they can gain. When we are giving something up, we feel deprived. This is why I encourage my clients to make a list of what has happened when they were in high-risk situations. Most are able to see that the consequences were not worth the short-term fun. Then I have them focus on other activities they would like to try and point out that they will meet like-minded people. It is hard for them to imagine the benefits when they have not yet experienced them. Therapists give perspective to clients in that they remember each clients' past but also help them see the possibilities for their future.

Avoid Heavy Drinkers

If moderators plan on consuming alcohol, they should anticipate the environment. When you are around people who are drinking heavily, you are more likely to go with the flow and keep pace with them.

Be the Designated Driver

There are times when a person does not feel they can miss a high-risk situation. Examples include a friend's wedding, a family member's birthday, an annual event, or a holiday gathering. In these situations, it can be helpful to offer to be the designated driver. Most people respect this and do not continue to offer alcohol. Many bars and restaurants will offer free nonalcoholic drinks to the person who is driving.

I have worked with a number of clients who were consistently nominated by their peers to be the designated driver because they were abstinent. After feeling used and seeing how intoxicated their peers were getting on a regular basis, many decided to establish new peer groups and different ways to socialize.

Plan an Early Event for the Next Day

Planning an event for early the next day can help when people are in risky situations, when they are sticking to a reduced amount, or are not drinking in an event. When people have something to look forward to in the morning, they will feel less like they are missing out. Additionally, it gives a good reason for why one is drinking less or remaining abstinent.

Focus on Conversation, Activity, or People

For successful moderation, the situation should not be about the alcohol but participating in the surroundings. Many may feel uncomfortable the first time they go when they stop or reduce their drinking, feeling like all eyes are on them, wondering what is wrong and why they are not drinking. This is why it is important to have a statement prepared, have a support person, know the levels of risk, understand and deal with their "why", etc., prior to attending a drinking situation. After going once or twice with their new relationship with alcohol, individuals realize that most people are having their own internal conversations, focusing on themselves and their experiences. If after going to the same type of event with the same people they still feel uncomfortable, it might be time to reevaluate their social circles and what they do with their time.

Tracking

Consumption Plan

Prior to leaving for an event, individuals should have a plan for how much they plan to consume. I recommend keeping alcohol consumption within moderate drinking guidelines: no more than a drink per hour, not on consecutive evenings, and no more than three drinks total for women or four for men. In addition to planning how much one will drink, I encourage knowing what type of drink one will consume as well as planning on eating something with alcohol.

Accountability Partner

Bringing an accountability partner when drinking is helpful in several ways. Communication and trust are important. The drinker should communicate his or her goals to the accountability partner. That person needs to be willing and able to step in if the plan is not being adhered to. Their job is one of support, not probation. If the drinker needs someone to count drinks and say when to stop, the drinker is not ready to be practicing moderation. They need more work to understand their "why," reduce risky situations, and learn more tools.

If one goes to an event on their own, he or she can check in with a friend both before and after the event. That person can predict risky situations and follow up on how they managed the drinking situation.

Use a Daily Counter

This can work for both abstinence and moderation. I suggest getting a calendar and hanging it in a prominent place in the house. For each day that the individual either has a day of not drinking or drinks within moderation guidelines, they put a check on the calendar. The counter helps people stay accountable and is a visual way to track successes. The calendar also helps people see if there are patterns. It is especially helpful when one uses a full annual calendar to see if there are patterns during a certain time of year, like holidays, seasons, birthdays, or annual remembrances. Having others see this tangible reminder is another way to get support, motivation, and accountability. Seeing the positive checks helps to regain trust from family members. When there are a number of blank spaces, loved ones can point out patterns, ask if they can be of help, and offer support.

Keep a Drink Diary

Paying attention to when one drinks, how much they drink, and how they feel before and after drinking is helpful. The drink diary gives us data. By writing this information down, people may start to see patterns. For example, a person may realize that whenever they spend time with a certain group of people, they tend to overdrink; or they may find that their willpower is not as strong when they are under a deadline; or that they were saying that they had a certain amount a week, but when they see it on paper, it is actually more than what they were admitting.

Pay Attention to Drinking Habits

It may seem like they develop and persist without thinking. However, with mindful attention, people can be in the moment and learn to do something different. Many are shocked at how they just did the same thing because it was how they always acted.

Avoid Back-to-Back Drinking Days

There are numerous reasons not to consume alcohol on a daily basis. By not drinking every day, one is more likely to reduce the amount they drink, reducing the overall health risks. Having off days from consuming alcohol requires people to have other tools for managing stress, relaxing, having fun, ending the day, etc. It also helps people to avoid getting into a habit. If someone does the same behavior every day, it can be very easy for the amount of alcohol to increase and hard to eventually break the pattern.

Drink Tracking

When practicing moderation, one can also use physical reminders to track drinks. Women can put on the corresponding amount of bracelets or rings for the drinks they plan to have and then move them to the other hand once the drink was ordered. Men can wear their watch on their opposite wrist as a way to be conscious when consuming alcohol. The brain notices when things are out of place and can help people be more intentional. There are hundreds of apps that assist people with tracking their alcohol consumption.[6] Nearly everyone carries a smartphone with internet access. They can convert and track intake quantities of alcohol consumed, send an alert when a limit is reached, track how much money is spent or calories consumed, send inspirational messages, or set off an alert when you go into a risky geographic boundary.

One study showed that most females used a notification service, such as reaching the specified drink amount or BAC, while males preferred an information component, such as how much they could drink in a specified time before they reach a certain BAC.[7]

Set an Alert

In addition to drink tracking, individuals can use their phones for moderation support. They can set an alert to go off at a predetermined time when they plan to leave an event. This should be prior to the point of intoxication, when judgment is not impaired and they are less likely to ignore the alert. Most people report that at a certain point in the evening, people have become loud, annoying, and obnoxious. When they are abstinent or drinking less, they realize that they are not enjoying themselves anymore and do not feel like they are missing out on anything.

Motivational

Tangible Reminders

I recommend using tangible reminders—things people can see, feel, touch, and hold—that remind them of why they are making changes to their drinking patterns. I help my clients identify something that they want more than alcohol. Often this has something to do with their loved ones, their health, financial situations, material possessions, or goals. It helps to make it personal.

Some positive reminders may include the following:

- A picture of the house you want to buy with your loved one if you resolve the problems related to your alcohol use.
- The car you want to drive once your license is reinstated.
- A photo of your kids on your last vacation when you were sober and got up early to play with them on the beach.
- A mug from the school you want to attend or the place you hope to work.

Motivational reminders could include these:

- Putting a sticky note of the Serenity Prayer on the dashboard of your car.
- Keeping a clean-date countdown on your phone.
- Listening to a recovery-related podcast each day.
- Reviewing an inspirational quote each morning.

While most of us are more motivated by positive reminders, remaining aware of the consequences of drinking is very important as time passes and we forget how bad it was. These are some of the negative tangible reminders that people can try:

- Keep the business card of your therapist or probation officer where you will see it before you open your wallet to pay for alcohol at the liquor store.
- Place the bracelet from your last hospital stay after your accident in the area where you keep your wine or highball glasses.
- Write down all the reasons you changed your drinking patterns, and review them the next time you experience a craving.

Glass Jar

Another tangible reminder that I recommend includes a technique that works well when people are going through a period of abstinence as well as moderation, is what I call the Glass Jar. I ask my clients to get a glass container. The reason for the glass is so that they can see the contents. I encourage them to put it in a common area of their home so that not only do they see it, but their loved ones see it as well and can offer accountability, motivation, and support.

Next, I have them calculate how much they typically spend on alcohol in a given day: perhaps $20 a day on wine or liquor or a $60 bar tab. Then I ask them to identify something that they would like to treat themselves with: a massage, a round of golf, clothes, a designer purse, or tickets to a game. Then I ask them to go to the bank and get $10 bills in the amount of what they would like to have in order to treat themselves. For each day or situation that they do not have a drink, they should put the amount of money they would have spent in the container. For every day that they drink when they were not supposed to, they take double the amount out of the container. At the end of a designated period of time, they can use the cash saved by making better choices to enjoy their special treat.

People report that this is a great tangible representation of how much they were spending on alcohol and how making small choices every day can add up to something positive. They also think twice when they know that overdrinking will cause them to lose double their savings.

Create New Traditions

It is important for clinicians to recognize that alcohol may have played a significant role in our clients' lives. For them to imagine New Year's Eve without champagne, a sports event without beer, a holiday dinner without wine, a cigar without bourbon, or a vacation without a cocktail is unimaginable. We can help them identify new traditions.

Maybe they can focus more on a new side dish for the holiday dinner instead of the wine. I remind them that they can save the calories they would have consumed on alcohol for a second helping or more dessert. They can do the Spanish tradition where you eat a grape for every strike of the bell at midnight instead of a champagne toast. When doing a toast, there is no rule that it has to be an alcoholic beverage. People can still raise a glass no matter what is in it. For a sporting event, they can have a competition on who makes the best chili, wings, or dip instead of downing beers. They may find that they may actually enjoy the event more when they are not constantly running to the bathroom, don't get into fights, or have a hangover. For other celebrations, I encourage them to focus more on daily activities. During get-togethers people can focus more on fitness and have a competition or race instead of waiting until the afternoon and looking forward to the open bar. Or try a high adventure activity to mark a celebration. Try ziplining, spelunking, rock climbing, whitewater rafting, swimming with sharks, or skydiving where alcohol is typically not present.

Healthy Transitions

For many, alcohol signals the end of the day or a reward for a job well done. I validate the need for both. Transitions are important to signal to our brain and body that it is okay to "turn it off." This is again why I encourage a four-month period of abstinence.

Courtney was in sales. She telecommuted for one of the major tech companies and was always pushing to meet her quotas. As soon as she woke up, she turned on her computer. Throughout the day the email notifications pinged constantly. If she got hungry enough between cups of coffee, she would silently shove some microwaved food in her face while on yet another conference call. This went on all day until her husband asked if she was coming to bed. She would down a few glasses of wine to "shut it down."

Courtney's situation is common for many people. She worked from home, so her brain never had time to transition from work to home mode. She was always "on." Additionally, Courtney was not eating well, artificially energized herself with numerous cups of coffee, and had stopped working out to be on calls in other time zones. She thought that the alcohol was helping her wind down and fall asleep. She was at her wit's end and willing to try something different. Courtney had gone to a few AA meetings but did not feel she fit in there.

I first educated her about sleep hygiene. Modern society is having more issues with insomnia and it is related to artificial lighting, especially what is emitted from our phones, pads, and computer screens. The light interrupts the body's production of melatonin, a natural hormone that affects sleep.[8] *Melatonin traditionally falls in the morning and rises in the evening. Artificial light blocks its production. The length of time in front of her screens and continued use into the evening was negatively affecting her sleep.*

Courtney had been a tennis player in college, so she knew about the importance of healthy proteins, fiber, and micronutrients. She was opting for convenience rather than quality in her food, always chasing the next commission.

As she began eating more whole foods, her energy level increased so she did not need to rely on coffee throughout the day. She also took a short break to eat, finding that fueling her body, clearing her head, and changing scenery actually increased her productivity more than pushing straight through. Early in her period of abstinence, her quantity of sleep improved. She also realized that she had been in a never-ending cycle: she was constantly working, drinking to relax and induce the onset of sleep, then having poor-quality sleep that affected her mood and motivation. She did not have the energy to see how much of a toll her job was taking on her. While she earned a high income, she realized that she did not have the time to enjoy it. Ultimately, she decided that a job change to a local company made more sense. Creating healthier transitions has allowed her to make time to enjoy dinner with her husband and resume her passion for playing tennis.

Identify Natural Highs

I ask my clients what they enjoyed doing as a child and encourage them to get back to doing those activities. Remember the days where you would spin in circles just to get a different feeling? Didn't you go outside and play? You did not have to have a plan; you could make an adventure out of a stick and a rock. Often, people forget how much they once enjoyed the outdoors. I ask them: Do you like to hike? Fish? Animal watch? Look at the stars? Stare at the water? Most of these are free and can be done alone or with people.

If people enjoy feeling a rush, I suggest they try skydiving, mountain biking, white water rafting, kayaking, ATV riding, or ziplining. If they are competitive, they should get involved with sports, enter a race, raise money for a cause, or volunteer. If they prefer a slower pace, they could listen to music, read, cook, explore the arts, do yoga, Tai Chi, or Pilates.

It makes me sad to see the blank faces on my clients when I ask them what they like to do for fun. Many have seen alcohol consumption as their source of having fun, socializing, rewarding, and managing stress. I work with my clients to get a sense of what they have enjoyed helping them reconnect and find new outlets.

Develop a List of 100 Things to Do Before I Die

Everyone should have one of these lists. Research has shown a variety of benefits from participating in novel and arousing experiences. When we do something that is different and exciting, the brain releases the feel-good neurotransmitter called dopamine.[9] This improves the quality of our long-term relationships.[10] New experiences also reduce the cognitive decline of aging.[11] I also recommend that all of my clients develop a List of 100 Things to Do Before I Die. On it should be big goals that may take time to complete, like earning a degree, speaking another language, developing a skill, or traveling abroad. There should be easily achievable goals like trying a new food, seeing a certain movie, or visiting a local attraction. I encourage a variety of activities that include adventure, travel, skills, and experiences and include work, spirituality, and relationships.

Review

Determine a time to periodically review the successes and failures of drinking habits. If individuals are having trouble moderating alcohol use, they may need to reconsider moderation. They might benefit from another period of abstinence or recognize that they are not able to successfully practice alcohol moderation. I also let my clients know that if the suggestions and tools mentioned in this chapter appear punitive, they may not be ready to try alcohol moderation. Moderation Management says it best: Take Responsibility. Acknowledge that drinking is something you do, not something that happens to you.[12]

Notes

1. National Highway Traffic Safety Administration (2016). *The ABC of BAC: A guide to understanding blood alcohol concentration and impairment.* Washington, DC: US Department of Transportation.
2. D. Cornett (2005). *Seven weeks to safe social drinking: How to effectively moderate your alcohol intake.* Santa Rosa, CA: People Friendly Books.
3. A. I. Cederbaum (2012). Alcohol metabolism. *Clinics in Liver Disease.* 16(4): 667–685. DOI: 10.1016/j.cld.2012.08.002.
4. Responsible Drinking (2019, June 1). *What happens when you drink.* Retrieved from www.responsibledrinking.org/what-happens-when-you-drink/how-you-drink-matters/.

5. Drinkaware (2019, June 1). *Alcohol and mental health.* Retrieved from www. drinkaware.co.uk/alcohol-facts/health-effects-of-alcohol/mental-health/alcohol-and-mental-health/.

6. O. Mubin (2016, July 13). Trying to cut down your drinking? There's an app for that. *The Conversation.* Retrieved from http://theconversation.com/trying-to-cut-your-drinking-theres-an-app-for-that-59386.

7. M. W. B. Zhang, J. Ward, J. J. B. Ying, F. Pan & R. C. M. Ho (2016). The alcohol tracker application: An initial evaluation of user preference. *BMJ Innovations.* 2(8): 8–13.

8. National Center for Complementary and Integrated Health (2019, May 23). *Melatonin: In depth.* Bethesda, MD. Retrieved from https://nccih.nih.gov/health/melatonin.

9. N. Dean (2018). The importance of novelty. *Brain World.* Retrieved from https://brainworldmagazine.com/the-importance-of-novelty/.

10. A. Aron, C. Norman, E. Aron, C. McKenna & R. Heyman (2000). Couples' shared participation in novel and arousing activities and experienced relationship quality. *Social Psychology.* 78(2): 273–284. DOI: 10.1037//0022-3514.78.2.273.

11. Y. Y. B. Cheng & U. M. Staduinger (2018). Novelty processing at work and cognitive aging: Evidence from the health and retirement study and MIDUS. *Innovation in Aging.* 2(1). https://doi.org/10.1093/geroni/igy023.1585.

12. F. Rotgers, M. F. Kern & R. Hoeltzel (2002). *Responsible drinking: A moderation management approach for problem drinkers.* Oakland, CA: New Harbinger Publications.

11 Developing and Monitoring an Alcohol Moderation Plan

This chapter gives a checklist of steps that should be taken prior to introducing an Alcohol Moderation Plan and identifies the necessary components of one. Examples of plans are included. The process of reintroducing alcohol is explored and relapse prevention tools are reviewed. The Quick Check tool assists clients in monitoring the effectiveness of the plan.

Prior to developing an Alcohol Moderation Plan, your clients should have done the following:

- Received education about the biological, psychological, and social consequences of drinking on self and others.
- Understand their "why."
- Have not developed a physical dependence on alcohol.
- Know the moderate drinking guidelines for their gender.
- Can commit to not engaging in unsafe behavior after drinking any amount of alcohol, such as driving a vehicle, operating machinery, caring for another person, and other such things.
- Do not misuse other mood-altering substances.
- Do not act in self-destructive ways after drinking even a small amount of alcohol.
- Experienced a period of abstinence.
- Identified triggers and made a plan to deal with risky situations.
- Experienced a range of emotions and learned how to cope with negative ones and enhance positive feelings in healthy ways.
- Determined that it is safe for to continue drinking.
- Know alcohol moderation tools.
- Chosen a support person to review the Alcohol Moderation Plan and assist with accountability.

Ideal Use Plan

After making sure each of the areas above is addressed, one of the first steps in creating an Alcohol Moderation Plan is to ask your client: If you could have your ideal drinking plan, what would it look like? From that we can work backward into a plan.

What follows is a sample Alcohol Moderation Plan.

ALCOHOL MODERATION PLAN

I am choosing moderation because:_____

_____

_____

I will not drink in these situations: _____

_____

_____

I will not drink until: _____

_____

_____

I will not drink after: _____

_____

_____

I will alternate an alcoholic beverage with:

My nonalcoholic drinks are:

I will have no more than _____ drink/s per: _____ For a total
of: _____ per: _____

I will review my plan with:_____

If I/we notice: _____

I/we will: _____

Signature: _____ *Date:* _____

Support Person: _____ *Date:* _____

Figure 11.1 Alcohol Moderation Plan

An explanation of why each of the components is listed on the Alcohol Moderation Plan are as follows:

I am choosing moderation because: I have my clients include this because it is another chance to explore their "why." Answers that are similar to those listed are positive predictors of success for the plan: I enjoy wine with my meal, I want to socialize with my friends, I like having a few beers during the game, I enjoy having a cocktail on vacation, or I'd like to toast to our success at the end of a project. These are all specific and add to a social situation, but are not the main focus. If someone is still looking to change their mood, wants to become intoxicated, or is miserable without alcohol, they are unlikely to be able to practice successful alcohol moderation.

I will not drink in these situations: Individuals should identify times when they will not consume alcohol at all. These typically correlate to people's risky situations and may include certain people, places, and things. These also should include areas where they have experienced problems in the past, safety reasons, and concerns expressed by loved ones. The safety ones tend to be the easiest to identify and may include: "I will not drive if I have had any alcohol," "I will not have alcohol if the kids are with me," "I will not do shots," etc. The problems in the past are dependent on the individual and require good memory on the therapist's part. Many people like to move on from the mistakes they made, so I may offer suggestions based on the work we did together: "What about when you are feeling anxious/depressed/stressed?" or "You mentioned that when you spend time with your single friends that you tend to drink more."

Developing a successful Alcohol Moderation Plan involves the family. They should have expressed their areas of concern. This is typically when there has been a pattern of problems. A spouse might notice that when his wife gambles, she consumes many of the free alcoholic beverages and spends money beyond the limits they set. Or a partner may notice when the significant other has a night out, that person is not available to help with housework. So the request may be that they don't drink alcohol on back-to-back nights or before a family event.

My most successful alcohol moderators do not drink on back-to-back evenings, drink only in social situations outside of their home, and generally do not drink more than once a week. Many successful moderators will include not drinking on back-to-back days, even during a holiday weekend or vacation.

I will not drink until: Remember that the Dietary Guidelines for Americans state that if alcohol is consumed, it should be in moderation; up to one drink a day for women/two for men.[1] While the National Institute on Alcohol Abuse and Alcoholism states that low-risk drinking is defined as no more than three drinks on any single day for women/four for men and no more than 7 a week for women and 14 for men.[2] Given these low amounts, alcohol consumption should be relegated to the event. I recommend against having a drink at home.

Most people's plans will state that they will not drink until they are at the event, game, party, wedding, restaurant, etc. Some go further to state that they will not order a drink until they have eaten or had a nonalcoholic beverage first. When we are hungry or thirsty, we tend to eat and drink more rapidly. This first drink or first course is consumed quickly. Sports fans write that they will not drink until after the first quarter, inning, or period.

Many note that "day drinking" will lead to serious consequences for them as they start early and go all day. Therefore, people designate a time of day like after work, chores are completed, dinner, kids go to bed, the weekend, etc.

I've worked with many retirees who have had challenges with increasing alcohol use. When there is no schedule and reduced responsibilities, they have to be more on guard. One gentleman was used to not drinking until he was finished with work. When there was no more employment, he found he was drinking earlier and earlier in the day. Another person stated that he would not drink until the sun went down. This worked well when we created the plan in June, but I had to help him decide what how to adjust in the winter months.

I will not drink after: This area identifies times and situations when a person will commit to not drinking. For example: "I will not use alcohol if I have had a fight with my significant other," "Once the event is over I will stop drinking," or "I won't continue drinking after getting home." Some people designate a time when they will stop consuming alcoholic beverages, like past 9:00 p.m. or after my spouse gives me the signal. This can be a tricky area if there is still tension between significant others. It works best once the drinker has earned back trust, has involved their spouse in the moderation process, identified warning signs, and mutually agreed on a signal if drinking may be getting out of control. Couples may have a predetermined gesture, like laying a hand on their partner's back, or a statement that signals that it is time to leave.

I will alternate an alcoholic beverage with: As has been previously reviewed, successful moderators keep their blood alcohol concentration below 0.06, which is where impairment typically begins. In order to slow rates of consumption and absorption, people should have both food and liquid in their stomachs. By switching between a nonalcoholic and an alcoholic beverage, individuals can prevent their BAC from rising too quickly. This is especially helpful if one will be at an event for several hours at a time.

My nonalcoholic drink is: I find that this is one of the easiest yet most commonly overlooked moderation tools. People need to find a nonalcoholic, "special occasion" beverage. Many nondrinkers report that they feel left out of the celebration because they are not drinking alcohol. When they are at home, they are fine drinking soda, tea, coffee, or water but struggle when they are in a social situation. I encourage them to pick a beverage that they would not have on a regular basis. Maybe this is a sweet tea, a flavored coffee, regular soda, tonic and lime, or sparkling water garnished with fruit.

I remind them of how fun it was to get a Shirley Temple as a kid. It's amazing how festive a cherry and a little grenadine can make one feel. Adults often need to re-program themselves that an alcoholic beverage does not equal celebration.

I will have no more than _____ *drink/s per:* _____ *For a total of:*_____ *per:*_____. These numbers are going to depend upon gender and weight. Males and those who weigh more can consume more alcohol with fewer effects. Regardless, I still recommend no more than one drink per hour. People also need to note the total amount they plan to consume in a setting and in a week. I recommend that women should have no more than two to three drinks in a setting, while men have no more than four to five. Any more than these amounts is considered a binge and should not occur more than once a month.

Each individual needs to identify the effects on themselves. If they have gone through the recommended period of abstinence, their tolerance levels should have decreased, and they will be affected by lower amounts of alcohol. My most successful moderators stick to one to two drinks for women and two to three for men and not more than once a week. Most have reported that they begin to feel the effects after two drinks and have a harder time staying within their limits. Those who drink more than two have also reported that they notice an effect the next day as well.

I will review my plan with: Moderators should choose a person who will show support as well as accountability. This is often a significant other. Issues of trust should have been resolved. If the partner is still having concerns, it is not time to try moderation. Both partners should have good communication with each other. Any accountability should not be punitive. It should come in the form of noticing if someone is sticking to the Alcohol Moderation Plan, pointing it out if there is some slipping, and discussing what to do as a result. The person is more of a partner than a probation officer. Their statements should be more along the lines of: "I noticed . . ." than accusations.

It is important to assess whether the support person is able to fill this role. They should be willing to participate in treatment and to be open about their alcohol consumption. They do not have to be alcohol-free, but they should have a healthy relationship with alcohol. If you remember from Chapter 2, donuts who drink within moderation will make the best support people. Cucumbers and pickles who are currently struggling with their alcohol use are unlikely to be able to offer support. Waters, those who do not drink alcohol at all, also may not be good support people as they may not understand the desire to drink and struggle to cut down.

If I/we notice: The therapist, person attempting alcohol moderation, and the support system should all have input. Each one will be individualized. What is typically included is on the Quick Check, described in further detail in the next section. It includes the amount, frequency, intent, and impact of alcohol use.

I/we will: All three should participate in determining what to do if the areas above are observed. I find that it is helpful to determine how to best confront the drinker if they begin to deviate from their Alcohol Moderation Plan. They may say something like: "I notice that you are drinking more frequently that you said you wanted to on your plan. You agreed that if that happened you would take a break for a month."

Many people include going through another period of abstinence if they are not sticking to their plan. This may be for a shorter time, like 30 days to recalibrate. Some may agree to check back in with their therapist. Others may commit to participating in an online forum, journaling, or getting more information through reading or listening to podcasts. It is helpful to plan ahead for risky situations. Some develop a situation-specific moderation plan, such as for a vacation or special event like a wedding.

It can also help to review the patterns. Is there something that stands out? Do they overdrink whenever they go to a certain place or are with specific people? Are they not managing their mood? Or did life circumstances change, like switching jobs, getting sick, or having children? Not following through on the plan is not a failure; it means that something was not working and needs to be adjusted. A good support system will help the moderator rework the plan, not responding with anger or withholding affection. If the subtle changes are caught quickly and renegotiated, these issues are less likely to arise.

Signature, Date, and Support Person: I include the signatures of both the person attempting alcohol moderation and the support person as well as the date because it takes the form of a contract so that people will take it seriously. Both have made commitments, and both are witnesses to it.

While it is a contract, an Alcohol Moderation Plan is not written in stone. The plan should be a fluid document that adapts as life changes. Both the moderator and the support person should be involved in any updates to the plan to address the reality of the situation.

Having a lapse in problematic drinking is not always a bad thing. It is an opportunity to address areas that they may not have considered or been realistic about when they first developed the plan. A lapse is a signal that something is not working and another strategy is needed. Sometimes lapses help everyone to take the situation more seriously. It is easy to fall back into old patterns. We need to monitor if the plan is working effectively. I developed the Quick Check to do so.

Quick Check of Alcohol Moderation Plan

A simple check when evaluating the success of your Alcohol Moderation Plan is to ask the following questions:

1. *What is the amount that I have been consuming?*
2. *How frequently have I been drinking?*
3. *What is the intent of my moderate drinking?*
4. *What is the impact of my current alcohol use?*

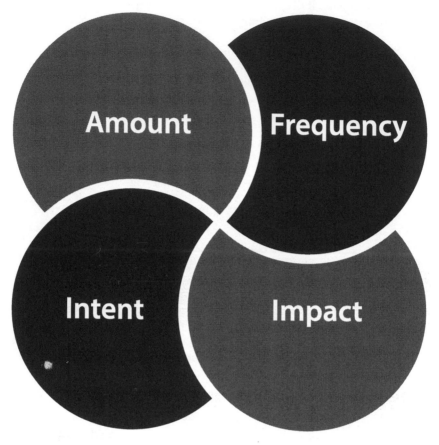

Figure 11.2 Quick Check

Amount

Keep in mind the guidelines for amount and frequency of alcohol consumption. For men, that means no more than 14 drinks a week, and for women no more than 7 a week, and not all at the same time. Remember that recent studies have shown that no amount of alcohol is considered safe or healthy. Each individual needs to determine what their safe level is. I have found that the people who experience the greatest success with alcohol moderation usually drink no more than once a week, never drink alone, and consume no more than three drinks at a time.

I ask my clients to ask themselves the following questions:

* How many nights a week do you drink?
* Do you drink more than two drinks a night (if you are a woman), or more than three (if you are a man)?

- Do you feel an effect from the alcohol?
- How do you feel in the days you drink and the few days after?
- How much you are focusing on your "drinking days"?

Paying attention to how they feel on a drinking day is helpful. If that is the one day they look forward to all week, they still have work to do. Explore what is so bad about their day-to-day life that they crave this outlet. See what other activities they can look forward to doing.

Some may be tempted to make regular exceptions to their Alcohol Moderation Plan. Holidays, graduations, weddings, birthdays, free tickets to a game, and sports playoffs will come up. However, there is no reason they cannot enjoy these events without alcohol. Find something other than drinking to focus attention on: the people, the game, the food, or the celebratory aspect of the event.

Frequency

Checking frequency of alcohol use is similar to monitoring the amount. It should fall within the moderation guidelines. Individuals need to watch out for how often they are drinking and if they are seeking out increasing situations where alcohol will be present. I also ask them what it is like when they do not drink. Many surprise themselves when they realize that they do not miss drinking as much as they thought and enjoy the benefits of an alcohol-free event.

Intent

People need to be aware of *why* they are drinking. As noted previously, if they are looking to change their mood or to cope with emotions, they will need to develop alternative ways to manage. I suggest identifying someone who has his or her life together. It can be someone they know or even a television, movie, or book character. Observe what they do and how they do it. Then emulate what they do.

If individuals are feeling an effect from the alcohol they consume, they should reevaluate the amount they are taking in. Identify why they place such a high priority on drinking. Pay attention to how they feel when they drink. If this is the only time they are happy or feel normal, they have more work to do. I typically recommend returning to a period of abstinence to get distance from alcohol and establish a new baseline.

I ask people to notice how they feel on nondrinking nights. If they feel bored, miserable, or left out, they may be focusing only on what they are losing, not on what they are gaining. We would identify other ways to relax, socialize, and have fun. This takes time, especially if past alcohol consumption has damaged some of the neurotransmitters in the brain that allow people to feel pleasure and happiness. It can take several months to repair the effects that alcohol has had on body chemistry.

Also, if people are struggling on nondrinking nights, they likely have not allowed enough time to adjust to the new lifestyle. Any change takes time to feel normal. It may take several months to feel normal, but most people report feeling significantly better after six months, and certainly by a year.

Impact

My goal is not to have clients relive all the bad times related to problematic drinking patterns, but to be honest about whether they are still occurring once they returned to alcohol use. They should explore what happens now when they drink. I tell them if you are not getting the "stink eye" from your family members, no one is complaining, and you are happy, you may have developed a very good plan. I encourage them to take a risk and ask loved ones for their observations on your current drinking. They may be pleasantly surprised to hear what those loved ones have to say about them now. They should also be realistic with whose opinions they consider. Asking their old drinking buddies how they are doing with their new drinking pattern will yield very different responses from those of the people they live with and may have hurt.

Box Matter 11.3

DID YOU KNOW? There is a way to test for alcohol use from three to four days prior. A Breathalyzer, urine screen, or blood test measures how much alcohol is in your system. There is a new test that measures the amount of ethyl glucuronide (ETG) in your system. ETG is a direct metabolite of the alcohol that you drink and remains in the body even after the alcohol itself can no longer be detected. The presence of ETG in urine indicates recent alcohol consumption, often up to 80 hours, even though the alcohol may no longer be in the system.[3]

Relapse Prevention Tools

As noted earlier, a relapse is an opportunity to learn what was not working. People use a number of terms when they talk about returning to problematic alcohol use: relapse, lapse, slip, or reoccurrence. I define relapse as a process of thoughts, behaviors, patterns, and emotions that can lead back to the original problem. For alcohol moderators, returning to drinking is not a relapse. The relapse is when consequences begin to occur. The most important word that I want people to remember is *process*. A relapse is not an event; it's a progression that is typically observable and, therefore, preventable. When people have a structure for how to observe the process, they can course correct faster and reduce consequences. I have listed several of the tools I use with clients to prevent relapses from progressing:

HALT

HALT is an acronym that stands for: Hungry, Angry, Lonely, Tired. HALT translates to "stop" in German. I encourage people to stop, take a moment to reflect, and take action if they need to address any of these areas. If any of them are out of balance, they are more likely to make poor choices.

Hungry: Think about how poorly you feel when you are hungry. When my blood sugar gets low, I get a headache, am irritable, and can't concentrate. If when people are physically hungry, make sure to refuel with some healthy food. If clients know they are going to have a long workday, car ride, or carpool, they should plan ahead for meals and healthy snacks like fruits, nuts, cheese, yogurt, or protein bars. I remind them to stay hydrated.

Hungry can also refer to how we feel emotionally—hungry for something more or different. If people are bored with their routine, I encourage them to do something to mix it up. Spend time with someone you have not seen in a while, take a trip, or try an activity you have never done before.

Angry: When we are angry or experiencing negative emotions, we often do not think rationally. If someone feels angry, they can take some time to calm down, talk with a friend, and then address the problem. If it is a chronic issue, break it down into manageable tasks. Just taking even one step forward can make individuals feel less hopeless and helpless about a situation. I also recommend waiting at least two hours and talking to another person before touching technology. This means no texting, tweeting, e-mailing, or posting. People don't want to put something out in cyberspace that they will regret later.

Lonely: We all experience loneliness at times in our lives. Though we may be surrounded by people, we often are not interacting with them. Despite all of our modern technology, many of us are plugged in but not connected. Think about the number of times you have made a problem much worse in your head, turning the situation into a catastrophe. However, once you talked it out, you gained a much more positive perspective. I encourage individuals to reach out every day and connect face-to-face with other people. Isolation can be a breeding ground for depression and unhealthy choices.

Tired: When we are physically and emotionally tired, we tend to engage in more negative thinking patterns and interactions. I work with individuals to make sure they get enough sleep at night. Practice good sleep hygiene. Sleep hygiene is a funny phrase, as if people are dirty sleepers, but it actually refers to developing habits that make restful sleep more conducive. This includes getting up and going to bed around the same time each day, reducing distractions that interrupt sleep (pets, television, or the phone), monitoring caffeine and sugar intake, managing stressors, and limiting exposure to bright lights, which interrupts the biological process that allows melatonin levels to rise and help us drift off to sleep.

Tangible Reminders

As I described in a previous chapter, tangible reminders are things that we can see, feel, touch, and hold that remind us of the changes we are trying to make in our lives regarding alcohol. I recommend individuals keep reminders in convenient areas such as on the bathroom mirror, on their physical person, in the car, on the phone, and in the workspace. People can have both positive and negative reminders to help them stay focused and accountable to their Alcohol Moderation Plan.

Daily Checks

I encourage my clients to pick a specific time each day to reflect on their mood, goals, and achievements. Notice that I did not say to look at where they did not do well. Most of us do this to ourselves anyway, agonizing over what we said or did or didn't do. Classic behavioral reinforcement notes that the behaviors we pay attention to are the ones that get reinforced. Think about that. If all we focus on is what we did wrong, we will keep doing it. But if we look at our successes, we can figure out how to build upon them and will be much happier as a result.

I ask them to pick a specific time each day to reflect. Some people choose times such as when they are on their way home from work, when they exercise, or when they shower. However, I point out that they may not do these activities every day. So I suggest reflecting when they brush their teeth or right before bed. A daily check takes just a few moments. If they are experiencing a negative emotion, consider proactive ways of dealing with the issue. See if HALT is in balance or how they are doing on their Quick Check. If areas need attention, identify a plan to address it.

Another type of daily check is scaling. It's not how much you weigh, but how you feel. I ask: On a scale of 1 to 10, with 10 being the best day ever and 1 being the worst, where are you today? If they are anywhere from a 7 to a 10, identify the factors that helped create this feeling and repeat them if they are healthy behaviors. If they are below a 4, it might be important to reach out to a friend or a professional. It is completely normal to have a bad day occasionally, sometimes for no apparent reason. But if the bad days continue for more than a week, try to identify the stressor and what can be done to correct it. If the bad days last for more than two weeks or start affecting activities of daily living, it may be time to seek professional help.

Some people like to keep a journal or a mood tracker. There are also many great apps on smartphones that can help with this. Note that people should not compare to anyone but themselves. Ask, "Am I feeling better or worse today than I did yesterday?" When people track their numbers, thoughts, and feelings, they may notice trends and patterns. That way they can identify the triggers that lead to negative moods and increase the actions that prompt the healthy ones.

Weekly Checks

Performing weekly checks is important at the beginning of abstinence as well as once an Alcohol Moderation Plan has been implemented. Again, I recommend selecting a specific day and time to review. In the first few months, this may be a therapist, support group, or online posting. Eventually, people may transition to a friend, partner, or other support people. By having a specific day, person, and time scheduled, people are more likely to review successes and struggles. Additionally, if the person does not show, the support person should come looking, increasing accountability.

Monthly Checks

I suggest picking a specific day each month for a planned meeting or activity such as meeting with a counselor, attending a support group, driving by the site where the DUI occurred or reviewing the Alcohol Moderation Plan with a support person. When people say they will do it once a month, they may not follow through. When they chose a date that is significant to them, like the anniversary of the last binge, the date they implemented their Alcohol Moderation Plan, or when they began therapy and share it with their support person, they are more likely to stick to it.

Preparing to Drink Again

This is one of the strangest techniques I teach clinicians to do: preparing your client to drink again. We have been so programmed that abstinence is the only way drinkers experiencing problems can be healthy and is the way most programs determine success. Remember that people tend to have better outcomes in alcohol moderation when they go through a period of abstinence. We have trained them on how to stop drinking, now we need to teach them how to handle resuming alcohol use so that their old problems and patterns do not re-emerge. The goal has been to create a new relationship with alcohol.

Hillary was in her late 20s. After a period of significant emotional and relationship turmoil resulting from her cocaine, marijuana, and alcohol use, she entered therapy and went through a period of complete abstinence. Hillary understood the role drugs played in her life and worked hard to find new ways to have fun, utilize the coping skills she had learned, and develop relationships with people who were advancing in their adult lives.

After she had been substance-free for over six months, we used therapy sessions to prepare her to try alcohol moderation. She consistently reported that cocaine was the chemical she'd had the most problems with. She chose a specific drink that she actually enjoyed the taste of, met with a healthy friend who supported her drinking goals, and chose an environment where she had never had a bad drinking or emotional episode.

Hillary was not prepared for the emotions stirred up by losing her clean date (the day after last substance use). She no longer felt the special feeling that sobriety had brought to her life. She had been keeping track of the days that marked the end of her unhealthy life and the start of a new one.

Hillary was also not prepared for the feelings of guilt that surfaced. During the time when she was not using any substances, she had felt as if she were making up for all the poor decisions and actions that had hurt her friends and family. Once she had the first drink, however, she felt as though she had lost their forgiveness.

Through unexpected tears, Hillary realized she had more work to do. She decided to remain alcohol-free for a few more months while she worked on her feelings about her past, repaired her relationships, and identified who she would like to be in the future.

In this scenario, Hillary was going through a process that I call *integration*. Integration is accepting who you were and what you did when you were drinking in an unhealthy way. It means not only seeking forgiveness from those you hurt but also forgiving yourself.

People in early recovery tend to spend a lot of time reliving the past, which was often destructive, unhealthy, and emotionally painful. While it is important to acknowledge the mistakes of the past, we cannot live there if we are going to stay healthy in the long run. The same is true for the present. It is important to stay connected and mindful of what is happening in the moment, but we also need to prepare for a healthier, happier future. Only once we integrate our past self into who we are in the present do we really begin to move forward emotionally. When I see people feeling comfortable with who they are right now and getting excited about something in the future, I know they have completed the integration process.

Notes

1. National Institute on Alcohol Abuse and Alcoholism (2019, June 4). *Drinking levels defined*. Bethesda, MD. Retrieved from www.niaaa.nih.gov/alcohol-health/overview-alcohol-consumption/moderate-binge-drinking.
2. U.S. Department of Health and Human Services and U.S. Department of Agriculture (2015). *2015–2020 dietary guidelines for Americans* (8th ed.). Retrieved from http://health.gov/dietaryguidelines/2015/guidelines/
3. L. Shukla, P. Sharma, S. Ganesha, D. Ghadigaonkar, E. Thomas, A. Kandas, P. Murthy & V. Benegal (2017). Value of ethyl glucuronide and ethyl sulfate in serum as biomarkers of alcohol consumption. *Indian Journal of Psychological Medicine*. 39(4): 481–487.

12 Including the Family

This chapter reviews some of the challenges that support systems face when their loved one is struggling with alcohol use. It teaches clinicians how they can include the family in the alcohol moderation process. This chapter will look at the role of denial, enabling, and codependency and then give ways to set boundaries and practice self-care. This chapter also reviews what questions the support system typically has and how to address them. Family members, support systems, friends, and loved ones will be used interchangeably throughout.

People who experience problems related to their alcohol use are usually also experiencing significant conflict with their loved ones. Numerous studies have shown that parental and family support is one of the strongest factors in successful treatment and recovery from substance use disorders.[1] It is critical that loved ones are involved in the process.

There are three main areas that should be addressed for those who are affected by someone else's alcohol use. These include denial, enabling, and codependency.

Denial

Denial happens when loved ones are unable or unwilling to admit that alcohol use is causing serious health, work, school, relationship, financial problems. It is often easier to ignore or pretend that these issues do not exist. To recognize there is a problem can be overwhelming. It means there is something wrong in the family system. Admitting that means that we have to do something about it. Where do we start? It has become cliché, but admitting there is a problem is often the first step. Once it becomes real, then we can begin to develop a plan.

Box Matter 12.1

DID YOU KNOW? Saliva regenerates every 10 to 15 minutes. Law enforcement and treatment providers know this. The excuses of "I just used mouthwash" or "I took some cough syrup" are not accurate explanations for testing positive for alcohol on a breath test. A person would have to actually drink the mouthwash or consume a large quantity of cold medicine to register positive. Initially, a Breathalyzer would read very high if a person had just used rinsed their mouth or swallowed, but then 15 minutes later, nothing readable would remain—unless the person had drunk it.[2]

Enabling

The Merriam-Webster definition of enabling is: "to provide with the means or the opportunity; to make possible, practical, or easy."[3] If you ask most family members, they would be angry or shocked to hear that some of their actions are making the very behavior that they are hurt by or fear possible, yet their behaviors often do just this. Examples of enabling alcohol use include:

- Protecting the alcohol user from natural consequences, such as cleaning up after the person, making excuses for absences or lateness, doing that person's responsibilities, and paying a bill they missed due to overspending on alcohol.
- Keeping secrets, including how much the family member may be drinking or how negatively it affects those around them.
- Covering up behaviors such as drinking and driving, or excusing verbal abuse or neglect of responsibilities.
- Bailing the person out of trouble, including paying debts, hiring lawyers, and covering up an accident where alcohol was involved.
- Making threats, then not following through: If this happens again, I will leave you (but then remaining in the home).
- Staying quiet to keep the peace and prevent an argument.
- Excusing behaviors and labeling it something else.

Codependency

Author Melodie Beattie introduced the term codependency in her famous book *Codependent No More: How to Stop Controlling Others and Start Caring for Yourself.* She defines a codependent person as someone who has let another person's behavior affect him or her and who is obsessed with controlling that person's behavior.[4] While Beattie's traditional advice has been to detach and expect abstinence, she still offers a good foundation for understanding some of the dynamics in families where alcohol use has caused problems.

People who are codependent tend to be overinvolved in the alcohol user's life, to the detriment of both people. If the nondrinker pays too much attention to the drinker, the nondrinker is ignoring his or her needs, responsibilities, and goals. As a result, the drinker avoids the natural consequences of his or her behavior and continues unhealthy behaviors.

Therapy can help the person engaging in codependent behaviors learn that:

- I did not cause the drinker to experience problems.
- I am not responsible for their problems.
- I cannot fix the problems.
- I can only control myself.

Boundaries

Often friends, family, or loved ones initiate therapy after an incident has occurred and they want a solution *right now*. Their goal is typically to get their loved one help. This may be part of the healing process, but it is not required for the family system to get better. In this chapter, we are focusing more on how to help those around the drinker experiencing problems. After examining the family's denial, enabling, and codependency, we can examine the boundaries within the system. There may be unhealthy, unclear boundaries when there is frequent alcohol use.

One of the most helpful behaviors that we can teach those affected by someone else's alcohol use is to set appropriate boundaries. Boundaries keep us safe and are about feelings, wants, and needs. Effective boundaries are clear and change as circumstances change. Loved ones may have firmer boundaries as someone is just entering treatment and making lifestyle changes. As those changes occur, boundaries may change, sometimes loosening and sometimes becoming more firm as the person gets healthier.

Author Brené Brown gives a straightforward definition for boundaries: a boundary is what's ok and what's not ok.[5]

Healthy boundaries require self-awareness and self-acceptance. People need to realize that their self-worth is not dependent upon the alcohol user. This is especially hard for parents and spouses to acknowledge. Parents often believe that they are still responsible for their children's choices, even when they have reached adulthood. Spouses get stuck in the belief that they took a vow of "for better or worse" to mean that they have to stand by and accept the unhealthy behaviors the drinker may be doing. Boundaries mean those affected by out of control alcohol use can, and should, express how it affects them. Healthy boundaries also mean that they do not engage in unhealthy patterns.

Effective boundaries occur when loved ones understand that they are separate from the alcohol user. Oftentimes, spouses, partners, parents, and even children feel responsible for the choices their loved one is making. You can't love someone into a healthy choice. Nor can you threaten, withhold, educate, or shame someone into making better decisions. However, communicating the impact that their choices are having helps the alcohol user realize their patterns of drinking are not working for those around them.

In order to set a healthy boundary, I ask family members to keep track of how they are feeling when their loved one talks about, uses, and recovers from alcohol. That gives us a starting point. From there, I suggest that we focus on two areas: one is the area that is most important to them, and the second is an area that might be easier to get a resolution. I do this because we cannot address all of their hurts and concerns at once. Everyone will get overwhelmed and frustrated.

The boundary that is most important to families tends to do with safety: "I will take your keys if you are drinking"; "If you are drinking, you can't be around the kids"; or "Before you try moderation, I want you to meet with a therapist." Then I suggest an easier one so that all involved can feel a degree of success. These may include: "I'm not going to pick up beer at the grocery store anymore"; "You need to pay for your bar tab"; or "I'm not going to call in for you if you oversleep." Notice that all of those had to do with what the family member was going to do. They were about their behaviors, not the drinker's. We cannot control that. They can only influence an outcome by staying firm with their boundaries.

Additionally, when we focus on solutions rather than problems, we can yield more positive results. It is better to look at what we can do rather than just what we will not do.

I recommend avoiding all-or-nothing ultimatums. They are unrealistic. Change takes time. The problem did not develop overnight. Also, people make mistakes. I role-play scenarios so that the family can prepare for them. What will they do when the loved one violates a boundary? What will they say? Does a relapse in the first week mean the same thing at one year?

Boundaries should be clear and communicated in a calm manner. Families should talk to the person after calming down following the incident, disappointment, or fight. When people are emotional, they are not thinking with their logical brain and are more likely to give ultimatums that they will not follow through on later. It helps to practice what they will say prior to speaking with their loved one so it comes out clearly.

An example of blurred boundaries occurred with Allison and Pierce:

Allison's older brother Pierce was a party boy. He was athletic with a charming smile who could talk himself out of any trouble he got into, which was frequent over the years. He never quite settled into adulthood. Allison tended to be quieter, with a strong moral compass. She went to college, secured a good job, and got married. While she was four years younger than Pierce, she was the one who watched out for her brother and helped him with a few legal and romantic situations.

As a result, Allison suffered with constant worry, never sure if Pierce would make it home or, as they got older, get a call in the middle of the night to pick him up after a binge. She did everything right as a kid, but all the attention went to her brother. Even as an adult, she was covering for him if he had an issue with his latest girlfriend, assisting him financially, picking him up when he'd had too much, and letting him stay at her house when he was in between jobs. She had difficulty with insomnia and had regular fights with her newlywed husband about how often she was bailing Pierce out of an alcohol-related problem. Her parents both had their own mental health issues and were never available emotionally for the kids, so she felt it was her job to mother him.

I worked with Allison to see the pattern that she and her brother had been in for years. She thought that the way to show love was to fix problems. With a non-emotionally involved perspective, she was able to see that by rescuing him from the consequences when he overdid it with alcohol, he never had to learn how to be responsible. She was able to see the role that she was playing and identify how she can be a sister, not an enabler. Now Allison regularly tells her brother that she loves him but that she will not answer his calls between midnight and 7:00 a.m., that he is welcome to visit but can't stay with them, and that her money is going towards saving for a nursery now that the tension between her and her husband dissipated.

Even though family members may be hurt, scared, and angry by their loved one who is misusing alcohol, good communication involves listening. Keep in mind that most alcohol users are not drinking just for fun; there is often some form of mental health or trauma. Alcohol has become their coping skill, however unhealthy. Family can be the biggest support to the alcohol user, offering love and accountability.

Just because the alcohol user may be hurting does not mean that family members should ignore their feelings. Families tend to put their focus on the one struggling, ignoring their own needs and emotions. Support systems should be honest about how damaging their alcohol use is to them. Denial and silence help no one. Therapy can teach people how to communicate in an effective way. Saying, "I hate you; you ruined my life" is very different from saying, "When you drink to the point of intoxication, you say mean things to me and I don't want to be around you."

Finally, loved ones can pay attention to cues. The alcohol user often may not want to talk about their drinking and its impact. Sometimes, the person may not even remember what they said or did when they were drinking. I teach families the term "active in their use." This means that the very effects of alcohol often impair the user's thinking, memory, and judgment. The drinker does things that they would never do if alcohol was not in their system. They look at their mother, child, or friend and think, "How could you do this?" I remind them that while their loved one did actually do the thing, they were impaired. They were active in their use. This concept helps them separate the behavior from the person. When they don't take it as a personal attack, they are better able to work through the issues.

As the relationships are changing, the alcohol user may pull away. It is important to continue to reach out and make contact. This may be the father who has asked his son to move out of the house but still invites him out to dinner once a week. It could be the wife who is angry with her husband's infidelity while he was intoxicated but allows him to stay in the house. Rather than the wife staying angry and giving him the cold shoulder, they remain in the same home because they have three children. She may tell him that she does not want to fight every day but that she is still working through anger and betrayal. We can teach family members that they can still love the alcohol user without approving of what they do.

Self-Care

For years, the only support for family members has been Al-Anon. It is a mutual support program for people who have been affected by someone else's drinking and is based on 12 steps that ask them to find a "Power greater than ourselves" who can help solve problems and find serenity.[6] As is true for many who do not find AA helpful, those who are not religious struggle with the concept of Higher Power. Many of my clients who have attended felt like the participants were more focused on helplessness than on finding a solution. Meetings introduce the concept of codependency. Family members are advised to practice "tough love" and "loving detachment." The takeaway for some is that when they try to help the person suffering, they are being codependent and enabling the drinker's behavior. In some cases this is true, but we need to educate our clients about what is helpful and what is not for their unique situation.

Many family members have felt they had been given the brush-off when Al-Anon was recommended to them. Most treatment tends to be focused on the drinker, and family members take a back seat while their loved one gets help. While I have had many families find great support within their Al-Anon groups, it is important to also teach self-care.

Support groups can be helpful. Many treatments recognize the importance of including the alcohol user's support system in the treatment process. I encourage all of my families to attend whatever family weekend or group that a program offers. They offer a confidential, safe place to share experiences. A lot of the families I work with try to hide that there is an alcohol problem. As a result, they are left without support. They fear judgment from outsiders and experience shame that they could not "fix it." Groups also reduce isolation, letting them know that they are not alone and are not "crazy."

Regarding self-care, I use what I call the "Airplane Analogy." I ask them if they have ever taken a flight on an airplane. If they have, I ask them to remember what the flight attendant said during the safety briefing about the oxygen masks. When they do the briefing, they say something along the lines of: "In the event of an emergency an oxygen mask will drop down. If you are sitting next to a child or older person, you must put your oxygen mask on first." The idea is that if you are not breathing, you cannot help anyone else. Therefore, you must help yourself before you can help others.

Self-care puts the focus back on oneself, rather than solely the alcohol user. It provides emotional support and practical tools and tips for coping. Self-care also restores a balance of power, showing families that there is something that they can do. Self-care will look different for all support systems and depends on the length and severity of the alcohol use, the damage that has occurred, and the age of the alcohol user. Going through the denial, codependency, and enabling behaviors will help identify the patterns and set forth a plan of action. Setting and enforcing boundaries through ongoing communication is self-care. Once those actions occur, it gets loved ones out of crisis mode. They are then able to focus on the future. Working through the hurt and wreckage of the past takes time. When families focus more on their needs, goals, and pleasurable pursuits, all tend to be more relaxed and are able to heal faster.

The following suggestions for self-care are based on From Grief to Action, a Vancouver support group:[7]

- Remember that you did not cause your loved one's struggles with alcohol. Do not blame yourself. Guilt is not a useful emotion.
- Recognize negative feelings like anger, hurt, and disappointment. Communicate them when you are calm.
- Admit when you have made a mistake, apologize for it, and move on.
- Focus on what you can do. Let go of what you cannot. You cannot make anyone do anything.
- Educate yourself on the signs and symptoms of your loved one's alcohol problem. Learn your role in it.
- Stay connected. Face-to-face is best.
- Get support. Humans do not function well in isolation.
- Make sure you are getting enough sleep, healthy food, and time to relax and have fun. All of your time and energy cannot and should not be spent on your loved one.
- Pursue your goals and dreams. You need to keep living your own life. You may even become an example of what is possible with healthy, balanced living.

Siblings

While most treatment focuses on the alcohol user, most family work tends to be with parents and spouses. Brothers and sisters are affected by alcohol use, even if they never touch a drop. In my treatment groups, parents have reported some common occurrences. Sometimes siblings became the "secret keepers." They know that their brother or sister is using alcohol in an unhealthy way. They feel bound to secrecy by the unwritten code that siblings don't tell on each other. The siblings may begin to show signs of anxiety as a result. They also can experience depression and low self-esteem because so much attention goes to the alcohol user.

On the other hand, older siblings may introduce alcohol to their younger brother, sister, or cousin earlier than it is appropriate. This consumption pattern is generally not about enhancing flavors in food or enjoying the taste. It is about feeling an effect. Binging on alcohol can lead to accidents, assaults, and higher rates of addiction.

Many siblings have poor relationships with the alcohol user. They are scared and hurt by their loved one's choices and are resentful at the impact their actions are having on the family.

Much of the time and attention goes to the one in trouble, not the "good one." There are court hearings, probation meetings, school visits, discussion on what to do, and therapy appointments all focused on the one experiencing problems. I encourage parents to make sure that they are spending individual time with each child. Make sure to give time to both children; otherwise, feelings of resentment can occur.

Sometimes the non-alcohol user feels the pressure to be perfect, not causing any more problems for Mom or Dad. As a result, they may develop depression or an anxiety disorder. Conversely, they may learn that the only way to get their parents' attention is to act out.

Family therapy can be helpful for all members to understand their roles in the system and find solutions. Therapy can also increase healthy communication. Individual therapy may also be beneficial for siblings to resolve current issues in the family and reduce the likelihood of future problems occurring.

Accountability Versus Paroling

As noted in the Alcohol Moderation Plan, I recommend that the drinker pick a support person for support and accountability. This is different from acting like a probation officer. The support person should be in agreement with the plan. If the drinker is choosing moderation and the support person is expecting abstinence, the process will fail at the outset. Part of the agreement is in the Alcohol Moderation Plan itself that has amounts, frequency, and action if the plan is violated. The approach is more about finding ways to help the person stick to the plan than catching them if they are not. It is proactive rather than reactive. The support person may say things like, "I see you struggling. How can I help?" rather than "You messed up. Here is your consequence." It is not their job to control, but to observe and communicate.

Common Questions

Below are some of the most common questions that I get from people who love the alcohol user.

Should I Cut Off Contact?

There are no right or wrong answers here. All answers should be based on the family's situation. However, I give general guidelines when practicing a harm reduction approach. Other programs recommend a tough love approach that views support as enabling. I find that people are not consciously contributing to their loved one's drinking. Often their behaviors are motivated by love or fear. They mistakenly believe that if they set a limit, the drinker will not want to have anything to do with them. So they keep quiet, thinking that they would change if they really wanted to, or that if they knew how bad it was hurting them, then they would just stop.

Sometimes, family members have their own issues with alcohol and are not ready to face them. We need to understand the role it plays in the entire family system. We may also need to distinguish how it affects each member. Some manage alcohol use without any issues, and for some it is catastrophic. Some families give mixed messages: it's okay for me, but not for you.

Depending on the severity and impact of the alcohol use, sometimes family members need a break from each other. It may be appropriate for the alcohol user to leave the home or reduce contact. Notice I did not say to end the relationship. Very rarely do parents, spouses, or siblings cut off blood relatives. This is a very special bond that keeps people connected.

Even if someone does decide to end a relationship or disconnect from someone, I remind them that it does not have to be permanent. Relationships do not come with a set of rules. What works today may not work a month or year from now. And, people change! By not having contact with loved ones, sometime the alcohol user may change their patterns and bring their drinking to a healthier level that all can accept. Sometimes people do choose to cut off contact. There should be no judgment on what is right for each family. They just need to be comfortable with the decision they chose.

Should I Kick Him/Her Out of the House?

There are many factors to consider when asking someone to leave their home. Is it a young adult who has not yet launched into his or her life? If they are living in the parental home, not working, and not pursuing a future, it makes sense for them to move out and start their own life. Sometimes you need to "kick them out to kick it in." On the flip side, asking someone to leave the family home and then paying for all living expenses is sometimes worse. That is freedom without responsibility.

I generally recommend a graduated process. This includes giving the person time and specifics of what behavior needs to change. Things may include: pursuing education or a trade to become economically independent, financially contributing to expenses, participating in family dinners, completing household chores, communicating whereabouts, not drinking and driving, consuming alcohol only on the weekends, not having more than three friends over, etc. The process may take an initial discussion that things will be changing, with more and more responsibility being transferred to the person over time.

If the young adult does not adhere to the expectations that are set, then the parents can give notice of time. You have a month to make changes, or you need to move out. Parents ask how to handle finances when the young adult may need to move out but is unable to afford it. Many parents worry that their child will live on the street, begin selling drugs, or turn to prostitution. I reality-test the parents' fears. Did they show signs of drug use? Have they ever engaged in this type of behavior? Or do they have skills but lack motivation? I remind them: they need you more than you need them. Often the balance of power has shifted where the child holds the power instead of the parents. I remind parents that they have, often, decades more experience, wisdom, education, and income. Adult children still rely on their parents for guidance. And, they need their money. Parents actually have more influence than they think. Once the adult child stops holding their parents' emotions hostage, they can set boundaries and have a healthy relationship with them again.

How Do We Handle Money?

Money is complicated. It is not just about purchasing power. Some strong emotions may be under the surface. For some, money equals love. For others, money is freedom or self-worth. Therapy can help families understand what role money plays in their lives. I have worked with families where the older generations had financial struggles and never wanted their children to experience the same deprivation that they did. While for another family, money was a sign of status. To have their child work meant that they were not successful. For another family, money was the way that they showed their love. Both parents held full-time jobs to be able to afford their extras. They gave their children money and things as a way to relieve their guilt for not being as present in their kids' lives. We need to understand the role money plays prior to giving any feedback.

If a loved one is using alcohol, I generally recommend against giving them easy access to money. Monitoring money is increasingly challenging in that it can be accessed in cash, credit, debit, virtual transfers, gift cards, etc. The concerns include money going directly towards purchasing alcohol, but more concerning is taking away personal responsibility. Part of maturing is learning how to make healthy decisions. Do I want to eat dinner or buy liquor? Should I pay this bill or go out tonight? If I reduce my drinking, can I save up for a trip? How can I save up for the designer clothes I want? If the more financially secure people give away their resources, how will the younger generation ever learn the value of money, earning, saving, and spending? Easy access deprives them of a learning opportunity.

I have a few general suggestions on handling money when there has been an issue with spending:

- Ask for receipts when cash is given.
- Give service-specific gift cards for services (like groceries, gas).
- Pay directly for things you agreed upon (rent, education, therapy).
- Offer opportunities to earn (extra household chores, helping out).

What Should We Pay For?

Each family has its unique circumstances, but I generally recommend that families assist only with expenses for:

- Education.
- Health insurance.
- Treatment/therapy.
- Medication.

Families may help with transportation. However, there is no reason to purchase a car. Maybe they match dollar for dollar to fund a loan for a used car. Maybe they purchase bus or metro vouchers. If the dependent is traveling a distance, might buy the less expensive train ticket rather than plane fare. The family has earned the right to purchase a luxury vehicle or direct flights; the young adult has not—yet!

Should We Stop Drinking Around Him/Her?

It depends. The most important thing people can do as a family is to have a discussion about it. Get it out in the open. Ask the person what works best for him or her. When individuals are early in their change process, it might help to not have alcohol present when the person is visiting or in the house if you are living together. Sometimes people's willpower is not as strong in the beginning. They may be triggered by the sights or smells of alcohol. Do not be offended if your family member chooses not to attend events where alcohol is present. They are working hard at making changes. Support them. Maybe they don't come to the gathering where all are imbibing, so offer to do something with them during the day or the morning after the event.

If a loved one is going through a period of abstinence or reducing their consumption, ask what nonalcoholic beverages they like. Make sure to have it available for them. Offer that beverage instead of just "Would you like a drink?"

Some enjoy the solidarity of going through a period of abstinence with them; some don't want to impose their lifestyle choices on others. Talk as a family as to whether alcohol will be present in the home. It may make sense to be "dry" for a period of time. If there is a liquor cabinet, they may want to lock it or even give the alcohol to a friend for safekeeping. I recommend to my clients that they change their environment and make it harder to get alcohol. I encourage them to get rid of all alcohol in the house and to remove or make it harder to get to glasses from which they drink.

What if I Suspect He/She Is Drinking?

This depends on the goals of the alcohol user. Did they plan to go through a period of abstinence? Are they committed to total sobriety? Do they have an Alcohol Moderation Plan? What was the frequency to which they agreed? The amount?

Again, the best way to handle this concern is by being proactive. All who are part of the Alcohol Moderation Plan should be aware of the goal and the plan for what to do if they are not sticking to the goal. I tell family members to listen to their gut. If they suspect that there is drinking, there probably is. They have had a history with the drinker, so their instincts are usually based on previous patterns. Loved ones are often in tune with subtle shifts in mood and behaviors. Sometimes it is obvious; they can see bottles or glasses, or they can smell alcohol. I recommend against turning a blind eye.

Many families say they do not want to start a fight. They should not ignore signs or symptoms until things are out of control. It is always easier to deal with a problem in the early stages. I let family members know that their job is to bring their concerns into the open. Family members mistakenly believe that by saying something, they may make it worse. Rather, they need to express it. They may also believe that there has to be an outcome. This is for the alcohol user to decide, not the family member. Sometimes it is pointing it out so the alcohol user knows they are not getting away with it.

Boundaries should have been identified and discussed. If a boundary is crossed, the job of the family member is to let them know that it has been crossed and set the agreed-upon limit. Make sure this is done when they are calm. Emotions such as anger, fear, and disappointment are common when there is a relapse, but a screaming match or a tearjerker is not necessary to convey the message "I notice that you are drinking and I don't approve of it." By addressing it the first time they notice or suspect it, they will not be in the position of sending mixed messages that sometimes it is okay and sometimes it is not. When they stick to their word, they are strengthening their boundaries.

What if He/She Is Not Sticking to the Alcohol Moderation Plan?

Remember that support people should be part of the Alcohol Moderation Plan. Someone should have heard what the plan entails. Clearly, all family members cannot be present. Have a conversation about who will know that a plan is in effect. The person with the plan should have identified the best way to be confronted. Some prefer a direct question, some prefer a softer approach. Most importantly, they should not ignore their concerns. Suspicion may breed resentment. No one should have to walk on eggshells in their own homes. It may be best to say: "On your Alcohol Moderation Plan you said that you were only going to have something to drink one night a week, but I noticed the last two weekends you drank both Friday and Saturday nights." Or: "When we talked in therapy, you agreed that you would not drink to the point of intoxication, but last night you were slurring your words and slept past noon. I really need you be available to help with the kids."

Notes

1. Substance Abuse and Mental Health Services Administration (2004). *Substance abuse treatment and family therapy* (Treatment Improvement Protocol (TIP) Series, No. 39). Rockville, MD: Substance Abuse and Mental Health Services Administration.
2. M. Tiwari (2011). Science behind human saliva. *Journal of Natural Science Biology and Medicine*. 2(1): 53–58. DOI: 10.4103/0976-9668.82322.
3. Merriam-Webster.com (2019, January 13). Retrieved from www.merriam-webster.com/dictionary/enabling.
4. M. Beattie (1992). *Codependent no more: How to stop controlling others and start caring for yourself*. Center City, MN: Hazelden.
5. B. Brown (2015). *Rising strong: How the ability to reset transforms the way we live, love, parent, and lead*. New York: Penguin.
6. Al-Anon Family Headquarters, Inc. (2019, May 30). Retrieved from https://al-anon.org/newcomers/what-is-al-anon-and-alateen/.
7. From Grief to Action (2018). *When addiction hits home: Coping kit* (4th ed.). Vancouver: FGTA.

13 Gender Differences, Special Populations, and Alcohol Use Around the World

This chapter examines the gender differences related to alcohol use. It also reviews the impact on special populations and alcohol consumption around the world.

Gender Differences

Women

One of the main differences between men and women's drinking has to do with the enzyme dehydrogenase.[1] It is a metabolizing enzyme that helps remove alcohol from the body. This enzyme helps men process alcohol faster, allowing them to drink more and not feel the effects as rapidly. In women, dehydrogenase plays a different role. Women have less of this enzyme than men, so more of what women drink enters their bloodstream as pure alcohol, causing their blood alcohol concentration to rise faster.

Women also usually weigh less than men, have more fatty tissue, and less water than a man's body. Because fat retains alcohol while water dilutes it, alcohol remains at higher concentrations for longer periods of time in a woman's body, exposing her brain and other organs to more alcohol.

It would seem that feeling the effects faster just leads to not being able to drink as much as fast. However, a dangerous biological process also happens in the female body.

Women are at greater risk than men for developing alcohol-related physical problems.[2] Once a drink passes her lips, it goes through the digestive tract where it is dispersed through water in the body. The more water that is available, the more diluted the alcohol gets. But women tend to weigh less than men. As a result, women's bodies are exposed more to the toxic byproducts that the body releases when it breaks down alcohol. Thus, a female is at higher risk for developing organ damage such as alcoholic hepatitis and cirrhosis.

The damage does not stop at the liver. Because women's bodies are more exposed to alcohol's toxins, they are more likely to experience alcohol-related brain damage and loss of mental function. Women who drink heavily also have an increased risk of thinning bones, falls, hip fractures, infertility, miscarriages, premature menopause, high blood pressure, heart disease, and cancer.[3]

While men have higher rates of alcohol use disorders, women experience the physical damage from drinking faster than men do. Take a man and a woman who both drink heavily. Over time, the woman will begin to have more severe health problems within five years, while it may take 20 years for it to develop in a man.

Another biological factor that affects the sexes differently is with hormones.[4] The natural fluctuations in hormone levels that occur during a woman's menstrual cycle also affect how she metabolizes and experiences alcohol's effects. The intoxicating effects of alcohol will occur faster when a female's estrogen is higher. This usually occurs just before her period. Alcohol also increases her estrogen levels. A woman taking estrogen added birth control pills will become intoxicated faster and stay drunk longer. The pills slow down the rate at which the body eliminates alcohol.

Social stigmas regarding women drinking are starting to fade and their rates of consumption are increasing, exposing themselves to greater risks. Women now consume about 57% of the wine in the United States. A new phenomenon is the "wine mom."[5] There have been countless social media posts, advertisements, and products making light of mothers drinking as a way to deal with parenting. "I wine because they whine." Women are drinking increasingly at home, alone. Once children are born, there is less time to go out. So the alcohol comes home. Having a glass of wine becomes a way to relax and unwind and a reward at the end of the day. The concern comes when this becomes a daily pattern and the amount increases. When people are in their own home, it can be harder to track consumption. Mothers are stressed, so they are not as cautious with their pours. In a bar or restaurant, the pour is limited for cost control. At home, you can pour as much as you want. And as wine glasses are getting to be the size of water goblets, what seems like one may actually count as two or three drinks.

Women's' increased alcohol consumption also puts them at greater risks for assaults. Rates of binge drinking in college-aged females have more than doubled between 1993 and 2001. Each year 1 in 20 women are sexually assaulted. Research confirms that the likelihood increases when both the attacker and the victim have consumed alcohol.[6]

Men

While women have their fair share of problems related to alcohol consumption, men experience different types of consequences. Several of these have to do with gender expectations.[7] Men tend to drink more frequently and in larger amounts than their female counterparts; thus, they are more likely to develop an alcohol use disorder (AUD). Alcohol consumption is often seen as a rite of passage. Excessive alcohol use is often pardoned as "boys will be boys." Consequences are excused and alcohol use progresses. The gender roles for men have traditionally been to be independent, self-sufficient, stoic, and invulnerable. These expectations cause men to tend to struggle more with the expression of emotions. Alcohol becomes an ineffective way to cope.

Another area that alcohol affects men is with their sexual function.[8] As noted previously, alcohol is a central nervous system depressant. Drinking decreases blood flow to the penis. As a result, men can experience erectile dysfunction and less satisfying orgasms. Alcohol also decreases mood and desire. Over time, excessive alcohol use interferes with testicular function, resulting in impotence, and reduces facial and chest hair.[9]

Research shows that men have dramatically higher rates of alcohol-related problems than female drinkers and are 50% more likely to binge drink. Because males tend to feel the effects slower than females, they may drink a larger amount in a shorter period of time. As a result of binge drinking, males experience more short-term risks to their health and safety. Men are much more likely to be injured or to die from alcohol use. Excessive alcohol use increases aggression, which leads to more fights and potential legal involvement. Men are also much more likely to complete suicide while under the influence of alcohol.[10]

A Columbia and Yale study hypothesizes an additional reason why men are twice as likely to develop severe alcohol use disorders.[11] The researchers reviewed positron emission tomography (PET) scans and found that men experience a far greater "pleasure rush" when drinking than women do. The PET scans showed a higher dopamine release, the feel-good neurotransmitter that is found in the area of the brain that is associated with pleasure, reinforcement, and addiction formation. When this process occurs in men's brains, there is an increased risk of habit formation that can lead to physical dependence on alcohol.

Other research shows that men derive another important benefit from drinking: socialization. When drinking, men experience what researchers call "emotion contagion."[12] This is a process that leads to social cohesion in groups. Guys are actually bonding over alcohol. However, drinking reinforces a social reward process that again leads to a higher likelihood of developing alcohol-related problems, especially if other outlets and connections are not found.

Men also respond to alcohol differently from women, especially in regards to stress.[13] Researchers found that stress depletes glucose levels, which impacts the ability to maintain self-control. When stressed, men drink four times as much women do. They believe that men under tension experience less self-control and make more impulsive decisions, increasing their risks related to alcohol. This is another reason that it is important for men to develop other ways to manage stress than using alcohol.

Alcohol is an area where gender plays a significant role. Men's and women's bodies are biologically different. Because of weight, water concentration, body fat, enzymes, and hormones, females will experience physical problems more quickly than males will. On the flip side, because men can consume more, they may do so faster, exposing themselves to greater short-term consequences and development of alcohol use disorders. Each sex has certain risk factors. Hopefully, armed with knowledge, both genders can make more educated decisions regarding their relationships with alcohol and ward off any consequences.

Special Populations

Adults Over 50

As we age, we become more sensitive to the effects of alcohol.[14] Older adults metabolize alcohol more slowly. Our cartilage and tendons lose water as we get older. This causes the body to hold less water. As a result, there is less liquid to dilute the alcohol, thereby increasing its toxic effects. Alcohol also affects balance, leading to increased accidents and injury. Older adults also tend to be on more medications. Alcohol impacts their effectiveness, and being on medications can affect alcohol's effects.

Women who enter menopause are also negatively affected by drinking.[15] This appears to be a pivotal point in women's alcohol use. I have worked with countless women who drank at levels that did not cause them any problems for years. However, once they experienced the hormonal shifts that menopause brings, they began to experience consequences from their alcohol use.

Trauma

One of the main predictors for having an alcohol use disorder is experiencing trauma.[16] There are many definitions of trauma. I think the simplest is: an emotional response to a terrible event. Note that I did not specify what type of event and what type of response. These are all individualized. What might be traumatic for me may have little to no impact on you. The person experiencing the trauma will have the best definition based on what they are thinking, feeling, and experiencing.

Traditionally, more than 70% of adolescents receiving treatment for substance use have a history of trauma exposure. Teens who experienced physical or sexual abuse are three times as likely to use substances as those who have not. And 59% of young people with PTSD develop substance use disorders.[17]

The National Center for PTSD reports that 60% to 80% of Vietnam veterans seeking PTSD treatment have alcohol use problems, and that up to three quarters of people who survived abuse or violent events and up to a third of those who survived traumatic accidents, illness, or disaster will experience drinking problems.[18] It is critical to ask about trauma as a part of the assessment process as well as including alternative ways to cope in the treatment process. Clinicians can ask questions found in the Adverse Childhood Experiences Study (ACES), including whether a client has dealt with physical, sexual, or emotional abuse, physical or emotional neglect, domestic violence, a household member's substance use, mental illness or incarceration, or divorce or separation.[19]

People who suffer from trauma and PTSD often turn to alcohol and other drugs to manage the intense flood of emotions and traumatic reminders. They may also use it to try to numb themselves. Alcohol initially dulls the effects that they are experiencing from the trauma and help them manage the distress. But a dangerous cycle may begin.

After a traumatic event, people may drink to deal with anxiety, depression, and irritability. But it may be the worst thing they can do. Alcohol initially seems to relieve these symptoms. When we experience a traumatic event, our brains release endorphins that help numb the physical and emotional pain of the event. This is our body naturally helping us cope. Those endorphin levels will eventually decrease over the next several days. Drinking actually increases our endorphin levels. Sounds good, however, this interrupts the natural protective function that the body was already doing. As a result, a type of emotional withdrawal is created, both increasing and prolonging the emotional distress.[20]

Drinking can increase PTSD symptoms of irritability, depression, and feeling off guard. Some drink to deal with insomnia that results from anxiety, anticipating nightmares, circular thinking, yet it impairs the quality of sleep, setting people up for a never-ending cycle with the increased difficulty of emotional and behavioral regulation. Trying to avoid memories of trauma can make it come out in sleep. Those who suffer from PTSD and alcohol use are also more likely to engage in risky behaviors that would lead to additional trauma.

The combination of trauma and drinking can also lead to challenges with getting close to people and increased conflicts with the people those around them. Drinking leads to a confused and disorderly life. The very thing a person needs is support and connection, yet those are often damaged as a result of their behaviors.

LGBTQ+

LGBTQ+ most commonly stands for Lesbian, Gay, Bisexual, Transgender (or Transitioning), and Questioning (or Queer). Despite recent strides in gay rights, many still face social prejudice in the form of discriminatory laws and practices in employment, housing, relationship recognition, and health care as well as challenges with family, friends, and religious practices. The LGBTQ+ community experiences more violence and harassment than the majority of the population. As a result, they tend to have higher rates of mental health struggles and substance use disorders than their heterosexual counterparts.[21] Assessing sexual identity and their experiences is crucial when working with LGBTQ+ persons.

Alcohol Use Around the World

It would be nearly impossible to identify alcohol use and its impact in every part of the world. Even within a country, regions can have vastly different patterns and problems. Age, income level, poverty, laws, religion, and government all play a role. This section gives a generalized overview of the main regions in the world.

The World Health Organization puts out a Global Status Report on Alcohol and Health. Some of the key findings from the 2018 report include:[22]

- More than half of the world's population over the age of 15 abstains from alcohol use.
- Rates of abstinence are higher in poorer societies than in richer ones, but those who drink tend to drink at heavier levels.
- The highest rates of alcohol consumption occur in the European region, while the heaviest drinkers are in parts of Africa.
- Harms from drinking are higher in poorer areas than in richer areas.
- More than half of the alcohol consumed comes from three regions: Europe, America, and the Western Pacific.
- Spirits account for 44.8%, beer is 34.3%, and wine is 11.7% of the type of alcohol drank.
- A quarter of the alcohol consumed worldwide is in the form of unrecorded alcohol including homemade spirits, especially in low-income countries like Southeast Asia and Eastern Europe.

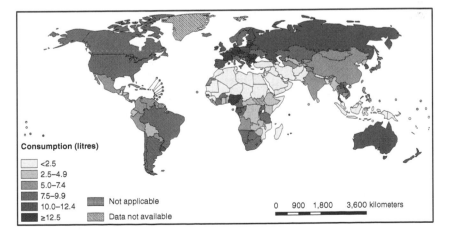

Figure 13.1 Alcohol Use Around the World

Source: Reproduced with the permission of the authors, from the Global Status Report on Alcohol Health 2018. https://www.who.int/substance_abuse/publications/global_alcohol_report/gsr_2018/en/Page 64

Lowest Alcohol Consumption

Overall, the regions that consume the least amount of alcohol tend to be Asia and Africa. The areas that have the least per capita alcohol consumption are Muslim states, where the sale and consumption of alcohol of prohibited. The countries with the lowest are Indonesia and Bangladesh, where the average person drinks less than a bottle of wine a year. The lowest is Pakistan, which is almost at zero.[23]

Highest Alcohol Consumption

The top ten countries that drink the most are all located in Eastern Europe. Regularly topping the list are Russia, Lithuania, Moldova, and Belarus. They tend to be colder climate regions with fewer hours of sunlight. A recent study found that there were two reasons for this.[24] The first is that alcohol is a vasodilator. It increases blood flow to the skin, increasing feelings of warmth. Additionally, these regions have fewer hours of sunlight, which is known to increase levels of depression. People are drinking more alcohol as a way to cope.

Africa

Alcohol consumption throughout Africa varies widely.[25] In many regions, alcohol is made from indigenous plants, such as bananas and palm trees, as well as from honey. The alcohol content of these fermented drinks tends to be very high, ranging from 30% to 60%. Nigeria has the highest consumption patterns, with about 84% coming from home-brewed beverages. The reason for this is that religious laws make it expensive to produce and sell alcohol.

American Indians and Alaska Natives (AI/AN)

AI/AN have the highest rates of AUDs in the United States. Nearly half, about 46.6%, will meet DSM-5 diagnostic criteria for an alcohol use disorder in their lifetime.[26] The group tends to be a population that has suffered economic disadvantage, cultural loss, and a history of abuse. All of these have contributed to challenges in mental and physical health where the use of alcohol may become an unhealthy coping skill. Providers who work with this group need to understand the implications of these factors on functioning and potentially spend more time on case management than on traditional therapy.[27] Additionally, AI/AN may have allelic variants that alter their ability to process alcohol that increase rates of AUDs.[28]

Asia

Asia is the largest and most populated continent in the world. Countries in this region face significant political unrest, natural disasters, and socioeconomic problems. Yet alcohol dependence is not as high as in other parts of the world. Lower availability of resources and biological factors are two potential reasons.[29] Genetically, Asians have a gene variant that causes more acetaldehyde to be accumulated in their systems during alcohol metabolism. This results in heightened effects and is accompanied with a burning redness in their faces and chests known as a "flush." As a result, many people of East Asian decent tend to drink less than in other cultures.[30] The World Health Organization Global Health Data Repository 2015 found that in Asia, the country that drinks the most is South Korea, with Vietnam and Thailand as close seconds.

Australia

Alcohol misuse is a major social and public health issue in Australia. It is estimated that it costs the country $30 billion a year.[31] Australia is usually one of the top ten drinking countries, according to the World Health Organization. Alcohol use is traditionally a part of most social events, including household parties, pubs, clubs, sporting events, meals, celebrations, and funerals. Some have said that to turn down alcohol is to be "un-Australian." Over 80% of Australian have had their first sip by age 14. However, the 10% of the population that drinks the most consumes over half of the alcohol in the country.[32]

Latin America

Alcohol consumption in Latin America tends to be relatively low at 5.5 liters per capita, which is considerably less than in Europe and the United States. El Salvador tends to have the lowest rates of drinking alcohol, while Venezuela has the highest. Socioeconomic factors are likely a factor in this. The age group that consumes the most is ages 25–35, and as income levels rise, so does the rate of alcohol use. Other studies show that since the 1960s, urbanization and modernization are increasing escapist tendencies and recreational reasons for increasing alcohol use.[33]

Portugal

I mention Portugal specifically because the country decriminalized the use of all drugs in 2001.[34] They take a harm reduction approach. Possession is no longer a criminal offense. Individuals go through a panel that includes legal, health, and social work professionals. While substance users may still be punished with a fine or community service, they are also given education and information about treatment options.[35]

Portugal now has one of Europe's lowest rates of drug, alcohol, and tobacco use and lowest infection rates for HIV/AIDS and hepatitis. It was not decriminalization that did this, but their approach of viewing drug use as a health problem, not a crime.[36]

United Kingdom

In 2016 the chief medical officers of the United Kingdom recommended keeping alcohol use to lower than 14 units a week, not on a regular basis, and to spread it out evenly over three or more days to reduce the risk of long-term illness and injury.[37] This is a reduction from the 1995 guidelines where the Royal College of Physicians said that up to 21 drinks a week was considered safe. This was before they understood the link between alcohol use and mortality rates form cancer and other diseases. Since this time, alcohol use in the United Kingdom has been decreasing.[38]

Box Matter 13.2

DID YOU KNOW? Countries in which people drink regularly tend to have less alcohol-related violence, and fewer accidents, deaths, and suicides. The reason for this is that a binge causes more impairment than regular use. It is worse to have four glasses of wine in one sitting than it is to have the same amount of alcohol over the course of a week.[39]

Notes

1. M. S. Mumenthaler, J. L. Taylor, R. O'Hara & J. A. Yesavage (1999). Gender differences in moderate drinking effects. *Alcohol Research and Health.* 23(1): 55–64.
2. National Institute on Alcohol Abuse and Alcoholism (2015). *Alcohol: A women's health issue.* NIH Publication No. 15–4956.
3. 3 Centers for Disease Control and Prevention (2016). *Fact sheets: Excessive alcohol use and risks to women's health.* Atlanta, GA. Retrieved from www.cdc.gov/alcohol/fact-sheets/womens-health.htm.
4. S. M. Evans & F. R. Levin (2011). Response to alcohol in women: Role of the menstrual cycle and a family history of alcoholism. *Drug Alcohol Dependence.* 114(1). DOI: 10.1016/j.drugalcdep.2010.09.001.
5. K. Mascia (2019). Parenting with a buzz: When does alcohol as self-care become a problem? *Parents Magazine.* Retrieved from www.parents.com/parenting/better-parenting/style/parenting-with-a-buzz-alcohol-as-self-care/.
6. M. Mohler-Kuo, G. W. Dowdall, M. Koss & H. Wechsler (2004). Correlates of rape while intoxicated in a national sample of college women. *Journal of Studies on Alcohol and Drugs.* 65(1): 37–45.
7. Substance Abuse and Mental Health Services Administration (2013). *Addressing the specific behavioral health needs of men* (Treatment Improvement Protocol (TIP) Series 56. HHS Publication No. (SMA) 13–4736). Rockville, MD: Substance Abuse and Mental Health Services Administration.
8. S. B. Arackal & V. Benegal (2007). Prevalence of sexual dysfunction in male subjects with alcohol dependence. *Indian Journal of Psychiatry.* 49(2): 109–112.
9. Centers for Disease Control (2016). *Fact sheets—excessive alcohol use and men.* Atlanta, GA. Retrieved from www.cdc.gov/alcohol/fact-sheets/mens-health.htm.
10. J. Suokas, K. Suominen & J. Lonnqvist (2005). Chronic alcohol problems among suicide attempters—post mortem findings of a 14-year follow up. *Nordic Journal of Psychiatry.* 59(1): 45–50.

11. N. B. Urban, L. S. Kegels, M. Slifstein, X. Xu, D. Martinez, E. Sakr, F. Castillo, T. Moadel, S. S. O'Malley, J. H. Krystal & A. Abi-Dargham (2010). Sex differences in striatal dopamine release in young adults after oral alcohol challenge: A positron emission tomography imaging study with [11C] raclopride. *Biological Psychiatry*. 68(8): 689–696.

12. C. E. Fairbarn, M. A. Sayette, O. O. Aalen & A. Frigressi (2015). Alcohol and emotional contagion: An examination of the spreading of smiles in male and female drinking groups. *Clinical Psychological Science*. 3(5). https://doi.org/10.1177/2167702614548892.

13. R. Otten, M. B. Cladder-Micus, J. L. Pouwels, A. A. T. Schurmanns & R. C. J. Hermans (2014). Facing temptation in the bar: Counteracting the effects of self-control failure on young adults' *ad libitum* alcohol intake. *Addiction*. 109(5): 746–753.

14. National Institute on Ageing (2017). *Facts about aging and alcohol*. Bethesda, MD. Retrieved from www.nia.nih.gov/health/facts-about-aging-and-alcohol.

15. North American Menopause Society (2019). *Drink to your health at menopause—or not?* Pepper Pike, OH. Retrieved from www.menopause.org/for-women/menopauseflashes/exercise-and-diet/drink-to-your-health-at-menopause-or-not.

16. K. T. Brady & S. E. Back (2012). Childhood trauma, posttraumatic stress disorder, and alcohol dependence. *Alcohol Research: Current Reviews*. 34(4): 408–413.

17. L. Khooury, Y. L. Tang, B. Bradley, J. F. Cubells & K. J. Ressler (2010, December). Substance use, childhood traumatic experience, and post traumatic stress disorder in an urban civilian population. *Depression and Anxiety*. 27(12): 1077–1086.

18. National Center for PTSD (2019, June 6). *PTSD and problems with alcohol use*. White River Junction, VT. Retrieved from www.ptsd.va.gov/understand/related/problem_alcohol_use.asp.

19. V. J. Felitti, R. F. Anda, D. Nordenberg, D. F. Williamson, A. M. Spitz, V. Edwards, M. P. Koss & J. S. Marks (1998). Relationship of childhood abuse and household dysfunction to many of the leading causes of death in adults. *American Journal of Preventative Medicine*. 14(4): 245–258. DOI: https://doi.org/10.1016/S0749-3797(98)00017-8.

20. J. Volpicelli, G. Balaraman, J. Hahn, H. Wallace & D. Bux (1999). The role of uncontrollable trauma in the development of PTSD and alcohol addiction. *Alcohol Research and Health*. 23(4): 256–262.

21. G. Medley, R. N. Lipari, J. Bose, D. S. Cribb, L. A. Kroutil & G. McHenry (2016). *Sexual orientation and estimates of adult substance use and mental health: Results from the 2015 national survey on drug use and health*. NSDUH Data Review. Retrieved from www.samhsa.gov/data/.

22. World Health Organization (2018). *Global status report on alcohol and health 2018*. Geneva: World Health Organization. License: CC BY-NC-SA 3.0 IGO.

23. World Atlas (2017). 14 countries where drinking is illegal. *World Atlas.com*. Retrieved from www.worldatlas.com/articles/14-countries-where-drinking-alcohol-is-illegal.html.

24. M. Ventura-Cots, A. E. Watts, M. Cruz-Lemini, N. D. Shah, N. Ndugga, P. McCann, A. S. Barritt, A. Jain, S. Ravi, C. Fernandez-Carrillo, J. G. Abraldes, J. Altamirano & R. Bataller (2018). Colder weather and fewer sunlight hours increase alcohol consumption and alcoholic cirrhosis worldwide. *Hepatology*. DOI: 10.1002/hep.30315.

25. G. Mukamaon (2015). *10 Biggest alcohol drinking countries in Africa*. Lifestyle.

26. C. J. Mulligan, R. W. Robin, M. V. Osier, N. Sambuughin, L. G. Goldfarb, R. A. Kittles, D. Hesselbrock, D. Goldman & J. C. Long (2003). Allelic variation at alcohol metabolism genes (ADH1B, ADH1C, ALDH2) and alcohol dependence in an American Indian population. *Human Genet*. 113(4): 325–336.

27. M. A. Emerson, R. S. Moore & R. Caetano (2019). Correlates of alcohol-related treatment among American Indians and Alaska natives with lifetime alcohol use

disorder. *Alcoholism: Clinical and Experimental Research.* 43(1): 115–122. http://dx.doi.org/10.1111/acer.13907.

28. N. R. Whitesell, J. Beals, C. B. Croy, C. M. Mitchell & D. K. Novins (2012). Epidemiology and etiology of substance use among American Indians and Alaska natives: Risk, protection, and implications for prevention. *The American Journal of Drug and Alcohol Abuse.* 38(5): 376–382.

29. C. Chiao-Chicy & Y. Shih-Jiun (2008). Alcohol abuse and related factors in Asia. *International Review of Psychiatry.* 20(5): 425–433. DOI: 10.1080/09540260802344075.

30. L. Tamara, T. L. Wall, S. E. Luczak & S. Hiller-Sturmhöfel (2016). Biology, genetics, and environment: Underlying factors influencing alcohol moderation. *The Journal of the National Institute on Alcohol Abuse and Alcoholism.* 38(1).

31. A. Laslett, P. Catalano, T. Chikritzhs, C. Dale, C. Doran, J. Ferris, T. Jainullabudeen, M. Livingston, S. Matthews, J. Mugavin, R. Room, M. Schlotterlein & C. Wilkinson (2010). *The range and magnitude of alcohol's harm to others.* Fitzroy, Victoria: AER Centre for Alcohol Policy Research, Turning Point Alcohol and Drug Centre, Eastern Health.

32. M. Livingston & S. Callinan (2019). Examining Australia's heaviest drinkers. *Australian and New Zealand Journal of Public Health.* DOI: 10.1111/1753-6405.12901.

33. D. W. Coombs & G. Globetti (1986). Alcohol use and alcoholism in Latin America: Changing patterns and sociocultural explanations. *International Journal of the Addictions.* 21(1): 59–81. DOI: 10.3109/10826088609063438.

34. N. Bajekal (2018, August 1). Want to win the war on drugs: Portugal might have the answer. *Time* magazine. https://time.com/longform/portugal-drug-use-decriminalization/.

35. Transform (2019, June 7). *Drug decriminalization in Portugal: Setting the record straight.* Retrieved from https://transformdrugs.org/drug-decriminalisation-in-portugal-setting-the-record-straight/.

36. D. Braham (2018). Daphne Bramham: Decriminalization is no silver bullet, says Portugal's drug czar. *Vancouver Sun.* Retrieved from https://vancouversun.com/opinion/columnists/daphne-bramham-decriminalization-is-no-silver-bullet-says-portugals-drug-czar.

37. World Health Organization (2018). *United Kingdom: Trends in alcohol consumption 2016.* Geneva: World Health Organization.

38. *BBC News* (2016, January 8). New alcohol guidelines: What you need to know. Retrieved from www.bbc.com/news/uk-35252650.

39. S. Peele (2015, June 8). Studies show that drinking problems are increasing. Here's why. *The Fix.* Retrieved from www.thefix.com/content/we-have-more-drinking-problems-why/.

14 Typical Questions

This chapter answers the questions that clinicians, family members, and alcohol users typically ask regarding alcohol moderation. Some include how to verify abstinence, if moderation can apply to other drugs, and success rates. The chapter closes out with how some of the treatment community has responded to alcohol moderation.

What About Marijuana?

This is one of the most common questions that I receive in presentations as well as from all ages of clients and other professionals. While marijuana is decriminalized in a number of states, it is still currently illegal under federal law in the United States. Marijuana use is increasing as it is becoming more available, and there are proven medical benefits. Even so, I still do not teach moderation for marijuana. There are a number of reasons for this.

The main reason I do not teach moderation for marijuana has to do with dosage. The physiological effects of alcohol have been well studied. We know how the average person will respond to certain doses of alcohol, and we can predict what will happen at increasing blood alcohol concentrations. Part of this is because we know the proof (alcohol content by volume) of alcohol in the beer, wine, and spirits that are sold throughout the world. Some argue that this is an excellent reason to legalize marijuana—so it can be regulated.

Developing a standardized measure for the potency of marijuana would be beneficial; however, alcohol and marijuana are very different drugs. The half-life (how long it takes for half of the amount of the substance to be removed from the body) of marijuana is one of the longest.[1] Marijuana is stored in the boy's fat cells because it is not easily dissolved in water like alcohol is. The half-life is dependent upon several factors, including the frequency use, potency of the marijuana, and route of administration (ingested versus inhaled). The half-life of marijuana generally occurs over a period of three to four days but can take up to two weeks. The half-life of alcohol is drastically shorter, around four hours.

Another reason I do not teach moderation for marijuana has to with its potency. While potency is a debated topic, most studies concur that the strength of marijuana is significantly higher than it was 50 years ago.[2] Some strains can be as low as 4%, while others can be at a whopping 80%. There are also countless more strains that have varying effects. We would need to have a standardized "proof" for marijuana before moderation could be considered. Even so, it would be harder to moderate, as the half-life is much longer than alcohol. And as a colleague of mine who is a psychiatrist said when we were discussing this topic: "Nothing you smoke is good for you." Additionally, the rates of overdose and accidental injestion have increased as edibles look like treats and their effects take longer to occur so people take more than intended (National Institute on Drug Abuse).

Do You Teach Moderation for Other Drugs?

Keep in mind that there is a difference between harm reduction and alcohol moderation. Alcohol moderation is a type of harm reduction. I practice harm reduction when a client is struggling with other drug use. I cannot legally or ethically teach a person how to use less of a drug, as there are no safe levels approved for street drugs and their use carries legal consequences. Additionally, we do not know who is manufacturing these drugs, what the potency is, or what it has been cut with. I remind my clients that it is not likely manufactured or handled in a sterile environment.

If a client is using illegal drugs, we have a conversation about the risks and the potential legal consequences. While I cannot condone it, I certainly don't refuse treatment. I explore with the client why they are using the substance and offer coping skills to assist with those issues. I work with them on how to reduce the harms and celebrate successes when there is a reduction in amount, frequency, or consequences.

What About Prescription Drugs?

Substances like opioids, methamphetamines, benzodiazepines, and many sleep medications are being monitored by the Food and Drug Administration (FDA), the Drug Enforcement Administration (DEA), and professionals who prescribe them. In order to legally obtain these drugs, a medically trained professional performs an evaluation and then monitors symptoms, side effects, and dosage. They look for dependency and adjust the dosage.

To be considered for prescription use, these drugs have undergone a rigorous ten-year process. This includes research, laboratory, animal, and human testing, and data analysis before they are determined safe for use by the FDA.[3] Once approved, they continue to be monitored. None of the same can be said for drugs that are sold on the street.

These four classes of drugs are also monitored by the DEA. One of the DEA's jobs is to "schedule" drugs.[4] The United States has maintained the Controlled Substance Act since 1970. It was an effort to protect the general public from potentially dangerous and addictive drugs. Drugs, substances, and certain chemicals that are used to make drugs are classified into five categories, called schedules. The schedule depends upon the drug's acceptable medical use and the potential of its being abused or leading to dependency. Opioids and methamphetamines are considered Schedule II medications, meaning they have a high potential for abuse and dependence. Benzodiazepines and many sleeping medications are Schedule IV medications that have a lower rate of abuse and dependence.

Many of my younger clients struggle to see the problem with these types of drugs. They feel that because they are "legal" drugs, they cannot be problematic. The only time a person should be taking these medications is under medical supervision. Just because it is prescribed for one person does not make it safe, or even legal, for another person to take. However, if a person is taking them as prescribed, they are essentially practicing moderation.

Because of their ability to alter mood and high rate of addictive potential, these drugs can still be abused and sold on the street. In that case, I would take a harm reduction, not a moderation approach.

How Do You Handle Young Adults?

Parents and professionals alike ask this question regarding college-aged students and young adults. I respond that most individuals in their early 20s are not drinking for taste, they are drinking for effect. The exceptions for this age group may come in certain countries where alcohol is part of everyday use. Because alcohol is available to them at younger ages, it is not seen as a rite of passage or even as something that is forbidden. The culture in the United States often is one of excess. Many from other countries are shocked at the availability of food and the large portion sizes that are available.

In general, this age group engages in binge drinking, which is more than four to five alcoholic beverages in a short period of time with the intent of intoxication. Research has shown that the heaviest alcohol use tends to occur in the early to mid-20s and then begins to decrease. Those who are developing an alcohol use disorder (AUD) often increase their use during this time.[5] This is something to explore in the assessment process. It may be interesting to note that by age 70, only a small percentage of people will meet criteria for an AUD. About half will have died of normal life expectancy issues, one-third will be alcohol-free, and the remaining 20% will be able to successfully moderate their alcohol use.[6]

For young adults, I teach harm reduction, not moderation. I take more of an educational approach as to the risks and outcomes of the choices they make. I also focus more on a safety approach. We may discuss the importance of consuming food when drinking, having a glass of water for each alcoholic drink, determining how to get home safely, and practicing safer sex. I discuss the dangers of doing shots, keg stands, or drinking challenges as well as the increased likelihood of injuries, accidents, sexual assaults, and altercations.

Box matter 14.1

DID YOU KNOW? An occasional glass of red wine may have some health benefits. Red wine contains an ingredient called resveratrol that may help prevent damage to blood vessels, increase high-density lipoprotein (the good cholesterol), and prevent blood clots. But you can also get resveratrol from grapes and supplements without all of the risks that chronic alcohol use can bring.[7]

Do You Drink/Did You Have a Problem With Alcohol?

I get these questions from audience members, professionals, and clients of all ages. People want to know if I drink alcohol or if I ever had or have a problem with it. This is probably the only type of question that I do not answer.

My colleague calls this a trick question. There is no good answer. If I were to say that I dealt with a substance use disorder, people wonder what I did in my recovery. Treatment becomes about me, not my client. Sometimes it also excuses the behavior, as if "Well, you get it." Other times, clients want to trade using stories. What if my story is worse than yours, or not as bad? How does that help treatment?

On the flip side, if I say that I never had a problem, some might think that there is no way I could understand what they are dealing with. How could you get how hard abstinence is if you never tried it? What do you know about drinking too much or waking up after a binge?

When asked, I usually say something like: "That is probably the only question I don't answer. I have found that there is no good response." I may expand on some of the reasons above, but most importantly, I am not defensive.

More often than not, clients often respond with: "Yeah, I didn't think you would tell me." Usually, I go a little further and ask: "What's the question behind your question?"

They may be looking for some reassurance about my education or experience. What they are really asking me is: Are you able to help me? Some are concerned that I will judge them. Some have had previous therapists in recovery that focus solely on what worked for them. Remember that harm reduction is about meeting the client where he or she is and working with them to identify their goals. I let my clients know that they are the expert because it is their life and I am the expert because it is *not* my life so I have an unbiased, unemotionally involved perspective to offer them.

There are few other fields in which competence is assessed by whether you have had the problem that is being treated. We don't ask a surgeon if he has had surgery before. We don't ask the cardiologist if he has high blood pressure or the dermatologist if she has had skin cancer. In fact, we probably prefer that our health care provider is not dealing with a medical issue. We just want them to treat us and get us healthy.

How did it come to be that a drug and alcohol counselor has to have dealt with addiction for that person to be effective? We should focus more on education and clinical experience than on personal familiarity. I want to be judged on the work I am doing, not on my personal history.

How Do You Verify Abstinence?

Many providers wonder how we verify abstinence and if we only look at alcohol. My answer starts with letting them know that they may get the best results if they are free from all nonprescribed mood-altering substances during a period of abstinence. The exceptions are nicotine, caffeine, and prescribed medications. (There are still clinicians and programs that will not work with people if they are taking medication. As a result, health and lives are greatly put at risk). Nicotine and caffeine tend to alter mood less than alcohol and other drugs, so we make these a secondary issue. As people are going through their periods of abstinence, we begin to focus more on finding balance. In the first month or so, the use of these substances may increase, as well as their intake of sugar as they are dealing with any withdrawals and cravings. Once they begin dealing with their "why" and develop better coping skills, the use of all three usually decrease. Many often want to discontinue their use of nicotine products within several months.

The second part of my answer is that, just like any skill, the more you do it, the better you get at it. Those who provide dual diagnosis treatment are often able to sense shifts in behavior and are attuned to body language. Many therapists can sense if a person is telling the truth regarding their substance use based on what their client is and is not saying. However, we do not just rely on our senses and experience.

I regularly use alcohol and drug screening. I administer a Breathalyzer in the groups I run—in intake sessions, randomly in individual sessions, and when I suspect recent alcohol use. The limitation of a Breathalyzer is that it measures only blood alcohol concentration—the amount of alcohol that is present in the body at the time of the test. Newer technology has allowed us to test metabolites that are present when the body is processing alcohol. This is often called the "80-hour alcohol test."[8] The test picks up ethyl glucuronide (ETG) and ethyl sulfate (ETS), which are direct metabolites of ethanol alcohol. ETG and ETS are present only if alcohol has been consumed. They are typically detectable in urine for about three and a half days. Sometimes just letting people know that there are ways to verify their self-report increases honesty.

Another new technology is Soberlink. This is a portable device that combines a professional-grade Breathalyzer with a web-based portal.[9] The technology uses facial recognition to ensure who is taking the test. The device can be set to require testing at certain intervals. Results are sent to an identified person such as a probation officer, attorney, or treatment provider. This is useful technology, but it is more for those dealing with a severe alcohol use disorder and struggling to maintain abstinence. If someone needs this degree of alcohol monitoring, they are unlikely to be a candidate for alcohol moderation.

I also use family, friends, and support people to verify abstinence. Part of the alcohol moderation process is to identify support people. Their role is support as well as accountability. I help my clients choose someone they trust to be honest with as well as confront them. In the presence of my client, I invite the support person to leave me a message if they have concerns about continued alcohol consumption or a relapse. We then discuss how to handle it in session.

Keep in mind that the alcohol moderation process is typically voluntary. The *Alcohol Moderation Assessment* rules out anyone who is currently on probation for legal, employment, or familial reasons. Most of my clients are honest about their alcohol use because they want to make changes. If they are hiding, minimizing, or lying about their drinking, they may not be a good candidate for alcohol moderation.

What if a Person Cannot Make It Four Months Without Drinking?

If an individual is unable to achieve four months of abstinence from all mood-altering substances, they may not be a good candidate for alcohol moderation. This process can be a diagnostic tool. It is also part of the harm reduction process in which the client determines what the goals are, not the clinician or the program. Some clients need to attempt moderation, or moderation without abstinence, before they can accept that they are unable to keep drinking safely. They may be struggling with a severe AUD where total abstinence is warranted. They may need a higher level of treatment that includes detoxification. Harm reduction allows the client to choose the goal. Your job as a clinician is to give guidance and feedback in the process.

It is rare that a person enters treatment with me and immediately achieves four months of abstinence. If it was that easy for them, they would not need professional help. This will all depend upon many factors including the stage of change they are in, their internal and external motivations, the amount, frequency, and length of time they have been using alcohol, and the impact and intent of their use.

Clinicians who practice harm reduction and alcohol moderation need to be able to tolerate the client engaging in risky and unhealthy behaviors. I address them directly and make sure to document my concerns along with the recommendations I make. There may be weeks if not months of unsuccessful attempts before one determines their relationship with alcohol.

What if Someone Wants to Stay Abstinent Past the Four Months?

This is all dependent upon the client. Four months is a recommendation based upon what I have found that works for thousands of people in my practice over almost three decades of treatment. I have worked with people who chose not to do the four months and still are able to successfully practice alcohol moderation. Other clients chose to extend their period of abstinence. Some also chose complete abstinence. Their health and happiness determine what is considered a success.

What Are Your Success Rates?

Treatment providers and the person paying for treatment typically will ask about success rates. I say that this is a very hard question to answer. Traditional success rates were based on abstinence after completion of a program. If my work is being judged on abstinence, then most of the treatment I have provided has been a failure. There are thousands of individuals and their families that I have worked with over three decades who would disagree.

My success rates are based on the individual. What are their goals, and did they achieve them? Oftentimes the goal at the beginning of treatment is different from when they finish. The majority of the people who start treatment at my practice state that their goal is to be able to keep drinking. Many times after a period of abstinence, they prefer sobriety and chose it going forward without ever having to admit that they were an "alcoholic" or were powerless over their drinking. Others decide that the actual process of moderation with having to monitor and count drinks is not worth it. Some clients realize that it was not the alcohol that was the issue but something related to their mental health, a relationship, or their job. I get a kick out of it when people start therapy feeling shame about their alcohol use, but then we resolve those types of issues, and the drinking resolves itself as it is no longer needed as a coping skill. Many of my clients are surprised at how little we talk about their alcohol use after their evaluation but their drinking problem gets better. Some have exclaimed: I didn't have a drinking problem, I had a work/depression/anxiety/relationship problem!

In our data-driven society, I can't easily answer a question about success rates. The therapist in me seeks to identify why someone is asking me this seemingly simple, but really complicated question and answer those questions instead. I will probably engage in a discussion rather than just give a quick answer.

What About the Family?

I have found that involving the family greatly improves outcomes. As part of the alcohol moderation process, I encourage the person struggling with his or her alcohol use to invite their loved ones into the treatment process. A married person might include their spouse. Older people may include their adult children. Parents may bring their children. It can also be a neighbor, best friend, roommate, or another family member. I let my client decide.

Oftentimes loved ones have borne the brunt of the consequences from their family members' unhealthy drinking patterns. As noted previously, bringing family members into an early session can be beneficial for the whole system. The client's loved ones usually share their concerns and say things like: "Did he tell you . . .?" or "Did you know about . . .?" This process helps ease their anxiety. Coming into a session also verifies that the person really is getting help and can help to increase trust.

Many times, loved ones attend the evaluation process. I ask the client if they would like them present for part of the process; sometimes they want the moral support. I find that it can be helpful to observe their dynamics, seeing how they interact with one another and whether it changes once I ask them to leave the room to ask additional questions and complete their substance use and addictive behaviors history.

Prior to having anyone in the session, I obtain their permission and always prepare my client. We review confidentiality and I assure them that I will not reveal the content of the session. I encourage them to share their goals and insights. In the session, I prefer to guide rather than take the lead. I answer general questions about the process while encouraging my client to voice their experience.

What Should We Tell Children?

Children rely heavily on instinct and emotions as opposed to logic. They tend to be sensitive to their environments. I have found that some parents are hesitant to talk to their children about their drinking as if it was some kind of secret. I educate them that most children are aware of what is happening in the household and can sense when something is wrong. They may not know that it is specifically alcohol-related.

I remind parents that they are their children's first role models. Their behavior teaches them what is "normal" for their family. Acknowledging that their alcohol use is causing problems validates for children what they were already sensing. Talking about it opens up a line of communication. I encourage parents to share that they are doing something about their drinking. This is an invaluable life lesson: Adults sometimes make bad decisions and do unhealthy things, but we admit it and take action to make it better.

Obviously, the discussion should be age appropriate. A discussion with a 6-year-old is very different from that with a 16-year-old. The parent can take cues from their child. It helps to introduce the subject and ask if he or she has any questions or anything they would like to share. Children may be afraid to express their concerns, fears, or criticism of a parent for fear of getting in trouble. It is important that the parent let children know that they are allowed to speak freely and that there will not be a consequence if the parent hears something that they do not like. A conversation with kids who are verbal and have some insight may start like this: "Son, I want to talk to you about my drinking. I'm guessing it has affected you. I realized it was causing problems for our family so I went to go see a therapist who is helping me make healthier decisions. Would you like to tell me what has worried you about my alcohol use?"

For teenagers, I recommend talking with kids in the car. You have a captive audience but one that has some distractions like the radio that can make the talk less intense. Some kids prefer being able to talk without having to have direct eye contact. I use therapy to role play with my clients the best way to engage their child and prepare for possible outcomes.

I also recommend that parents bring their kids into a session or even stop by the office to see it and meet the therapist. It helps them to see where their mom or dad goes each week. It shows them that it is a real place and that someone exists to help their family. Actually seeing the setting and meeting the providers reduces children's anxiety, explains parents' absences, and makes it safer to ask questions.

How Do You Handle Relapse?

It depends! There are many factors that would determine my response. Did my client set an unrealistic goal? Did they say they were going to quit drinking tomorrow after drinking their entire adult life? Were they experiencing pressure from loved ones to stop completely? What stage of change are they in? Are they in an abstinence period or a moderation phase? Was the relapse a blackout binge? Was it drinking four glasses of wine instead of three at a wedding? Did it happen one night or did they go back to daily drinking?

My overall response to relapses is that it is an opportunity to learn. I would explore the following questions: What was not working? Do they need additional tools? Did we not prepare for that situation and need to come up with additional plans? How can we avoid that outcome in the future? I tell my clients that all they lose is their clean date, not all of the information they gained and the work that they have been doing.

Does My Loved One Need Rehab?

I have found that the term "rehab" is used incorrectly. Some use it to say that they are seeking treatment for a substance use disorder. But there are a variety of settings with varying frequency and intensity. In the treatment field, rehab usually refers to a rehabilitation facility. This is where a person typically is in a program that provides 24/7 care, often for several weeks at a time. This is for individuals with a severe AUD who need medical monitoring.

Clinicians who have training in substance use disorders should know how to determine if an individual needs the most intensive level of care. Remember that the general public and most generally trained professionals are still taught only to respond as if there was an addiction, not a mild or moderate AUD. They hear that there is a problem with alcohol and assume that AA, complete abstinence, and rehab are warranted. I know of many individuals who were recommended to inpatient, 30-day rehabilitation centers, who spent tens of thousands of dollars and whose lives were interrupted, who could have been treated at an outpatient level of care. This intensive level of care is needed only on rare occasions.

I recommend to family members that they have their loved ones get an evaluation from someone who is licensed and experienced in both mental health and substance use disorders and is aware of ASAM placement criteria (discussed briefly in Chapter 3). They should ask if they have heard of harm reduction or alcohol moderation. If they have not, they are likely to follow a 12-step, abstinence-only model. Many clinicians recommend higher levels of treatment, such a detoxification and residential treatment when they are not familiar with AUDs.

Generally, it is only when a person has developed a physical tolerance for alcohol that they will need a detoxification period. This often occurs in a hospital-based setting or can be the first phase of a residential treatment program. To assess this, I identify the amount and frequency of alcohol use. If someone is a daily drinker of several drinks a day, there is a chance they need detox. One of the best ways to determine if detoxification is needed is to ask when their last drink was. If it was more than three days ago, they are past the acute withdrawal stage.

In addition, I assess if they have had a period of abstinence in the past. I look for what happened then to see if they had any life-threatening withdrawal symptoms. However, if someone is experiencing delirium tremens ("the shakes"), erratic heart rate, or hallucinations, or is unable to be roused, they need medical attention immediately.

Do You Hate Alcoholics Anonymous?

I don't. Simply because I do not require all of my clients to attend AA meetings, do 90 in 90, work the steps, and obtain a sponsor does not mean I hate AA. Many of my clients are active in the program and derive great benefits. I recommend AA on a regular basis. Other clients have attended and decided it was not for them. This includes clients who chose not to drink again. Some flat out refuse to go. Others utilize different mutual support meetings like SMART, Celebrate Recovery, or Moderation Management, while some participate in online forums. A clinician should have basic knowledge about the varying programs in their area and be able to discuss how it is or is not benefitting them.

I simply believe that AA should not be the only recommendation. Just as I don't recommend that all of my clients struggling with depression start taking an SSRI, I don't recommend that all of my clients go to AA.

What Do You Do if Someone Tells You They Do Not Want to Drink?

I saved this question for last because it demonstrates the challenges you will face as a clinician who teaches alcohol moderation. This was an actual question. It came from a gentleman at the end of a half day training. He raised his hand during the question-and-answer period of the seminar. In a loud, accusatory voice, he challenged: "What do you do if a person says he does not want to drink?" He threw it out there as if he believed that I coerce nondrinkers into imbibing. It was like he was accusing me that I keep a bottle in my desk for these very occasions. The sarcastic part of me wanted to say that I wouldn't work with them unless they took a sip or that our next session would be at the local bar. I did not. At least I could see a number of audience members snicker and roll their eyes as this attacker spoke.

I politely stated that harm reduction techniques are about the treatment being geared towards the client's goals and that I would help them achieve abstinence. I reminded him that the best outcomes with alcohol moderation come when a client goes through a period of abstinence and that more than half of my clients who started out wanting moderation actually chose complete abstinence.

The moral of that question is that there will always be people entrenched in old beliefs no matter how many hours of education you may provide them. The abstinence-only model is still pervasive, and you will receive criticism as a clinician who teaches moderation.

Many treatment providers and programs have outright disdain for alcohol moderation despite years of research that support its efficacy. I've been called a criminal—on the air—by the medical director of a well-known treatment center. I was invited to speak about harm reduction and alcohol, but he believed his way was the only way of providing treatment.

I've also been told I was incompetent on an internationally known public forum. They had invited me to write a guest post about alcohol moderation, yet one of their members disagreed with my predictions for successful alcohol moderation. This population is so used to being criticized that they could not see me as a supporter despite my being a moderation-friendly therapist.

Three days before I was scheduled to speak at a conference sponsored by a national treatment program, I was asked to leave out the moderation portion in my presentation. They had their education program director call me to say that they did not want to confuse their clinicians with other approaches. In order to enter their program, clients had to admit that they were "alcoholics." When I arrived, they tried to move me to the afternoon session so fewer people would be in attendance and realized that they removed the lines of my biography from the program that mentioned anything about my previous book or moderation. Prior to my going on stage, a woman checked my PowerPoint presentation as if I was a naughty child, not an expert with almost three decades of experience. I was so shocked and offended that I almost did not speak. But I decided that it was more important for me to educate their clinicians. Little did they know that I have been presenting for so long that I do not need a slide show to speak. I taught them about alcohol moderation and just avoided the glares from the table where their administrators were.

I can't count how many conferences have turned down my application to speak about alcohol moderation. Their response is, "there is not enough scientific evidence to support your claims." Next time I will send them Chapter 1 that has over 50 years' worth of data. Many times when I do present, I am often the only one speaking about harm reduction and alcohol moderation in a four-day conference.

I share some of these stories to demonstrate the challenges you may face. Are you ready to be a criminal and practice alcohol moderation? It can be fun to be a rebel. It is even more amazing to get people the right kind of treatment to lead healthier, happier lives.

Questions

Do you have a question I did not answer? I would love to hear from you. You can email me at cturner@canIkeepdrinking.com.

Notes

1. P. Sharma, P. Murthy & M. M. S. Bharath (2012). Chemistry, metabolism, and toxicology of cannabis: Clinical implications. *Iranian Journal of Psychiatry.* 7(4): 149–156.
2. M. A. ElSohly, Z. Mehmedic, S. Foster, C. Gon, S. Chandra & J. C. Church (2016). Changes in cannabis potency over the last two decades (1995–2014)—analysis of current data in the United States. *Biological Psychiatry.* 79(7): 613–619. DOI: 10.1016/j.biopsych.2016.01.004.
3. U. S. Food and Drug Administration (2019, June 12). *The drug development process.* Retrieved from www.fda.gov/patients/learn-about-drug-and-device-approvals/drug-development-process.
4. United States Drug Enforcement Administration (2019, June 11). *Drug scheduling.* Retrieved from www.dea.gov/drug-scheduling.
5. D. B. Clark (2004). The natural history of adolescent alcohol use disorders. *Addiction.* 99: 5–22.
6. G. E. Vaillant (2003). A 60-year follow-up of alcoholic men. *Addiction.* 98: 1043–1051.
7. Mayo Clinic (2019, March 11). *Red wine and resveratrol: Good for your heart?* Retrieved from www.mayoclinic.org/diseases-conditions/heart-disease/in-depth/red-wine/art-20048281.
8. P. I. Jatlow, A. Agro, R. Wu, H. Nadim, B. A. Toll, E. Ralevski, C. Nogueira, J. Shi, J. D. Dziura, I. L. Petrakis & S. S. O'Malley (2014). Ethyl glucuronide and ethyl

sulfate assays in clinical trials, interpretation and limitations: Results of a dose ranging alcohol challenge study and two clinical trials. *Alcoholism: Clinical and Experimental Research.* DOI: 10.1111/acer.12407.

9. A. Gordon, A. Jaffe, T. McLellan, G. Richardson, G. Skipper, M. Sucher, C. F. Tirado & H. C. Urschell (2017). How should remote clinical monitoring be used to treat alcohol use disorders? Initial findings from an expert. Round table discussion. *Journal of Addiction Medicine.* 11(2): 45–153. DOI: 10.1097/ADM.0000000000000288.

15 Alcohol Moderation Resources

This final chapter outlines moderation-friendly programs and resources that are available throughout the world. Mutual support programs and dry month campaigns are included.

Mutual Support Groups for Alcohol Moderation

For decades AA has been the recommendation of choice for recovery from alcohol-related problems. However, many struggle with the concept of powerlessness and reliance on a Higher Power that is involved with the program. This has been especially difficult for those who do not have a spiritual or religious background.

There are increasing types of mutual support groups worldwide that assist people struggling with drinking. Most still encourage total abstinence, but several have developed for those attempting alcohol moderation. A recent study compared Women for Sobriety, LifeRing, and SMART Recovery.[1] Even though the researchers found less in-person meeting attendance, they found higher levels of satisfaction, participation, and cohesion in these groups compared to the traditional 12-step model of AA. The researchers also noted that these members tended to be older, married, and have less severe psychiatric and alcohol use severity. This is further support for the need of alternatives for individuals struggling with more mild and moderate alcohol use disorders. In this way, they can receive help before their use and consequences progress.

Below are the more established programs and mutual support groups that support alcohol moderation:

Moderation Management
www.moderation.org

Moderation Management (MM) is a lay-lead nonprofit dedicated to reducing the harm caused by the abuse of alcohol.[2] They focus on self-management, balance, moderation, and personal responsibility. The program encourages individuals to accept responsibility for maintaining their own recovery path.

MM promotes early recognition of risky drinking so that moderate drinking is more likely to be achieved. MM was the first moderation-based support group approved by the National Institute on Alcohol Abuse and Alcoholism and is included on SAMHSA's National Registry of Evidence-Based Programs and Practices (NREPP) website.

MM offers a mutual-help environment that encourages people who are concerned about their drinking to take action before drinking problems become severe. They offer a nine-step professionally reviewed program that includes information about alcohol, moderate drinking guidelines, monitoring exercises, goal setting tools, and self-management strategies. In addition, MM provides listings of moderation-friendly therapists, online forums, chat groups, and face-to-face meetings. They also run the Dryuary™ Challenge described later in this chapter.

Hello Sunday Morning
www.hellosundaymorning.org

Hello Sunday Morning (HSM) is an online support community with health campaigns and behavior change programs designed to help people who want to change their relationship to alcohol in a confidential environment.[3] It was started in 2009 by Australian Chris Raine, a nightclub promoter who began blogging about taking a year off from drinking goal. He wrote about how he would wake up each Sunday morning hangover-free, singing "Hello Sunday morning!"

HSM's mission is to change the world's relationship with alcohol. The relationship can be abstaining, taking a break, or understanding how to have a healthy relationship with alcohol. A recent study showed that participation in the HSM program reported a significant decrease in alcohol consumption, leading to decreased hazards.[4] Interestingly, with this program, those who had the highest levels of alcohol use experienced the largest decrease in harm, showing that even those experiencing severe alcohol use disorders may benefit from a moderation program.

In 2010, HSM released the Daybreak app for an annual fee. The app includes a peer support community, habit change experiments, and personal coaching from professionals. Users report a reduction in cravings, which leads to a reduction in alcohol use. The Daybreak Program is currently free for Australian residents, funded by the Australian Government, Department of Health.[5]

HAMS Harm Reduction Network
www.hamsnetwork.org

The HAMS Harm Reduction Network (HAMS) provides information and support for people who wish to reduce the harm in their lives caused by the use of alcohol or drugs.[6] HAMS stands for harm reduction, alcohol abstinence, and moderation support. They support the goals of safer drinking, reduced drinking, or quitting. Participants choose the goal and may switch it at any time. Hamsnetwork.org lists treatment providers who support safer alcohol use and also offers online forums, chat groups, written materials, podcasts, and live meetings. They neither encourage nor condemn alcohol use or alcohol intoxication, but recognize recreational use as a reality and see to reduce harms associated with it. HAMS believes in the autonomy of the individual and supports each individual's choice of a goal regarding their alcohol use.

SMART Recovery
www.smartrecovery.org

SMART Recovery is a self-empowering addiction-recovery support group. SMART stands for "self-management and recovery training."[7] They offer meetings around the world, including the United States, Canada, Denmark, Australia, Ireland, and the United Kingdom. Participants learn to use tools based on the latest scientific research and attend self-help groups. SMART offers a four-point program with tools and techniques for each. This includes building and maintaining motivation; coping with urges; managing thoughts, feelings, and behaviors; and living a balanced life. SMART is typically for those wanting to achieve abstinence, but people wanting to try moderation are still invited to participate.

Smartrecovery.org lists people who have completed 30 hours of training on SMART recovery principles, offers online resources, maintains lists of local meetings, and sponsors an online community. A recent study found that SMART helped to reduce the severity and consequences of problematic alcohol use.[8]

Alcohol Moderation Programs

CheckUp & Choices

Research shows that people tend to be more honest about their alcohol consumption when they have the anonymity of a computer.[9] Other advantages of using an internet-based program are that they are affordable, easy to access at any time, without having to get to a meeting. While it is hard to replace the face-to-face interaction with a professionally trained therapist or the in-person support from a group, apps can be a helpful supplement. It is important that you know what you are getting from it. Look for ones that are evidence-based. One of the few that has been researched, studied, and peer-reviewed is CheckUp & Choices.[10]

Reid Hester, PhD, cofounded CheckUp & Choices with Canton Burtwell. Their goal was to help individuals and organizations realize their potential by helping them reduce alcohol and drug problems. They developed the web-based program to be used on any internet device. The program is listed as an evidence-based program by the Substance Abuse and Mental Health Services Administration.[11]

The first phase, called CheckUps, includes a confidential alcohol self-assessment where participants receive feedback on their responses. The second phase, Choices, is a 3- to 12-month program and can be used for those who wish to abstain from alcohol as well as those who want to moderate. Individuals receive motivational exercises, drink, mood and urge trackers, guided emails, and change plans.

Seeking Safety

Lisa Najavits, PhD, developed Seeking Safety in the early 1990s with grant funding from the National Institute on Drug Abuse.[12] It is an evidence-based model that helps people attain safety from trauma and/or substance use by developing coping skills without having to delve in the past. Numerous research studies show that there is a strong comorbidity between substance use and experiencing trauma.[13]

Seeking Safety is present-focused and engages clients in a safe, optimistic way. The model is flexible and can be used in individual and group format and for all ages and genders in a variety of settings. Topics include setting boundaries, nurturing the self, developing honesty, creating meaning, and coping with triggers.

Dry Month Campaigns

Researchers in Europe have found rapid growth in people's participation in dry month campaigns.[14] Overall, Australia currently has the most available. These campaigns ask participations to commit to a month of being alcohol-free. Some raise money for public health concerns like cancer, while others focus on health benefits and offer education, motivation, and support. All have a form of warning that if an individual is a daily drinker of more than five alcoholic beverages, they should consult a medical professional as they might be at risk of withdrawals. Some of the most popular dry month campaigns are reviewed in this section.

Box matter 15.1

DID YOU KNOW? Withdrawal from alcohol can kill you. Many people mistakenly believe that coming off painkillers, stimulants, or heroin can be fatal. It generally is not. These withdrawals are extremely painful, with the acute symptoms lasting for several days, possibly up to a week. Alcohol is a central nervous system depressant. CNS depressants, often referred to as sedatives or tranquilizers, slow brain activity. This is why when people drink, they feel more relaxed and do not filter their thoughts, actions, or words as well. When a person no longer has alcohol in the body, the CNS begins to experience a rebound effect that can result in potentially life-threatening complications related to the heart, breathing, seizure, kidney, or liver.[15]

Dryuary™ Challenge

The Dryuary™ Challenge is an outreach program put out by Moderation Management. It is "all about Not Drinking in January." Experts, as well as Moderation Management forum members, post daily articles with inspirational quotes and music. Their goal is to offer a supportive environment for taking a month-long break from alcohol. For the first time, the Moderation Management team put together the *Dryuary 2019 Collection* that includes all of the posts so that people can receive support any time of the year. All proceeds go to support Moderation Management and future Dryuary campaigns.[16] I was proud to be an invited contributor.

Dry January

Dry January is a public health campaign started by Alcohol Concern, a British charity whose aim is to reduce the harms caused by alcohol.[17] They encourage a month without alcohol and offer education, online articles, and supportive postings throughout the month. Dry January has found to have significant improvements on lives, including reduced weight, increased energy, saved money, and improved sleep. Of greatest significance is that participants continued to reduce their alcohol intake for the following months after participating.[18]

Dry Feb

Dry Feb is a Canadian fundraiser that challenges its participants to be alcohol-free for the month of February.[19] The funds go to the Canadian Cancer Society. They focus on getting healthy and clearing your head while raising money for an important cause. In addition to the money raised and numerous health effects of a month off from alcohol, over 75% of their participants said they would drink less in the future.

febfast

febfast is an Australian program that asks participants to "pause for a cause." They take a month-long break from alcohol, sugar, and anything of your choice to raise money for disadvantaged youth.[20] It has been in existence since 2007, raising over $9 million and reporting over 14 million indulgence free days.

Dry July

Dry July is another fundraising campaign in Australia.[21] It started in 2008 by three friends who wanted to take a break from alcohol. They describe an easy four-step process: (1) sign up for the challenge, (2) go alcohol-free throughout July, (3) ask friends and family to sponsor you, and (4) raise money for cancer. The Dry July campaign has had outstanding success, raising over $37 million for people affected by cancer thus far.

Ocsober

Ocsober is run by Life Education in Australia.[22] Their goal is to raise awareness and funds to educate and empower the next generation of Australians. They report that one out of eight deaths for those under age 25 can be attributed to alcohol consumption. For over a decade Ocsober has been asking its participants to "lose the booze" for the month of October.

Go Sober for October

Go Sober for October is a program run in the United Kingdom.[23] Tens of thousands of "Soberheroes" commit to going alcohol-free for the month of October. Thus far they have raised almost $5 million for Macmillan Cancer support and report the health benefits of taking a month off from drinking.

Final Thought

Even though abstinence remains the traditional recommendation, there are many groups and programs that support alcohol moderation. It is encouraging to see that moderation is becoming an alternative to the status quo. My hope is that you now have the training and tools to confidently teach the harm reduction strategy of alcohol moderation to your clients. You now have the power to get the right kind of treatment to help those who are struggling with their alcohol use.

Notes

1. S. E. Zenmore, L. A. Kaskutas, A. Mericle & J. Hemberg (2017, February). Comparison of 12-step groups to mutual help alternatives for AUD in a large, national study: Differences in membership characteristics and group participation, cohesion, and satisfaction. *Journal of Substance Abuse Treatment.* 73: 16–26.
2. Moderation Management (2019, June 14). *What is moderation management?* Retrieved from www.moderation.org/about_mm/whatismm.html.
3. J. Elisabeth (2015). Hello Sunday morning: A different kind of online recovery community. *The Fix.* Retrieved from www.thefix.com/interview-chris-raine-founder-hello-sunday-morning-alternative-aa.

4. J. J. L. Kirkman, B. Leo & J. C. Moore (2018). Alcohol consumption reduction among a web-based supportive community using the hello Sunday morning blog platform: Observational study. *Journal of Medical Internet Research*. 20(5): e196. DOI: 10.2196/jmir.9605.

5. S. Parnell (2017). Hello Sunday morning helps build healthy relationships with drink. *The Weekend Australian*. Retrieved from www.theaustralian.com.au/life/hello-sunday-morning-helps-build-healthy-relationships-with-drink/news-story/dc75544a78d84b9ba504243ba3bfa9d2.

6. K. Anderson (2010). *How to change your drinking: A harm reduction guide to alcohol* (2nd ed.). New York: The HAMS Harm Reduction Network.

7. SMART Recovery (2019, June 14). *Sensible tools for addiction recovery*. Retrieved from www.smartrecovery.org/#.

8. A. K. Beck, E. Forbes, A. L. Baker, P. J. Kelly, F. P. Deane, A. Shakeshaft, D. Hunt & J. F. Kelly (2017). Systematic review of SMART recovery: Outcomes, process variable, and implications for research. *Psychology of Addictive Behaviors*. 31(1): 1–20. DOI: 10.1037/adb0000237.

9. J. Milward, Z. Khadjesari, S. Fincham-Campbell, P. Deluca, R. Watson & C. Drummond (2016). User preferences for content, features, and style for an app to reduce harmful drinking in young adults: Analysis of user feedback in app Stores and focus group interviews. *JMIR mHealth and uHealth*. 4(2): e47. DOI: 10.2196/mhealth.5242.

10. E. Williams (2016, October 8). Navigating the world of apps that claim to fix your drinking problem. *NPR*. Retrieved from www.npr.org/sections/alltechconsidered/2016/10/08/496742219/navigating-the-world-of-apps-that-claim-to-fix-your-drinking-problem.

11. R. K. Hester, H. D. Delaney & W. Campbell (2011). ModerateDrinking.Com and moderation management: Outcomes of a randomized clinical trial with non-dependent problem drinkers. *Journal of Consulting and Clinical Psychology*. 79(2): 215–224. DOI: 10.1037/a0022487.

12. L. Najavits (2001). *Seeking safety: A treatment manual for PTSD and substance abuse*. New York: The Guilford Press.

13. L. M. Najavits & D. Hien (2013). Helping vulnerable populations: A comprehensive review of the treatment outcome literature on substance use disorder and PTSD. *Journal of Clinical Psychology: In Session*. 69(5): 433–479. DOI: 10.1002/jclp.21980.

14. R. O. De Visser, E. Robinson, T. Smith, G. Cass & M. Walmsley (2017, October 1). *Eur Journal of Public Health*. 27(5): 929–931. DOI: 10.1093/eurpub/ckx124.

15. L. A. Trevisan, N. Boutrous, I. L. Petrakis & J. H. Krystal (1998). Complications of alcohol withdrawal: Pathophysiological insights. *Alcohol Health & Research World*. 22(1): 61–66.

16. Moderation Management (2019). *Dryuary 2019 collection: Inspirational posts and expert advice for a month of abstinence from alcohol*. Grandville, MI: Moderation Management Network, Inc.

17. University of Sussex (2018). How "Dry January" is the secret to better sleep, saving money and losing weight. *ScienceDaily*. Retrieved from www.sciencedaily.com/releases/2018/12/181228164834.htm.

18. B. Bold (2015). Government launches "Dry January" push with "Booze Black Friday" warning. *Campaign*. Retrieved from www.campaignlive.com/article/government-launches-dry-january-push-booze-black-friday-warning/1377544.

19. Dry Feb (2019, June 13). Retrieved from www.dryfeb.ca.

20. Feb Fast (2019, June 13). Retrieved from www.febfast.org.au.

21. Dry July Foundation (2019, June 13). Retrieved from www.dryjuly.com/about.

22. Life Education (2019, June 13). Retrieved from www.lifeeducation.org.au/support-us/ocsober.

23. A. Fleming (2018). Alcohol-free months are all the rage—but will a sober October lead to long-term health benefits? *The Guardian*. Retrieved from www.theguardian.com/lifeandstyle/2018/sep/17/alcohol-free-months-are-all-the-rage-but-will-a-sober-october-lead-to-long-term-health-benefits.

References

Al-Anon Family Headquarters, Inc. (2019, May 30). Retrieved from https://al-anon. org/newcomers/what-is-al-anon-and-alateen/.

Alcohol in Moderation. (2018, Updated September). *Sensible drinking guidelines.* Retrieved from www.drinkingandyou.com/site/pdf/Sensibledrinking.pdf.

Allen, J., Mohatt, G. V., Fok, C. C. T., Henry, D., & Burkett, R. (2014, June 21). A protective factors model for alcohol abuse and suicide prevention among Alaska native youth. *The American Journal of Community Psychology.* 54: 125–139. DOI: 10.1007/s10464-014-9661-3.

Almendrai, A. (2018, April 14). Alcohol companies are funding research to convince you drinking is healthy. *Huffington Post.* Retrieved from www.huffpost.com/entry/alcohol-companies-want-you-to-drink-more-and-theyre-funding-research-to-make-it-happen_n_5ad123bce4b077c89ce8a835.

Amato, F. M., & Davioli, M. (2006). Alcoholics anonymous and other 12-step programmes for alcohol dependence. *Cochran Database of Systemic Reviews.* (3). Art. No:CD005032. DOI: 10.1002/14651858.CD005032.pub2.

American Academy of Experts in Traumatic Stress website. (2016, December 14). *Effects of parental substance abuse on children and families.* Retrieved from www.aaets.org/article230.htm.

American Heart Association. (2014, August 15). *Alcohol and heart health.* Retrieved from www.heart.org/en/healthy-living/healthy-eating/eat-smart/nutrition-basics/alcohol-and-heart-health.

American Psychiatric Association. (2013). *Diagnostic and statistical manual of mental disorders* (5th ed.). Washington, DC: American Psychiatric Association.

American Society of Addiction Medicine. (2011, August 15). *Public policy statement: Definition of addiction.* Retrieved from www.asam.org/resources/definition-of-addiction.

American Society of Addiction Medicine. (2013). *American society of addiction medicine releases new treatment criteria, modernizing care for addictive disorders* [Press Release]. Retrieved from www.asam.org/docs/default-source/pressreleases/asam-releases-new-treatment-criteria_2013-10-25.

American Society of Addiction Medicine Board of Directors. (2011, August 15). *Public policy statement: Short definition of addiction.* Chevy Chase, MD: ASAM.

Anderson, K. (2010). *How to change your drinking: A harm reduction guide to alcohol* (2nd ed.). New York: The HAMS Harm Reduction Network.

Andréasson, S., Chikritzhs, T., Dangardt, F., Holder, H., Naimi, T., & Stockwell, T. (2014). Evidence about health effects of "moderate" alcohol consumption: Reasons for skepticism and public health implications. In *Alcohol and society.* Stockholm: IOGT-NTO & Swedish Society of Medicine.

Arackal, S. B., & Benegal, V. (2007). Prevalence of sexual dysfunction in male subjects with alcohol dependence. *Indian Journal of Psychiatry.* 49(2): 109–112.

Armor, D. J., Polich, M. J., & Braiker, H. B. (1976). *Alcoholism and treatment.* Santa Monica, CA: RAND Corporation.

Aron, A., Norman, C., Aron, E., McKenna, C., & Heyman, R. (2000). Couples' shared participation in novel and arousing activities and experienced relationship quality. *Social Psychology.* 78(2): 273–284. DOI: 10.1037//0022-3514.78.2.273.

Aubrey, A. (2015, March 23). Rethinking alcohol: Can heavy drinkers learn to cut back? *NPR.* Retrieved from www.npr.org/sections/health-shots/2015/03/23/393651417/ rethinking-alcohol-can-heavy-drinkers-learn-to-cut-back.

Bajekal, N. (2018, August 1). Want to win the war on drugs: Portugal might have the answer. *Time* magazine. Retrieved from https://time.com/longform/portugal-drug-use-decriminalization/.

Banerjee, N. (2014). Neurotransmitters in alcoholism: A review of neurobiological and genetic studies. *Indian Journal of Human Genetics.* 20(1): 20–31. DOI: 10.4103/0971-6866.132750.

BBC News. (2016, January 8). New alcohol guidelines: What you need to know. Retrieved from www.bbc.com/news/uk-35252650.

Beattie, M. (1992). *Codependent no more: How to stop controlling others and start caring for yourself.* Center City, MN: Hazelden.

Beck, A. K., Forbes, E., Baker, A. L., Kelly, P. J., Deane, F. P., Shakeshaft, A., Hunt, D., & Kelly, J. F. (2017). Systematic review of SMART recovery: Outcomes, process variable, and implications for research. *Psychology of Addictive Behaviors.* 31(1): 1–20. DOI: 10.1037/adb0000237.

Bold, B. (2015). Government launches "Dry January" push with "Booze Black Friday" warning. *Campaign.* Retrieved from www.campaignlive.com/article/government-launches-dry-january-push-booze-black-friday-warning/1377544.

Bombardier, C. H., & Turner, A. (2009). Alcohol and traumatic disability. In R. Frank & T. Elliott (Eds.), *The handbook of rehabilitation psychology* (2nd ed., pp. 241–258). Washington, DC: American Psychological Association Press.

Bowen, S., Chawla, N., & Marlatt, G. A. (2011). *Mindfulness-based relapse prevention for addictive behaviors: A clinician's guide.* New York: The Guilford Press.

Brady, K. T., & Back, S. E. (2012). Childhood trauma, posttraumatic stress disorder, and alcohol dependence. *Alcohol Research: Current Reviews.* 34(4): 408–413.

Braham, D. (2018). Daphne Bramham: Decriminalization is no silver bullet, says Portugal's drug czar. *Vancouver Sun.* Retrieved from https://vancouversun.com/opinion/columnists/daphne-bramham-decriminalization-is-no-silver-bullet-says-portugals-drug-czar.

Braiker, H. B., & Polich, M. J. (1977). *Some implications of the RAND alcoholism and treatment study for alcoholism research.* Santa Monica, CA: RAND Corporation.

Brody, J. E. (1980, January 30). Drinking problem dispute. *New York Times,* p. 20.

Brown, B. (2015). *Rising strong: How the ability to reset transforms the way we live, love, parent, and lead.* New York: Penguin.

Bush, B., & Hudson, T. (2010). The role of cortisol in sleep. *Natural Medicine Journal.* 2(6).

Byrne, S. P., Haber, P., Baillie, A. B., Costa, D. S. J., Fogliati, V., & Morley, K. (2019, March). Systematic reviews of mindfulness and acceptance and commitment therapy for alcohol use disorder: Should we be using Third wave therapies? *Alcohol and Alcoholism.* 54(2): 159–166. https://doi.org/10.1093/alcalc/agy089.

Cains, S., et al. (2017). Agrp neuron activity is required for alcohol-induced overeating. *Nature Communications.* 8: 14014. DOI: 10.1038/ncomms14014.

Carroll, A. E. (2018, August 28). Study causes splash, but here's why you should stay calm on alcohol's risks. *New York Times.*

Cederbaum, A. I. (2012). Alcohol metabolism. *Clinical Liver Disease.* 16(4): 667–685. DOI: 10.1016/j.cld.2012.08.002.

Center for Behavioral Health Statistics and Quality. (2015). *Behavioral health trends in the United States: Results from the 2014 national survey on drug use and health* (HHS Publication No. SMA 15–4927, NSDUH Series H-50). Retrieved from www.samhsa.gov/data/.

Centers for Disease Control. (2016). *Fact sheets-excessive alcohol use and men.* Atlanta, GA. Retrieved from www.cdc.gov/alcohol/fact-sheets/mens-health.htm.

Centers for Disease Control and Prevention. (2016). *Fact sheets: Excessive alcohol use and risks to women's health.* Atlanta: GA. Retrieved from www.cdc.gov/alcohol/fact-sheets/womens-health.htm.

Centers for Disease Control and Prevention. (2018, October 24). *Fact sheet: Binge drinking.* Retrieved from www.cdc.gov/alcohol/fact-sheets/binge-drinking.htm.

Cheng, Y. Y. B., & Staduinger, U. M. (2018). Novelty processing at work and cognitive aging: Evidence from the health and retirement study and MIDUS. *Innovation in Aging.* 2(1). https://doi.org/10.1093/geroni/igy023.1585.

Chiao-Chicy Chen & Shih-Jiun Yin. (2008). Alcohol abuse and related factors in Asia. *International Review of Psychiatry.* 20(5): 425–433. DOI: 10.1080/09540260802344075.

Chowdhury, P., & Gupta, P. (2006). Pathology of alcoholic pancreatitis: An overview. *World Journal of Gastroenterology.* 12(46): 7421–7427. DOI: 10.3748/wjg.v12.i46.7421.

Christian, C. (2016, April 29). TEDx London Business School: How I overcame alcoholism. Retrieved from https://www.youtube.com/watch?v=6EghiY_s2ts.

Clapp, P. C., Bhave, S. V., & Hoffman, P. L. (2009). *How adaptation of the brain to alcohol leads to dependence: A pharmacological perspective.* National Institute of Alcohol Abuse and Alcoholism. Retrieved from https://pubs.niaaa.nih.gov/publications/arh314/310-339.htm.

Clark, D. B. (2004). The natural history of adolescent alcohol use disorders. *Addiction.* 99: 5–22.

Commander, U.S. 2nd Fleet. (2011, March 14). 0-0-1-3 formula keeps alcohol-related incidents at bay. Story Number: NNS110314-10.

Cornett, D. (2005). *7 weeks to safe social drinking: How to effectively moderate your alcohol intake.* Santa Rosa, CA: People Friendly Books.

Cutler, R., & Fishbian, D. A. (2005). Are alcoholism treatments effective? The Project MATCH data. *BMC Public Health.* 5(75). https://doi.org/10.1186/1471-2458-5-75.

Davis, C. P., & Shiel, W. C. Jr. (2019, March 7.) Liver blood tests (normal, low, and high ranges & results). *MedicineNet.* Retrieved from www.medicinenet.com/liver_blood_tests/article.htm#what_are_the_basic_functions_of_the_liver.

David, W. C., & Globetti, G. (1986). Alcohol use and alcoholism in Latin America: Changing patterns and sociocultural explanations. *International Journal of the Addictions.* 21(1): 59–81. DOI: 10.3109/10826088609063438.

Dawson, D. A. (1996). Correlates of past-year status among treated and untreated persons with former alcohol dependence: United States. *Alcoholism: Clinical and Experimental Research.* 20(4): 771–779.

Dean, N. (2018). The importance of novelty. *Brain World.* Retrieved from https://brainworldmagazine.com/the-importance-of-novelty/.

Denning, P., & Little, J. (2012). *Practicing harm reduction psychotherapy: An alternative approach to addictions* (2nd ed.). New York: The Guilford Press.

Denning, P., & Little, J. (2017). *Over the influence: The harm reduction guide to controlling your drug and alcohol use* (2nd ed.). New York: The Guilford Press.

Department of Health and Human Services. (2017, January 18). Rules and regulations. *Federal Registrar.* 82(11).

Dermota, P., Wang, J., Dey, M., Gmel, G., Studer, J., & Mohler-Kuo, M. (2013). Health literacy and substance use in young Swiss men. *International Journal of Public Health.* 58(6): 939–948.

De Visser, R. O., Robinson, E., Smith, T., Cass, G., & Walmsley, M. (2017, October 1). *European Journal of Public Health.* 27(5): 929–931. DOI: 10.1093/eurpub/ckx124.

Dodes, L., & Dodes, Z. (2015). *The sober truth: Debunking the bad science behind 12-step programs and the rehab industry.* Boston, MA: Beacon Press.

Drinkaware. (2019, June 1). *Alcohol and mental health.* Retrieved from www.drinkaware.co.uk/alcohol-facts/health-effects-of-alcohol/mental-health/alcohol-and-mental-health/.

Drug and Alcohol Information and Support. (2019, May 31). Retrieved from www.drugs.ie/alcohol_info/worried_about_someone1/what_can_i_do_to_help/.

Dry Feb. (2019, June 13). Retrieved from www.dryfeb.ca.

Dry July Foundation. (2019, June 13). Retrieved from www.dryjuly.com/about.

Edenberg, H. J. (2003, June). *The collaborative study on the genetics of alcoholism: An update.* Bethesda, MD: National Institute on Alcohol Abuse and Alcoholism.

Egelko, B. (2007, September 8). Appeals court say requirement to attend AA unconstitutional. *San Francisco Chronicle.* Retrieved from https://www.sfgate.com/bayarea/article/Appeals-court-says-requirement-to-attend-AA-2542005.php.

Elisabeth, J. (2015). Hello Sunday morning: A different kind of online recovery community. *The Fix.* Retrieved from www.thefix.com/interview-chris-raine-founder-hello-sunday-morning-alternative-aa.

ElSohly, M. A., Mehmedic, Z., Foster, S., Gon, C., Chandra, S., & Church, J. C. (2016). Changes in cannabis potency over the last two decades (1995–2014)—analysis of current data in the United States. *Biological Psychiatry.* 79(7): 613–619. DOI: 10.1016/j.biopsych.2016.01.004.

Emerson, M. A., Moore, R. S., & Caetano, R. (2019). Correlates of alcohol-related treatment among American Indians and Alaska natives with lifetime alcohol use disorder. *Alcoholism: Clinical and Experimental Research.* 43(1): 115–122. http://dx.doi.org/10.1111/acer.13907.

Esser, M. B., Hedden, S. L., Kanny, D., Brewer, R. D., Gfroerer, J. C., & Naimi, J. C. (2014). Prevalence of alcohol dependence among US adult drinkers, 2009–2001. *Preventing Chronic Disease.* 11: 140329. http://dx.doi.org/10.5888/pcd11.140329.

Evans, S. M., & Levin, F. R. (2011). Response to alcohol in women: Role of the menstrual cycle and a family history of alcoholism. *Drug and Alcohol Dependence.* 114(1). DOI: 10.1016/j.drugalcdep.2010.09.001.

Facing Addiction with NCAAD. (2019, May 2). *Facts about alcohol.* Retrieved from www.facingaddiction.org/resources/facts-about-alcohol.

Fairbarn, C. E., Sayette, M. A., Aalen, O. O., & Frigressi, A. (2015). Alcohol and emotional contagion: An examination of the spreading of smiles in male and female drinking groups. *Clinical Psychological Science.* 3(5). https://doi.org/10.1177/2167702614548892.

Falcone, T. J. (2003). *Alcoholism: A disease of speculation.* Amsterdam, NY: Baldwin Research Institute.

Feb Fast. (2019, June 13). Retrieved from www.febfast.org.au.

Felitti, V. J., Anda, R. F., Nordenberg, D., Williamson, D. F., Spitz, A. M., Edwards, V., Koss, M. P., & Marks, J. S. (1998). Relationship of childhood abuse and household dysfunction to many of the leading causes of death in adults. *American Journal of Preventative Medicine.* 14(4): 245–258. https://doi.org/10.1016/S0749-3797(98)00017-8.

Fernandez, J. (2018). *Power over addiction: A harm reduction workbook for changing your relationship to drugs.* San Francisco, CA: Invisible Work Press.

Fleming, A. (2018). Alcohol-free months are all the rage—but will a sober October lead to long-term health benefits? *The Guardian.* Retrieved from www.theguardian.com/lifeandstyle/2018/sep/17/alcohol-free-months-are-all-the-rage-but-will-a-sober-october-lead-to-long-term-health-benefits.

Fouquereau, E., Fernandez, A., Mullet, E., & Sorum, P. C. (2003, June). Stress and the urge to drink. *Addictive Behaviors.* 28(4): 669–685. https://doi.org/10.1016/S0306-4603(01)00276-3.

From Grief to Action. (2018). When addiction hits home: Coping kit (4th ed.). Vancouver: FGTA.

General Service Office of Alcoholics Anonymous. (2019, April 23). *Historical data: The birth of A.A. and its growth in the U.S./Canada.* Retrieved from www.aa.org/pages/en_US/historical-data-the-birth-of-aa-and-its-growth-in-the-uscanada.

Glaser, G. (2015, April). The irrationality of alcoholics anonymous. *The Atlantic.* Retrieved from https://www.theatlantic.com/magazine/archive/2015/04/the-irrationality-of-alcoholics-anonymous/386255/.

Glaser, G. (2017, December 29). America, can we talk about your drinking? *New York Times Opinion.*

Gordon, A., Jaffe, A., McLellan, T., Richardson, G., Skipper, G., Sucher, M., Tirado, C. F., & Urschell, H. C. (2017). How should remote clinical monitoring be used to treat alcohol use disorders? Initial findings from and expert. Round table discussion. *Journal of Addiction Medicine.* 11(2): 45–153. DOI: 10.1097/ADM.0000000000000288.

Grandiean, P. (2016). Paracelsus revisited: The dose concept in a complex world. *Basic and Clinical Pharmacology and Toxicology.* 119(2): 126–132. DOI: 10.1111/bcpt.12622.

Grant, B. F. (1997). Prevalence and correlates of alcohol use and DSM-IV alcohol dependent in the United States: Results of the national longitudinal alcohol epidemiologic survey. *Journal of Studies on Alcohol.* 58(5): 464–473.

Grant, B. F., & Dawson, D. A. (1997). Age of onset of alcohol use and its association with DSM-IV alcohol use and dependence. Results from the national longitudinal alcohol epidemiological survey. *Journal of Substance Abuse.* 9: 103–110.

Griffin, K. (2010). Interview with G. Alan Marlatt: Surfing the urge. *Inquiring Mind.* 26(2).

Griswold, M. G., Fullman, N., Hawley, C., Arian, N., Zimsen, S., Tymeson, H. D., Venkateswaran, V., Tapp, A. D., Forouzanfar, M., Salama, J. S., Abate, K., Abate, D., Abay, S., Abbafati, C., Suliankatchi, R., Zegeye, A., Aboyans, V., Abrar, M. M., & Acharya, P. (2018). Alcohol use and burden for 195 countries and territories, 1990–2016: A systematic analysis for the global burden of disease study 2016. *Lancet.* 392: 1015–1035.

Hall, C. W., & Webster, R. E. (2007). Risk factors among adult children of alcoholics. *International Journal of Behavioral Consultation and Therapy.* 3(4): 494–511. http://dx.doi.org/10.

Hanson, D. J. (2019, April 16). *E. M. Jellinek: Disease theory of alcoholism promoter: Crook & liar?* Retrieved from www.alcoholproblemsandsolutions.org/e-m-jellinek-disease-theory-alcoholism-promoter/.

Hanson, D. J. (2019, April 17). *Beginnings of temperance in America.* Retrieved from www. alcoholproblemsandsolutions.org/beginnings-of-temperance-in-america/.

Hari, J. (2015). *Chasing the scream: The first and last days of the war on drugs.* New York: Bloomsbury Publishing.

Harm Reduction Coalition. (2011). Edith Springer: Goddess of harm reduction. *Interview.* Retrieved from http://harmreduction.org/publication-type/podcast/forty-two/.

Hasin, D. S., Stinson, F. S., Ogburn, E., &Grant, B. F. (2007). Prevalence, correlates, disability, and comorbidity of DSM-IV alcohol abuse and dependence in the United States: Results from the national epidemiologic survey on alcohol and related conditions. *Archives of General Psychiatry.* 64(7): 830–842.

Hastings, G., Stead, M., & Webb, J. (2004). Fear appeals in social marketing: Strategic and ethical reasons for concern. *Psychology and Marketing.* 21(11): 961–986.

Herrine, S. K. (2018, January). Liver structure and function. *Merck manual professional version.* Retrieved from www.merckmanuals.com/professional/hepatic-and-biliary-disorders/approach-to-the-patient-with-liver-disease/liver-structure-and-functi on/?msclkid=2382e46601c815879deeb8e4bc76ef56&utm_source=bing&utm_ medium=cpc&utm_campaign=EDL_MERCKUSA_Hepatic%20and%20Bil iary%20Disorders-C-S_SE_SEM_N_MIX_NTL_US_EN_M&utm_term=what%20 is%20liver%20function%20test&utm_content=Liver%20Structure%20and%20 Function%20(Exact).

Hesse, M. (2006). The readiness ruler as a measure of readiness to change poly-drug use in drug abusers. *Harm Reduction Journal.* 3(3). DOI: 10.1186/1477-7517-3-3.

Hester, R. K., Delaney, H. D., & Campbell, W. (2011). ModerateDrinking.Com and moderation management: Outcomes of a randomized clinical trial with non-dependent problem drinkers. *Journal of Consulting Clinical Psychology.* 79(2): 215–224. DOI: 10.1037/a0022487.

Hester, R. K., Lenberg, K. L., Campbell, W., & Delaney, H. D. D. (2016). Overcoming addictions, a web-based application, and SMART recovery, an online and in-person mutual help group for problem drinkers, Part 2 six-month outcomes of a randomized controlled trial and qualitative analyses. *Journal of Medical Internet Research.* Retrieved from www.jmir.org/2013/7/e134.

Hester, R. K., & Miller, W. R. (2002). *Handbook of alcoholism treatment approaches: Effective alternative* (3rd ed.). Needham Heights, MA: Allyn & Bacon.

Hester, R. K., & Miller, W. R. (2003). *Handbook of alcoholism treatment approaches: Effective alternatives* (pp. 148–159). Needham Heights, MA: Allyn & Bacon.

Hodgson, R. (1979, October). Much ado about nothing much: Alcoholism treatment and the rand report. *The British Journal of Addiction to Alcohol and Other Drugs.* 74(3): 227–234. DOI: 10.1111/j.1360-0443.1979.tb01343.x.

Horvath, G. (Producer) & Finberg, A. (Director). (2015). *The Bu$iness of recovery.* United States.

Huebner, R. B., & Kantor, L. (2011). Advances in alcoholism treatment. *Alcohol Research and Health.* 33(4): 295–299.

Institute for Behavior and Health, Inc. (2014). *Creating a new standard for addiction treatment outcomes.* Rockville, MD: A report from the Institute for Behavior and Health, Inc.

Institute of Medicine (IOM) (1990). *Broadening the base of treatment for alcohol problems: Report of a study by a committee of the institute of medicine, division of mental health and behavioral medicine.* Washington, DC: National Academy Press.

Jaffe, A. (2018). *The abstinence myth: A new approach for overcoming addiction without shame, judgement, or rules.* Los Angeles, CA: IGNTD Press.

Jatlow, P. I., Agro, A., Wu, R., Nadim, H., Toll, B. A., Ralevski, E., Nogueira, C., Shi, J., Dziura, J. D., Petrakis, I. L., & O'Malley, S. S. (2014). Ethyl glucuronide and ethyl sulfate assays in clinical trials, interpretation and limitations: Results of a dose ranging alcohol challenge study and two clinical trials. *Alcoholism Clinical and Experimental Research.* DOI: 10.1111/acer.12407.

Johnston, L. D., O'Malley, P. M., Bachman, J. G., & Schulenberg, J. E. (2007). *Monitoring the future: National results on adolescent drug use: Overview of key findings, 2006.* Bethesda, MD: National Institute on Drug Abuse.

Kadam, M., Sinha, A., Nimkar, S., Matcheswalla, Y., & De Sousa, A. (2017). A comparative study of factors associated with relapse in alcohol dependence and opioid dependence. *Indian Journal Psychological Medicine.* 39(5): 627–633. DOI: 10.4103/IJP-SYM.IJPSYM_356_17.

Keller, M., & Valliant, G. E. (2019, April 24). Alcoholism. *Encyclopedia Britannica.* Retrieved from www.britannica.com/science/alcoholism.

Khooury, L., Tang, Y. L., Bradley, B., Cubells, J. F., & Ressler, K. J. (2010, December). Substance use, childhood traumatic experience, and post traumatic stress disorder in an urban civilian population. *Depression and Anxiety.* 27(12): 1077–1086.

Kirkman, J. J. L., Leo, B., & Moore, J. C. (2018). Alcohol consumption reduction among a web-based supportive community using the hello Sunday morning blog platform: Observational study. *Journal of Medical Internet Research.* 20(5): e196. DOI: 10.2196/jmir.9605.

Kodjak, A. (2016, June 16). Inventors see big opportunities in opioid addiction treatment. *NPR.* Retrieved from www.npr.org/sections/health-shots/2016/06/10/480663056/investors-see-big-opportunities-in-opioid-addiction-treatment.

Kranzler, H. R., Tennen, H., Armeli, S., Chan, G., Covault, J., Aria, A., & Oncken, C. (2009). Targeted naltrexone for problem drinkers. *Journal of Clinical Psychopharmacology.* 29(4): 350–357. DOI: 10.1097/JCP.0b013e3181ac5213.

Laslett, A., Catalano, P., Chikritzhs, T., Dale, C., Doran, C., Ferris, J., Jainullabudeen, T., Livingston, M., Matthews, S., Mugavin, J., Room, R., Schlotterlein, M., & Wilkinson, C. (2010). *The range and magnitude of alcohol's harm to others.* Fitzroy, Victoria: AER Centre for Alcohol Policy Research, Turning Point Alcohol and Drug Centre, Eastern Health.

Lesser, L. I., Ebbeling, C. B., Goozner, M., Wypij, D., & Ludwig, D. S. (2007). Relationship between funding source and conclusion among nutrition-related scientific articles. *PLoS Medicine.* 4(1): e5. https://doi.org/10.1371/journal.pmed.0040005.

Life Education. (2019, June 13). Retrieved from www.lifeeducation.org.au/support-us/ocsober.

Lincoln, P. (2013, September). *Low-risk drinking guidelines: Where do the numbers come from?* Retrieved from https://ireta.org/resources/low-risk-drinking-guidelines-where-do-the-numbers-come-from/.

Livingston, M., & Callinan, S. (2019). Examining Australia's heaviest drinkers. *Australian and New Zealand Journal of Public Health.* DOI: 10.1111/1753-6405.12901.

MADD. (2019, May 3). *Statistics.* Retrieved from www.madd.org/statistics/.

Mann, K., Aubin, H-J., & Witikiewitz, K. (2017, September 22). Reduced drinking in alcohol dependence treatment, what is the evidence? *European Addiction Research.* 23: 219–230. DOI: 10.1159/000481348.

Marlatt, G. A. (1987). Research and political realities: What the next twenty years hold for behaviorists in the alcohol field. *Advances in Behavior Research and Therapy.* 9(2–3): 165–171. https://doi.org/10.1016/0146-6402(87)90013-0.

Mascia, K. (2019). Parenting with a buzz: When does alcohol as self-care become a problem? *Parents Magazine.* Retrieved from www.parents.com/parenting/better-parenting/style/parenting-with-a-buzz-alcohol-as-self-care/.

Mate, G. (2010). *In the realm of hungry ghosts: Close encounters with addiction.* Berkeley, CA: North American Books.

May, P. A., & Gossage, J. P. (2011). Fetal alcohol spectrum disorders. *Alcohol Research and Health.* 34(1): 16–23.

Mayo Clinic. (2019, March 11). *Red wine and resveratrol: Good for your heart?* Retrieved from www.mayoclinic.org/diseases-conditions/heart-disease/in-depth/red-wine/art-20048281.

Mclellan, A. T. (2017). Substance misuse and substance use disorders: Why do they matter in healthcare? *Transactions of the American Clinical and Climatological Association.* 128: 112–130. PMCID: PMC5525418. PMID: 28790493.

Medley, G., Lipari, R. N., Bose, J., Cribb, D. S., Kroutil, L. A., & McHenry, G. (2016). *Sexual orientation and estimates of adult substance use and mental health: Results from the 2015 national survey on drug use and health.* NSDUH Data Review. Retrieved from www.samhsa.gov/data/.

Mee-Lee, D., Schulman, G. D., Fishman, M. J., Gasfriend, D. R., & Miller, M. M., (Eds.) (2013). *The ASAM criteria: Treatment criteria for addictive substance-related, and co-occurring conditions, third edition.* Carson City, NV: The Change Companies.

Merriam-Webster.com. (2019, January 13). Retrieved from www.merriam-webster.com/dictionary/enabling.

Miller, W. R. (2019, July 7). Personal communication.

Miller, W. R., & Munoz, R. F. (2013). *Controlling your drinking: Tools to make moderation work for you* (2nd ed.). New York: The Guilford Press.

Miller, W. R., & Rollnick, S. (2002). *Motivational interviewing: Preparing people for change* (2nd ed.) New York: The Guilford Press.

Milward, J., Khadjesari, Z., Fincham-Campbell, S., Deluca, P., Watson, R., & Drummond, C. (2016). User preferences for content, features, and style for an app to reduce harmful drinking in young adults: Analysis of user feedback in app stores and focus group interviews. *JMIR mHealth and uHealth.* 4(2): e47. DOI: 10.2196/mhealth.5242.

Moderation Management. (2019). *Dryuary 2019 collection: Inspirational posts and expert advice for a month of abstinence from alcohol.* Grandville, MI: Moderation Management Network, Inc.

Moderation Management. (2019, March 27). Retrieved from www.moderation.org/about_mm/whatismm.html.

Moderation Management. (2019, June 14). *What is moderation management?* Retrieved from www.moderation.org/about_mm/whatismm.html.

Mohler-Kuo, M., Dowdall, G. W., Koss, M., & Wechsler, H. (2004). Correlates of rape while intoxicated in a national sample of college women. *Journal of Studies on Alcohol and Drugs.* 65(1): 37–45.

Monteiro, M. G. (2007). *Alcohol and public health in the Americas: A case for action.* Washington, DC: Pan American Health Organization.

Morin, J-F. G., Harris, M., & Conrod, P. J. (2017). A review of CBT treatments for substance use disorders. *Clinical Psychology.* DOI: 10.1093/oxfordhb/9780199935291.013.57.

Mubin, O. (2016, July 13). Trying to cut down your drinking? There's an app for that. *The Conversation.* Retrieved from http://theconversation.com/trying-to-cut-your-drinking-theres-an-app-for-that-59386.

Mukamaon, G. (2015). *10 Biggest alcohol drinking countries in Africa.* Lifestyle.

Mulligan, C. J., Robin, R. W., Osier, M. V., Sambuughin, N., Goldfarb, L. G., Kittles, R. A., Hesselbrock, D., Goldman, D., & Long, J. C. (2003). Allelic variation at alcohol metabolism genes (ADH1B, ADH1C, ALDH2) and alcohol dependence in an American Indian population. *Human Genetics.* 113(4): 325–336.

Mumenthaler, M. S., Taylor, J. L., O'Hara, R., & Yesavage, J. A. (1999). Gender differences in moderate drinking effects. *Alcohol Research and Health.* 23(1): 55–64.

Munroe, D. (2015, April 27). Inside the $35 billion addiction treatment industry. *Forbes.* Retrieved from www.forbes.com/sites/danmunro/2015/04/27/inside-the-35-billion-addiction-treatment-industry/#42574e2117dc.

Najavits, L. M. (2001). *Seeking safety: A treatment manual for PTSD and substance abuse.* New York: The Guilford Press.

Najavits, L. M., & Hien, D. (2013). Helping vulnerable populations: A comprehensive review of the treatment outcome literature on substance use disorder and PTSD. *Journal of Clinical Psychology: In Session.* 69(5): 433–479. DOI: 10.1002/jclp.21980.

National Alliance on Mental Illness. (2019, May 14). Retrieved from www.nami.org/Find-Support/Living-with-a-Mental-Health-Condition/Taking-Care-of-Your-Body/Drugs-Alcohol-Smoking.

National Association of Social Workers. (2013). *NASW standards for social work practice for clients with substance use disorders.* Washington, DC: National Association of Social Workers.

National Center for Complementary and Integrated Health. (2019, May 23). *Melatonin: In depth.* Bethesda, MD. Retrieved from https://nccih.nih.gov/health/melatonin.

National Center for PTSD. (2019, June 6). *PTSD and problems with alcohol use.* Junction, VT: White River. Retrieved from www.ptsd.va.gov/understand/related/problem_alcohol_use.asp.

National Child Traumatic Stress Network. (2008). *Understanding links between adolescent trauma and substance abuse: A toolkit for providers* (2nd ed.). Washington, DC: American Psychiatric Publishing, Inc.

National Health Service. (2018, May 30). *Sleep and tiredness: Why lack of sleep is bad for your health.* Retrieved from www.nhs.uk/live-well/sleep-and-tiredness/why-lack-of-sleep-is-bad-for-your-health/.

National Highway Traffic Safety Administration. (2016). *The ABC of BAC: A guide to understanding blood alcohol concentration and impairment.* Washington, DC: US Department of Transportation.

National Highway Traffic Safety Administration. (2018). *Traffic safety facts 2016 data: Alcohol-impaired driving.* Washington, DC: U.S. Department of Transportation. Retrieved from https://crashstats.nhtsa.dot.gov/Api/Public/ViewPublication/812450External.

National Institute on Ageing. (2017). *Facts about aging and alcohol.* Bethesda, MD. Retrieved from www.nia.nih.gov/health/facts-about-aging-and-alcohol.

National Institute on Alcohol Abuse and Alcoholism. (1998, July). *Alcohol alert no. 41.* Bethesda, MD: National Institute on Alcohol Abuse and Alcoholism.

National Institute on Alcohol Abuse and Alcoholism (NIAAA). (2000). *Tenth special report to the U.S. Congress on alcohol and health: Highlights from current research, from the secretary of health and human services, national institute of health, national institute on alcohol abuse and alcoholism.* NIAAA: Rockville, MD.

National Institute on Alcohol Abuse and Alcoholism. (2006, October). *National Epidemiologic survey on alcohol and related concerns.* (70).

National Institute on Alcohol Abuse and Alcoholism. (2015). *Alcohol: A women's health issue.* NIH Publication No. 15-4956.

National Institute of Alcohol Abuse and Alcoholism. (2016, May). *Rethinking drinking: Alcohol and your health.* Bethesda, MD: Department of Health and Human Services, NIH, National Institute on Alcohol Abuse and Alcoholism.

National Institute on Alcohol Abuse and Alcoholism. (2018, October). *Understanding the dangers of alcohol overdose.* Retrieved from https://pubs.niaaa.nih.gov/publications/AlcoholOverdoseFactsheet/Overdosefact.htm.

National Institute on Alcohol Abuse and Alcoholism. (2019, March 11). *Alcohol calorie calculator.* Retried from www.rethinkingdrinking.niaaa.nih.gov/Tools/Calculators/Calorie-Calculator.aspx.

National Institute on Alcohol Abuse and Alcoholism. (2019, March 20). *Alcohol and your health.* Retrieved from www.niaaa.nih.gov/alcohol-health/overview-alcohol-consumption/alcohol-use-disorders.

National Institute on Alcohol Abuse and Alcoholism. (2019, June 4). *Drinking levels defined.* Bethesda, MD. Retrieved from www.niaaa.nih.gov/alcohol-health/overview-alcohol-consumption/moderate-binge-drinking.

National Institute on Drug Abuse. (2018, July). *The science of drug use and addiction: The basics.* Retrieved from www.drugabuse.gov/publications/media-guide/science-drug-use-addiction-basics.

National Institute on Drug Abuse; National Institutes of Health; U. S. Department of Health and Human Services. (2003). *Preventing Drug use among children and adolescents* (In brief). Rockville, MD.

National Sleep Foundation. (2019, May 5). *How alcohol affects the quality—and quantity of sleep.* Retrieved from www.sleepfoundation.org/articles/how-alcohol-affects-quality-and-quantity-sleep.

Newman, T. (2017, December 22). All about the central nervous system. *Medical News Today.* Retrieved from https://www.medicalnewstoday.com/articles/307076.php.

Newman, T. (2018, March 2). What does the liver do? *Medical News Today.* Retrieved from www.medicalnewstoday.com/articles/305075.php.

Nordqvist, C. (2018, February 6). What's to know about liver disease? *Medical News Today.* Retrieved from www.medicalnewstoday.com/articles/215638.php.

North American Menopause Society. (2019). *Drink to your health at menopause—or not?* Pepper Pike, OH. Retrieved from www.menopause.org/for-women/menopauseflashes/exercise-and-diet/drink-to-your-health-at-menopause-or-not.

Ojehagen, A., & Berglund, M. (1989). Changes of drinking goals in a two-year outpatient alcoholic treatment program. *Addictive Behaviors.* 14(1): 1–9. https://doi.org/10.1016/0306-4603(89)90011-7.

Ostafin, B. D., & Marlatt, G. A. (2008). Surfing the urge: Experiential acceptance moderates the relation between automatic alcohol motivation and hazardous drinking. *Journal of Social and Clinical Psychology.* 27(4): 404–418. https://doi.org/10.1521/jscp.2008.27.4.404.

Otten, R., Cladder-Micus, M. B., Pouwels, J. L., Schurmanns, A. A. T., & Hermans, R. C. J. (2014). Facing temptation in the bar: Counteracting the effects of self-control failure on young adults' *ad libitum* alcohol intake. *Addiction.* 109(5): 746–753.

Parnell, S. (2017). Hello Sunday morning helps build healthy relationships with drink. *The Weekend Australian*. Retrieved from www.theaustralian.com.au/life/hello-sunday-morning-helps-build-healthy-relationships-with-drink/news-story/dc75544a78d84b9ba504243ba3bfa9d2.

Pedery, M. L., Maltzman, I. M., & West, L. J. (1982, July 9). Controlled drinking by alcoholics? New findings and a reevaluation of a major affirmative study. *Science*. 217(4555): 169–175. DOI: 10.1126/science.7089552.

Peele, S. (1987). Why do controlled-drinking outcomes vary by investigator, by country, and by era? *Drug and Alcohol Dependence*. 20: 173–201.

Peele, S. (1996). Denial—of reality and of freedom—in addiction research and treatment. *Bulletin of the Society of Psychologists in Addictive Behaviors*. 5(4): 149–166, 1986.

Peele, S. (1997). Bait and switch in Project MATCH: What NIAAA research actually shows about alcohol treatment. *PsychNews International*. 2 (May–June).

Peele, S. (1997, September 16). A brief history of the national council on alcoholism through pictures. *The Stanton Peele Addiction Website*, September 16.

Peele, S. (2000, August 13). Everything in moderation the debate over alcohol: Is one too many? *Star Ledger* (NJ), p. 1 (Perspective Section).

Peele, S. (2015, June 8). Studies show that drinking problems are increasing. Here's why. *The Fix*. Retrieved from www.thefix.com/content/we-have-more-drinking-problems-why/.

Piano, M. R. (2017). Alcohol's effects on the cardiovascular system. *Alcohol Research*. 38(2): 219–241.

Powers, T. (2015, September 13). Recognizing the stages of alcoholism: The Jellinek curve. *The Fix*.

Probst, C., Manthey, J., Martinez, A., & Rehm, J. (2015). Alcohol use disorder severity and reported reasons not to seek treatment: A cross-sectional study in European primary care practices. *Substance Abuse Treatment Prevention Policy*. 10(32). DOI: 10.1186/s13011-015-0028-z.

Prochaska, J. O., DiClemente, C. C., & Norcross, J. C. (1992). In search of how people change: Applications to the addictive behaviors. *American Psychologist*. 47: 1102–1114. PMID: 1329589.

Prochaska, J. O., Norcross, J. C., & DiClemente, C. C. (1994). *Changing for good*. New York: Morrow. ISBN: 0-380-72572-X.

Project MATCH Research Group. (1997). Matching alcoholism treatments to client heterogeneity: Project MATCH posttreatment drinking outcomes. *Journal of Studies on Alcohol*. 58: 7–29.

Rabin, R. C. (2018, March 17). Federal agency courted alcohol industry to fund study on benefits of moderate drinking. *New York Times*. Retrieved from https://www.nytimes.com/2018/03/17/health/nih-alcohol-study-liquor-industry.html.

Raistrick, D. S., Dunbar, G., & Davidson, R. J. (1983). Development of a questionnaire to measure alcohol dependence. *British Journal of Addiction*. 78: 89–95.

Responsible Drinking. (2019, June 1). *What happens when you drink*. Retrieved from www.responsibledrinking.org/what-happens-when-you-drink/how-you-drink-matters/.

Rice, P. (2017, January 24). *Should dependent drinkers always try for abstinence?* Retrieved from https://findings.org.uk/docs/cont_drink_findings.pdf?s=eb&r=&sf=fpd.

Rifkin, R. (2015, July 28). One in five Americans say alcohol use is healthy. *Gallup News*. Retrieved from https://news.gallup.com/poll/184382/one-five-americans-say-moderate-drinking-healthy.aspx.

Roan, S. (2009, November 16). You can cut back on alcohol. *LA Times*. Retrieved from www.latimes.com/health/la-he-alcohol16-2009nov16-story.html.

Rotgers, F., Kern, M. F., Hoeltzel, R. (2002). *Responsible drinking: A moderation management approach for problem drinkers*. New Harbinger Publications: Oakland, CA.

Roth, S. (2017, April 17). *Light-to-moderate alcohol consumption can reduce risk of death, while heavy alcohol consumption can have opposite effect*. Retrieved from www.acc.org/about-acc/press-releases/2017/08/14/14/04/light-to-moderate-alcohol-consumption-may-have-protective-health-effects.

Rothschild, D. (2015, February 6). The "third wave" of substance use treatment. *The Fix*. Retrieved from www.thefix.com/content/third-wave-substance-use-treatment.

Royal College of Physicians, Royal College of Psychiatrists, Royal College of General Practitioners. (1995, June). *Alcohol and the heart in perspective—Sensible limits reaffirmed. Report of a joint working group*. ISBN 1 86016 019 0.

Rush, B. (1808). *An inquiry into the effects of ardent spirits upon the human body and mind: With an account of the means of preventing, and of the remedies for curing them*. Philadelphia: Thomas Dobson.

Saladin, M. E., & Santa Ana, E. (2004, May). Controlled drinking: More than just a controversy. *Addictive Disorders*. 17(3): 175, 187.

Sanchez-Craig, M. (2013). *Saying when: How to quit drinking or cut down*. Toronto, Canada: Center for Addiction and Mental Health.

Sanchez-Craig, M., Annis, H. M., Bronet, A. R., & MacDonald, K. R. (1984). Random assignment to abstinence and controlled drinking: Evaluation of a cognitive-behavioral program for problem drinkers. *Journal of Consulting and Clinical Psychology*. 52(3): 390–403. http://dx.doi.org/10.1037/0022-006X.52.3.390.

Sarkar, D., Jung, M. K., & Wang, H. J. (2015). Alcohol and the immune system. *Alcohol Research Current Reviews*. 37(2): 153–155.

The SASSI Institute. (2019, May 10). Retrieved from https://sassi.com.

Saunders, J. B., & Aasland, O. G. (1987). *WHO collaborative project on identification and treatment of persons with harmful alcohol consumption*. Report on phase I. Development of a screening instrument. Geneva: World Health Organization.

Schomer, A. (2014). *One little pill*. Proven Entertainment.

Scott, H. K., & Tatarsky, A. (2012). Re-envisioning addiction treatment: A six-point plan. *Alcoholism Treatment Quarterly*. 30(1): 109–128. DOI: 10.1080/07347324.2012.635544.

Selk, J. (2013, April 15). Habit formation: The 21-day myth. *Forbes.com*. Retrieved from www.forbes.com/sites/jasonselk/2013/04/15/habit-formation-the-21-day-myth/#48ee9dcddebc.

Seville, L. R., Schecter, A., & Rappleye, H. (2017, June 25). Florida's billion-dollar drug treatment industry is plagued by overdoses, fraud. *NBC News*.

Shahre, M., Roeber, J., Kanny, D., Brewer, R. D., & Zhang, X. (2014). Contribution of excessive alcohol consumption to deaths and years of potential life lost in the United States. *Preventing Chronic Disease*. 11(13): 130293. http://dx.doi.org/10.5888/pcd11.130293.

Sharma, P., Murthy, P., & Bharath, M. M. S. (2012). Chemistry, metabolism, and toxicology of cannabis: Clinical implications. *Iranian Journal of Psychiatry*. 7(4): 149–156.

Shukla, L., Sharma, P., Ganesha, S., Ghadigaonkar, D., Thomas, E., Kandasamy, A., Murthy, P., & Benegal, V. (2017). Value of ethyl glucuronide and ethyl sulfate in serum as biomarkers of alcohol consumption. *Indian Journal of Psychological Medicine*. 39(4): 481–487.

Sinclair, J. D. (1998). New treatment options for substance abuse from a public health viewpoint. *Annals of Medicine*. 30(4): 406–411.

Sinclair, J. D. (2001). Evidence about the use of naltrexone and for different ways of using it in the treatment of alcoholism. *Alcohol and Alcoholism*. 36(1): 2–10. https://doi.org/10.1093/alcalc/36.1.2.

SMART Recovery. (2019, June 14). *Sensible tools for addiction recovery*. Retrieved from www.smartrecovery.org/#.

Smolen, J. (2018, October 6). Binge drinking and blackouts: The sobering truth about lost learning in students. *The Conversation*. Retrieved from https://theconversation.com/us/search?utf8=√&q=%29.+Binge+drinking+and+and+blackouts%3A+The+sobering+truth+about+lost+learning+in+students.+.

Sobell, L. C., & Sobell, M. B. (2011). *Group therapy for substance use disorders: A motivational cognitive-behavioral approach*. New York: The Guilford Press.

Sobell, M. B., & Sobell, L. C. (1973). Individualized behavior therapy for alcoholics. *Behavior Therapy*. 4(1): 49–72.

Sobell, M. B., & Sobell, L. C. (1984). The aftermath of the heresy: A response to Pendery et al.'s 1982 critique of "Individualized behavior therapy for alcoholics." *Behavior and Research Therapy*. 22(4): 413–440. https://doi.org/10.1016/0005-7967(84)90084-6.

Sobell, M. B., & Sobell, L. C. (2005). Guided self-change model of treatment for substance use disorders. *Journal of Cognitive Psychotherapy*. 19(3). DOI: 10.1891/jcop.2005.19.3.199.

Springer, E. (1991). Effective AIDS Prevention with active drug users: The harm reduction model. In M. Shernoff (Ed.), *Counseling chemically dependent people with HIV illness* (pp. 141–158). New York: Harrington Park Press.

Stinchfield, R., & Owen, P. (1998). Hazelden's model of treatment and its outcome. *Addictive Behaviors*. 23(5): 669–683. https://doi.org/10.1016/S0306-4603(98)00015-X.

Stockwell, T., Zhao, J., Panwar, S., Roemer, A., Naimi, T., & Chikritzhs, T. (2016). Do "moderate" drinkers have reduced mortality risk? A systemic review and meta-analysis of alcohol consumption and all-cause mortality. *Journal of Studies on Alcohol and Drugs*. 77(2): 185–198.

Substance Abuse and Mental Health Services Administration. (2004). Treatment Improvement Protocol (TIP) Series, No. 39. *Substance abuse treatment and family therapy*. Rockville, MD.

Substance Abuse and Mental Health Services Administration. (2012, February). *What's recovery? SAMHSA's working definition*. Publication ID: PEP12-RECDEF.

Substance Abuse and Mental Health Services Administration. (2013). *Addressing the specific behavioral health needs of men*. Treatment Improvement Protocol (TIP) Series 56. HHS Publication No. (SMA) 13–4736. Rockville, MD: Substance Abuse and Mental Health Services Administration.

Substance Abuse and Mental Health Services Administration (SAMHSA). (2015). National Survey on Drug Use and Health (NSDUH). Table 2.41B—Alcohol Use in Lifetime, Past Year, and Past Month among Persons Aged 12 or Older, by Demographic Characteristics: Percentages, 2014 and 2015. Retrieved January 18, 2017, from www.samhsa.gov/data/sites/default/files/NSDUH-DetTabs-2015/NSDUH-DetTabs-2015/NSDUH-DetTabs-2015.htm#tab2-41b.

Substance Abuse and Mental Health Services Administration. (2018). *Key substance use and mental health indicators in the United States: Results from the 2017 national survey on drug use and health* (HHS Publication No. SMA 18–5068, NSDUH Series H-53).

Rockville, MD: Center for Behavioral Health Statistics and Quality, Substance Abuse and Mental Health Services Administration. Retrieved from www. samhsa.gov/data/.

Substance Abuse and Mental Health Services Administration, Center for Behavioral Health Statistics and Quality. (2014, September 4). *The NSDUH report: Substance use and mental health estimates from the 2013 national survey on drug use and health: Overview of findings.* Rockville, MD.

Suh, S., & Ikeda, M. (2015). Compassionate pragmatism on the harm reduction continuum: Expanding the options for drug and alcohol addiction treatment in Japan. *Communication-Design.* 13: 63–72.

Sullivan, E. V., Harris, A., & Pfefferbaum, A. (2010). Alcohol's effects on brain and behavior. *Alcohol Research & Health.* 33(1–2): 127–143.

Suokas J., Suominen K., & Lonnqvist J. (2005). Chronic alcohol problems among suicide attempters—post-mortem findings of a 14-year follow up. *Nordic Journal of Psychiatry.* 59(1): 45–50.

Sweeney, D. F. (2011). Take blackouts seriously. *Addiction Professional.* 9(4): 54–57.

Tamara, L., Wall, T. L., Luczak, S. E., & Hiller-Sturmhöfel, S. (2016). Biology, genetics, and environment: Underlying factors influencing alcohol moderation. *The Journal of the National Institute on Alcohol Abuse and Alcoholism.* 38(1).

Tatarsky, A. (2007). *Harm reduction psychotherapy: A new treatment for drug and alcohol problems.* Lanham, MD: Rowman & Littlefield Publishers.

Tatarsky, A., & Marlatt, A. (2010). State of the art in harm reduction psychotherapy: An emerging treatment for substance misuse. *Journal of Clinical Psychology: In Session.* 66(2): 117–122. DOI: 10.1002/jclp.20672.

TED. (2010, June) *Brené Brown.* www.ted.com/talks/brene_brown_on_vulnerability.

TED. (2015, June). *Johann Hari: Everything you think you know about addiction is wrong.* Retrieved from www.ted.com/talks/johann_hari_everything_you_think_you_know_about_addiction_is_wrong.

Tiwari, M. (2011). Science behind human saliva. *Journal of Natural Science, Biology and Medicine.* 2(1): 53–58. DOI: 10.4103/0976-9668.82322.

Transform. (2019, June 7). *Drug decriminalization in Portugal: Setting the record straight.* Retrieved from https://transformdrugs.org/drug-decriminalisation-in-portugal-setting-the-record-straight/.

Trevisan, L. A., Boutrous, N., Petrakis, I. L., & Krystal, J. H. (1998). Complications of alcohol withdrawal: Pathophysiological insights. *Alcohol Health & Research World.* 22(1): 61–66.

Turner, C. (2017). *Can I keep drinking? how you can decide when enough is enough.* New York: Morgan James Publishing.

Turner, C., & James, C. (2013). *How do I know if I can keep drinking quiz* (Author).

United States Census Bureau. (2019, March 11). Retrieved from www.census.gov.

United States Drug Enforcement Administration. (2019, June 11). *Drug scheduling.* Retrieved from www.dea.gov/drug-scheduling.

University of Sussex. (2018). How "Dry January" is the secret to better sleep, saving money and losing weight. *ScienceDaily.* Retrieved from www.sciencedaily.com/releases/2018/12/181228164834.htm.

Urban, N. B., Kegels, L. S., Slifstein, M., Xu, X., Martinez, D., Sakr, E., Castillo, F., Moadel, T., O'Malley, S. S., Krystal, J. H., & Abi-Dargham, A. (2010). Sex differences in striatal dopamine release in young adults after oral alcohol challenge: A positron emission tomography imaging study with [11C]raclopride. *Biological Psychiatry.* 68(8): 689–696.

U.S. Department of Health and Human Services (HHS), Office of the Surgeon General. (2016). *Facing addiction in America: The Surgeon General's report on alcohol, drugs, and health.* Washington, DC: Health and Human Services.

U.S. Department of Health and Human Services (HHS), Office of the Surgeon General. (2016, November). *Facing addiction in America: The Surgeon General's report on alcohol, drugs, and health.* Washington, DC: Health and Human Services.

U.S. Department of Health and Human Services and U.S. Department of Agriculture. (2015). *2015–2020 dietary guidelines for Americans: External* (8th ed.). Washington, DC: Office of Disease Prevention and Health Promotion.

U. S. Food and Drug Administration. (2019, June 12). *The drug development process.* Retrieved from www.fda.gov/patients/learn-about-drug-and-device-approvals/drug-development-process.

Usman, M. (2109, February 2). *How does alcohol consumption affect your weight and shape?* Retrieved from www.weightlossresources.co.uk/body_weight/alcohol-effect.htm.

Vaillant, G. E. (2003). A 60-year follow-up of alcoholic men. *Addiction.* 98: 1043–1051.

Ventura-Cots, M., Watts, A. E., Cruz-Lemini, M., Shah, N. D., Ndugga, N., McCann, P., Barritt, A. S., Jain, A., Ravi, S., Fernandez-Carrillo, C., Abraldes, J. G., Altamirano, J., & Bataller, R. (2018). Colder weather and fewer sunlight hours increase alcohol consumption and alcoholic cirrhosis worldwide. *Hepatology.* DOI: 10.1002/hep.30315.

Volkow, N. D., & Koob, G. (2015, August). Brain disease model of addiction: Why is it so controversial? *The Lancet Psychiatry.* 2(8).

Volpicelli, J., Balaraman, G., Hahn, J., Wallace, H., and Bux, D. (1999). The role of uncontrollable trauma in the development of PTSD and alcohol addiction. *Alcohol Research and Health.* 23(4): 256–262.

Walters, G. D. (2000). Behavioral self-control training for problem drinkers: A meta-analysis of randomized control studies. *Behavior Therapy.* 31(1): 135–149. https://doi.org/10.1016/S0005-7894(00)80008-8.

Washton, A., & Ascher, M. (2017, April 11). Mindful moderate drinking—how to drink less, enjoy it more, and reduce the risks. *Huffingtonpost.com.* Retrieved from www.huffingtonpost.com/entry/mindful-moderate drinking-how-to-drink-less-enjoy_us_58ed8744e4b0ea028d568e13.

Weathermon, R., & Crabb, D. W. (1999, November 1). Alcohol and medication interactions. *Alcohol Research and Health.* 23(1): 40–54.

Wells, S., Graham, K., & West, P. J. (2000 July). Alcohol-related aggression in the general population. *Journal of Studies on Alcohol.* 61(4): 626–632.

White, A. M. (2003). What happened? Alcohol, memory, blackouts, and the brain. *Alcohol Research and Health.* 27(2): 186–196.

White, W. (1998). *Slaying the Dragon: The history of addiction treatment and recovery in America.* Bloomington, IL: Chestnut Health Systems.

White, W. (2000). Addiction as a disease: Birth of a concept. *Counselor.* 1(1): 46–51, 73.

White, W. (2012). The history of secular organizations for sobriety—save our selves: An interview with James Christopher. Retrieved from www.williamwhitepapers.com and www.facesandvoicesofrecovery.org.

White, W. (2013). *The history of LifeRing secular recovery: An interview with Marty Nicolaus.* Retrieved from www.williamwhitepapers.com.

Whitesell, N. R., Beals, J., Croy, C. B., Mitchell, C. M., & Novins, D. K. (2012). Epidemiology and etiology of substance use among American Indians and Alaska Natives: Risk, protection, and implications for prevention. *The American Journal of Drug and Alcohol Abuse.* 38(5): 376–382.

Williams, E. (2016, October 8). Navigating the world of apps that claim to fix your drinking problem. *NPR*. Retrieved from www.npr.org/sections/alltech considered/2016/10/08/496742219/navigating-the-world-of-apps-that-claim-to-fix-your-drinking-problem.

Winter, C. (2017, January 11). Why does alcohol make you hungry? Biological link between drinking and binge eating discovered. *ABC.net.AUNews*. Retrieved from www.abc.net.au/news/2017-01-11/why-does-alcohol-make-you-hungry/8176220.

Witikiewitz, K., Bowen, S., Harropt, E. N., Douglas, H., Enkema, M., & Sedgwick. (2014). Mindfulness-based treatment to prevent addictive behavior relapse: Theoretical models and hypothesized mechanisms of change. *Substance Use Misuse*. 49(5): 513–524. DOI: 10.3109/10826084.2014.891845.

Witte, K., & Allen, M. (2000). A meta-analysis of fear appeals: Implications for Effective public health programs. *Health Education and Behavior*. 27(5): 591–615.

World Atlas. (2017). 14 countries where drinking is illegal. *World Atlas.com*. Retrieved from www.worldatlas.com/articles/14-countries-where-drinking-alcohol-is-illegal.html.

World Health Organization. (2014). *Global status report on alcohol and health—2014 ed.* Retrieved from www.who.int/substance_abuse/publications/global_alcohol_report/msb_gsr_2014_1.pdf.

World Health Organization. (2018). *Global status report on alcohol and health 2018*. Geneva: World Health Organization; 2018. License: CC BY-NC-SA 3.0 IGO.

World Health Organization. (2018). *United Kingdom: Trends in alcohol consumption 2016*. Geneva: World Health Organization.

World Health Organization Brief Intervention Study Group. (1996). A cross-national trial of brief intervention with heavy drinkers. *American Journal of Public Health*. 86: 948–955.

Yeh, M-Y., Che, H-L., & Wu, S-M. (2009, November 27). An ongoing process: A qualitative study on how the alcohol-dependent free themselves of addiction through progressive abstinence. *BMC Psychiatry*. 99: 76. https://doi.org/10.1186/1471-244X-9-76.

Zakhari, S. (2019, March 9). *Overview: How is alcohol metabolized by the body?* National Institutes on Alcohol Abuse and Alcoholism. Retrieved from https://pubs.niaaa.nih.gov/publications/arh294/245-255.htm.

Zenmore, S. E., Kaskutas, L. A., Mericle, A., & Hemberg, J. (2017, February) Comparison of 12-step groups to mutual help alternatives for AUD in a large, national study: Differences in membership characteristics and group participation, cohesion, and satisfaction. *Journal of Substance Abuse Treatment*. 73: 16–26.

Zhang, M. W. B., Ward, J., Ying, J. J. B., Pan, F., & Ho, R. C. M. (2016). The alcohol tracker application: An initial evaluation of user preference. *BMJ Innovations*. 2(8): 8–13.

Zhao, X., Zhang, X., & Rong, J. (2014). Study of the effects of alcohol on drivers and driving performance on straight road. *Mathematical Problems in Engineering*. Article ID 607652. https://doi.org/10.1155/2014/607652.

Index

Page numbers in *italic* type indicate figures.